The Dangers of Knowing it all

From the Diaries of an Outsider

Acharya Nihal Paul

ISBN: 9798518041943

Acknowledgements

This book has been possible only, because of the gentle nudges, serious encouragement, and some judicious nagging by many kind friends.

My most sincere gratitude, is, first and foremost, to my mother, who taught her children, never to give up, but follow their dreams with unbending courage and compassion. Also, to my father, who passed away before I could get to know him but left a rich legacy of memories for us to remember him by.

I am grateful to all, whose lives adorn this narrative. I thank you for your contribution to the story/stories.

There are too many kind and generous individuals for me to thank them by name. You know who you are. I thank you sincerely.

Thank you, Wendy Ogilvy for your diligent and generous support in proofreading and editing my manuscript. Thank you, Paul Burridge for your patience and generosity in preparing and loading this onto Amazon publishing platform.

Nihal Paul
Basildon, May 20

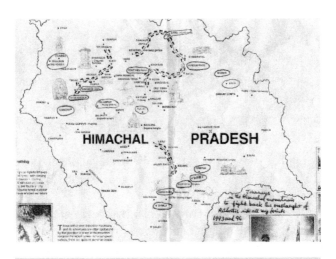

HIMACHAL PRADESH

Journeys in the Himachal mountains to fight back the onslaught of Activities with all my friends
1993 and 96

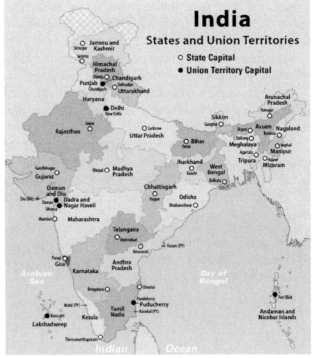

India

States and Union Territories

○ State Capital
● Union Territory Capital

Prologue

At the end of my friend's wedding ceremony in a village across the stream from my place, Sankhu and I were wondering which of the two routes might be the safer option for my return home that evening. Sankhu, a recognised expert on the movements of bears and leopards in that part of the world, had no doubt in his mind that I ought to take the longer route. "Along the longer route you will be running into a constant trickle of people at this time of the day." I weighed up the option for a moment or two and being the know-it-all teenager, chose the shorter route.

From the groom's veranda, I could clearly see my house, high up, across the stream, hanging on to the side of the rocky cliff by the skin of its foundation teeth. I said my farewells and walked down half a mile through terraced fields, into the dark pine forest. Five hundred or so yards further, I reached the shallow stream. Hopped from stone to stone over the water. Another hundred yards of moist and soggy earth uphill, and I reached the starting point of my ascent up the cliff face, directly below my house. From there, it was 2,500 plus feet up the 80–90 degrees climb. I calculated in my head, *an hour and some minutes, and I will be home.*

Halfway up, I was sweating and breathless in the muggy heat of mid-July. Constantly having to Zig-zag up the cliff face, the climb had been much slower than I had imagined. I sat on the edge of a rock jutting out from the face of the cliff. From my perch, I could see every inch of my journey so far. Back across the stream, my eyes roamed over wide spaces of layer upon layer of terraced fields, small villages, and hamlets resting in the shadows of thousands of apple trees. Branches of the trees gracefully bent over under the weight of their fruits in gratitude to their maker.

Farther up the sloping valley and beyond the apple orchards, were the rocky hills dotted with small farms and wooded patches of mainly pine trees. Farther and higher still, the snow-clad mountains on the eastern horizon stood proudly between me and Tibet, looking down upon the entire landscape. To the north-east of me the bare, rocky hills stretched beyond the pine trees to my left. Down the center of this wonderful picture, the blue river Satluj snaked along the Shimla-Tibet Road, on its way to the planes of the Punjab.

In the crevices of the white mountains before me, there were signs of the goddesses and the fairies getting ready to entertain the gods with their dazzling, flirtatious dances, before bedtime. The evening breeze was gently picking up pace. In the tall treetops above my head, I could hear the ghosts whispering their timetable for the night. The evening shadows were slowly moving towards the eastern horizon before me. Another hour at the most, I guessed, and the dark night would begin to take over my world. Sounds from the waterfall behind the forest to my right, were adding to my sense of isolation and impending dangers. *I wish I had listened to Sankhu.*

I imagined some hungry leopard or bear coming out to meet me before I got home. I stood up and hurriedly turned to continue my journey but lost my balance and fell into the vast empty space between my rock and the stream, 1,500 feet below, at the bottom of the cliff.

As my body floated downward into the empty space, I

heard human voices and saw shadowy figures and faint objects all around me, but no one seemed to hear my muffled screams for help. Then, from one of the human shadows, two strong hands reached out, grabbed me by the arms, and broke my fall. I heard a man's soft baritone voice calling my name. I opened my eyes and saw Mark sitting me up safely in the chair near the entrance to the dining area of our hotel in Tunisia.

Standing next to Mark was Nicky, joined by a dozen nosey strangers; all adding to my sense of embarrassment. Nicky sounded overly concerned. "What happened, Nihal? Your face has gone white! Are you alright?"

I briefly explained that I had placed myself in that chair by the door, waiting for some familiar faces to join me for dinner. I dozed off into dreamland, and found myself in the foothills of the Himalayas, climbing up the cliff face below my house. Halfway up the cliff, I lost my balance, fell into the empty space . . . and landed back here in the same chair.

A shrieky female voice reached me from over my left shoulder, "I thought you were Spanish! So, how far is your house from Mount Everest, then?" she asked mockingly. I turned to face her with a wicked grin dancing across my face, and said with a mock shiver, "Ooh, it's right up near the top. Even the birds up there suffer from vertigo. And you should see the monkeys climbing up the trees; the poor things look petrified." That started a round of chuckles and sniggers.

Luckily for me, someone mentioned dinner, and we attached ourselves to the back of the queue snaking in the direction of the food counters. Once there, we piled our plates high. Looking over us, were the overworked and hungry waiters – it was their festival of fasting. Mind you, not all of them had necessarily fasted all day. I say that, because the day before, I had climbed up the stairs onto the roof above my section of the building to get a better view of the hills behind the hotel. At the top of the stairs, in a sheltered corner of the roof, there were tell-tale signs of food and drinks and scores of cigarette-ends.

Mark, Nicky and I made our way to a table in the far corner. A Church of England rector from Bradford, by the name of Michael Weedon Frenching, whom we had run into the day before, joined us at the table.

Mark was a lecturer in psychology somewhere in Surrey. Nicky was a professor of history in some college in London. We had first met on the coach from the airport to the hotel three days before and happened to enjoy each other's company.

We had hardly settled down in our chairs when Michael referred to some discussion he and Mark had had earlier in the day. He turned to face Mark who was sitting on his right. "At the bar, earlier this afternoon, did you mean to say that the Bible is not the Word of God?"

"Yes. The Bible is a collection of stories, folklores, some religious as well as some political propaganda. If I am to say that the Bible is the 'Word of God' because someone says so, then I must also accept that the Quran too is the 'Word of God' because someone says so.

"Can we leave the discussion about religion and politics for another time, please fellows? Let's enjoy our meal in peace." I suggested calmly.

Michael turned his face in my direction and stared at me unnervingly, expecting some explanation, I guessed. I conceded, eventually. "I don't mean to offend you, Michael, I just look at things differently from the way you look at them. Can we talk about this another day? We have had plenty of discussions about religion in the past two days to last us a lifetime."

Nicky turned to Michael. "Sorry to interrupt. The problem with the God of the holy books is that, not only is he unable to make up his mind about what he wants to say to his creatures – his writings are so full of contradictions and confusions - but he is also not very wise in his choice of the ghost writers. All the writings in the Holy books, so called, were written by highly misogynistic and power-hungry men. It was all about what they wanted. Nothing to do with God, I am sure. Recently, archaeologists have found some manuscripts that were written by women about the same time as the Bible was being written. Women had to hide their writings away for fear of men burning them."

Michael's face was becoming redder by the second. I feared the purple veins on his face would burst open any moment. He carefully placed his knife and fork on his plate and burned his eyes onto Nicky's.

Before he could say something, Nicky put her hand up. "Let me finish Michael. I've been listening to you patiently since yesterday. Now it is my turn. I'll be brief. According to those recently discovered documents, this is how the story of Creation appears in the women's Bible...."

God first created a woman in her own image and in her own likeness. She named her Innocence, and placed her in a garden, in the centre of an 'Oasis' in the desert near Egypt. On one of Her evening walks in the Garden, God sees Innocence reclining against a tree. Her left arm was wrapped round the neck of a lion cub, and her left cheek resting on its head. With her free hand Innocence caressed the cub's face as she hummed softly. Innocence looked sad and forlorn. God feels sorry for her. God goes up to her and says, "Innocence, I am going to create a

5

companion for you. He will be big, strong and handsome. He may even be intelligent. He will cater for all your physical and emotional needs and desires, and will help with looking after this beautiful world I have created for you ... Innocence interrupts, "How soon can I have this thing . . . I mean, this companion?"

"Soon. But you get nothing for nothing in my world. He will cost you an arm and a leg."

Innocence ponders briefly, then turns to God and says, "That's too much. You only gave me two of each." Pointing to her chest, she says, "What about the ribs? I've got plenty of these. What can I have for the price of a rib?"

"The rest is history, as they say. You see my point, Michael? All Holy books were written by men, and they reflect their culture, habits, politics, and their personal take on life, based upon their extremely limited knowledge of the world."

"I bet you pinched that joke from somewhere. Come on, be honest," I said. Nicky winked cheekily and turned her attention to the food on her plate.

Michael turned to me. "Mark tells me you are an atheist. Is that right?" He looked at me with derision in his eyes.

I said I was not keen about 'ists' and 'isms'. "I am just 'me'. To me, God is the Spiritual Mystery that unites all existence. 'Isms' and 'Ists', by their very definition, are there to cause divisions. What? Who? or, Where? It is, I know no more than anyone else. A theist's God is an old man who lives on the top floor of a three-storey universe. All his creatures live on the ground floor, and all those whom God does not like, burn alive eternally in the basement with their friend, the Satan."

Michael asked quite angrily, "from our conversation over the past two days, I am assuming that you don't believe that Bible is the Word of God. You don't believe in Trinity, either. You don't believe that Jesus is the incarnation of God. Then what is it that you believe?"

"Those who invaded other peoples' lands. Destroyed many ancient cultures, forced the poor populations into subjugation. Bought and sold humans as slaves. Forcibly took their children away from them and put them in institutions for the pleasure of the Invaders. Wiped out their languages and dialects by forcing them to speak only the language of the invader. Committed cultural and physical genocides. Stole their natural resources to build cities and palaces for themselves. They were all Trinitarians. They seriously believed that their ancient folklores and legends were the 'Word of God'. They took pride in making the 'Son of God' do their bidding. The one thing they did not do, was, that did not take any notice of the young man of Nazareth, and paid no regard to what he wanted."

Michael looked at me with pitiful eyes. "I feel sorry for you, Nihal". I thanked him for his concern.

"I must also thank you", I said, "for spurring me on to complete a project that I've been procrastinating about for years. As soon as I get back to England, I will seriously get on with it."

Nicky asked me, "Any hints about what your long-awaited project is going to be?"

"I'll tell you it is finished"

We finished our dinner. Moved into the foyer. There we joined with some other 'holiday friends. Played a few games of cards and scrabble. Few minutes past midnight, we said, 'Goodnight' and shuffled in the direction of our rooms. On the way to my room, a cool whiff of breeze from the ocean gently ruffled my hair and whispered 'Sweet dreams' in my ear.

Chapter 1

The Surplus Child

The Tunisian Inquisition did finally help me to overcome my 'writer's block' and the curse of procrastination. Please join me on what I hope will be an interesting journey through some breathtakingly beautiful landscapes of the physical and the non-physical worlds. Some folklores from the ancient cultures, and a journey that may free us, to be who or what we are meant to be. Along the way, we will hopefully connect with the unfathomable mysteries all around us. We may have a few hair-raising, and some tearful, moments I suspect. A few laughs as well, I hope.

Most memories from before my seventh birthday faded away at the point of my father's death which happened under tragic circumstances. With your permission, may I start this project with the few memories that frequently resurface?

Let us start with this one: 22 May 1945 was a sunny Sunday afternoon in Dabi, and I was four years, ten months, and fourteen days old.

Our small plot of land, in the middle of nowhere, was surrounded by thick forests on three sides, and a sheer cliff to the front. The place came to be known as Dabi because of the shape of the first of the two houses built on the site towards the tail end of the nineteenth century. It was a large, square house. From the distant villages, it looked like a box. Box in the local language is 'Dabi' hence the name.

The three grown-up paid helpers of my parents (I don't like the word 'servants') were a mile or so away in the woods of Saroga, to the south of Dabi, gathering fodder for the animals, firewood, dry pine leaves, and whatever else people gathered from the forest in that part of the world, at that time of the year. Shankru, a young helper and I, had been instructed to stay away from the house at a safe distance. Under no circumstance was anyone to enter the house until invited by the old lady, who was presumably attending to Mother's needs inside the house. Shankru did gladly as instructed. I obeyed under protest. We made our way to one of the four large ancient apple trees on site. By the way, this apple tree had nothing to do with the downfall of the human race.

Shankru was seven years older than me, and along with some other members of his family, worked for my parents in various roles. He climbed a couple of yards up the leaning trunk and sat himself down, facing the sun. I followed him and sat down about two feet below him. Shankru took out his packed brunch, which consisted of four small pieces of dry-ish curried potatoes wrapped inside two dry *rotis* (like Mexican tortillas). I guessed his brunch was saved over from the previous night's meal. All mothers were heard telling their children that eating a little less at the evening meal than you desired, kept a person fit and well. It was, of course, a ruse to make the evening meal last into the next day.

Shankru was looking for distractions to keep my mind away from whatever was happening inside the house. He tried to teach me a ballad about the tragic death of a local boy who had been mauled to death by a bear some months before, not far from where we were sitting. After a few failed attempts, I gave up. "OK! Let us try something different," Shankru said hopefully. "We'll listen to the *lamans* people are singing in the woods of Saroga and see if we can identify the singers."

'*Lamans*'? Let me explain. From early spring, right through to the end of autumn, people from the villages took their cattle, sheep, and goats out to graze in the woods. While there, they gathered firewood, grass, dead pine needles, mushrooms of all sorts, and herbal flowers. Pine needles were used to cover cattle shed floors to keep the animals warm and dry. The mixture of cow dung and pine needles was eventually turned into compost for the land. Dry pine needles also came in handy as packing material for fruits.

While going about their chores, the men and women sang *lamans* (ad-libbed eight-liners), sung as solos or duets to only two or three set tunes. In a *laman*, a question, a riddle, or a message was sent out in the hope of attracting a reply from someone in other parts of the forest. Invariably, a reply would come back and thus the sequence of questions and answers, riddles, jokes, and sometimes romantic messages were exchanged all day long. On rare occasions, the *lamans* led to romance and even marriage. Or the breakup of one, depending on the sender and the receiver of the message, of course!

In those days, all the jobs in and around the house, including the fetching of firewood, hay, water, tending to the needs of the family and animals, were generally shared fairly between all genders – we knew of only two genders. There was a significant minority of men though, who did only the 'man's jobs', and only then if assisted by their women folk.

To be fair to the latter category of men, they did not always sit around the house doing nothing. They dutifully visited the nearest shops, most days of the year. Between the hours of late morning and early evening, they sat on the floors of the shop fronts in small groups, gossiping, smoking *hucka* (hubble-bubble), cigarettes, *beedis,* and some other mind-numbing stuff. They played cards and chess for hours on end. This second category of men saw the men in the first category, as *joru ke ghulaam* (slaves to their wives).

On the day in review, father and the three eldest of my siblings, Rup Chand, Vidya and Prabha were away from home. The other two, immediately above me, Pushpa and Khushal, were at school. Not having much success in identifying the *laman* singers, I decided to get up the tree to where Shankru was sitting. A spindly branch was determinedly obstructing my progress. At the third attempt, the branch pushed me off the tree, four/five feet below, onto the soft, grassy earth. I landed with a thud. While I lay there, debating between throwing a tantrum or ignoring the few minor bruises I might have sustained, we heard the noises we had been dreading all morning: two loud screams from Mother, followed by screechy noises that resembled the cries of an angry baby monkey.

Mother had given birth to her seventh and last child. At that moment I experienced something in my innermost being. Something that still pops up occasionally into the conscious mind at odd moments in my life – a weird sense of being an extra, an outsider.

The mental video of that Sunday afternoon in my head shows that: I jumped up off the ground, shook the bits of dust and grass off my clothes and said something to Shankru. Later that day, I heard him telling Mother, and everyone else within his hearing, that what I had said to him was, "Shankru, please get me my school bag!"

"Why? What for?" Shankru asked in surprise.

"Because I want to go to school!" My right arm at full stretch, the index finger at the end of which, he said, was pointing in the direction from whence the screams had emanated. I cried, "She won't want me now. She has got a new one! Come on, let us go." I was said to have reasoned quite decisively. They all made it sound funnier than it could possibly have been in its original script. To my embarrassment, the tale was repeated all the way into my teenage years, and a few times since.

Here is another one: It must be somewhere close to my sixth birthday. Father arrives home on an overcast, warm late morning. So, it must have been summertime. He is accompanied by a young man in his twenties. The young man is wearing a colourful *Bushehri* cap, a clean, white *khaddar* shirt under a home-spun and home-stitched long woollen coat, and a woolly *churhidar suthan* (looks like Jodhpurs). I cannot recall seeing any shoes on his feet. He is carrying a military-style heavy rucksack on his back. My father has an enormous bag hanging from his left shoulder. Father says that the two of them had set off from Narkanda (eleven miles to the south-west of Dabi), about seven o'clock that morning. Both men look and sound tired as they put their bags down on the veranda. There is no hugging and kissing between my parents. Physical contact in public was not a done thing. Public show of romance and tenderness were 'spit-spit, gooey, mushy' luxuries, that no respectable couple in our part of the world had ever been seen to indulge in – not in public, anyway.

Washed and freshened, both men are served platefuls of fried rice with cumin seeds and onion strips, lentils, vegetable curry, chapatis, and fresh salad, accompanied by a large brass tumbler of water each, on the shady veranda. When the young man is finished, Mama goes over and gives him some money, and thanks him for accompanying father on his journey. She asks him if he would like to stay the night. He says some polite words in return, which I cannot hear, and begs leave to return home. After another tumbler of tea, Mother asks Shankru to pick some ripe peaches and apricots to give to the young man for the long journey back home. He makes some overly exaggerated gestures of gratitude for the fruits, and we all bid him a cheerful farewell. Funny! I could recognise him anywhere, even after all these years.

The young man leaves, and mother gets on with the eagerly awaited task of unpacking the bags. The rucksack is full of dirty washing and some items for domestic use, including packets of fancy bars of soap and father's cigarette packets. What I am concentrating on clearly are the two large, oval-shaped tin boxes that come out of Papa's shoulder bag. The boxes have fancy-coloured pictures all over. The first box mother opens, has sweets of unusual shapes and colours. The second box has a variety of neatly packed biscuits. Those luxuries we saw only whenever Papa visited us from wherever he was based at work. We resented being required to share those sweets with the children of our paid helpers.

Here is one more:

A day or two after Papa's return with the sweet goodies, the time is about half past five on a crisp summer's morning. Everyone in Dabi is out of bed. The sun is winking from the top of the Praying Mountains. Papa is standing under an apple tree, where only a few years before the 'Dabi' house had clung onto the rock face. Khushal and I are summoned to join him. He picks two apples from under the tree, wipes them on a clean hand towel, and gives one to each of us. "Take small bites, chew it properly, and roll it round in your mouth at the same time. Do not swallow, spit it out and then repeat the exercise until the apple is finished." Then adds, "Don't do it near the house." We follow unsuccessfully. More giggles and shrieks of laughter than chewing and spitting. Once we finished the apples, Papa tells us to repeat the exercise if ever we run out of toothpowder in the future – most of our tooth powders were homemade, anyway. "Soon you will be perfect. Now, hurry up, go get a towel each and a bar of soap from the house. We will go to the spring in Khlawan and have a cold shower. That'll wake you up." He smiles as if that was the funniest thing he ever said in his whole life.

Khushal and I make eye contact. We are thinking, we have heard of, and even seen, some people indulging in this kind of madness, but we have never imagined doing it ourselves, especially not at this unearthly hour of the morning. We run into the house and gather the items as instructed. Papa gestures for us to follow him. Khushal and I jog along to keep up with him.

At the spring, all three of us undress, but Papa keeps his underpants on. I cannot recall any signs of protest from either of us for being stripped naked in a breezy, shady part of the earth, with temperatures not far from zero degrees. Papa suggests for us to sing out loud, as we splash icy cold water over our goose-pimpled bodies and pass the bar of Lifebuoy soap around. We watch father sideways, curious to see how he would wash himself inside his pants. We try to sing anything we can think of, but our lips are wearily clapping nineteen to the dozen under our runny noses – even the snot trickling out of our nostrils feels like icicles. We gig-gg-le, we try to siss-ii-ii-ng, but the cold appears to have frozen the 'think' cells. Finally, soaped and rinsed, father rubs us down with the towels, first me, then Khushal, and finally himself.

After we put our clothes back on, we head back, waving our wet towels in the air, siss-ii-ii-ng, jogging, and g-gig-gg-ling all the way home. I clearly remember getting back home to a hot cup of tea, sweetened with fresh honey, to help defreeze our bodies. I can still taste the fresh breakfast: hot *Prantthas* (fried roti) with a spicy dish of potatoes and onions and a big dollop of homemade yoghurt on the side.

Mention of summer conjures up another picture in my mind. In summer months, mainly in June, the one thing we all hate is when God breaks wind. For some weird reason, before God does that, lots of bright lights dance through the clouds above our heads with mesmerising speed followed by a huge bang, which seems to go on and on, scaring the children, cats, dogs, and other animals out of their wits! Luckily for us, the thunder is not followed by the pong, like that of some humans we know.

The granddad of one of my friends from the village behind the pine trees, once told him that the lights flashing in the clouds before the thunder are caused by the swords and the arrows of the gods and the demons fighting over who can get closest to the throne of God. And God breaks wind with a thunder, to scare them away.

The noise is at its scariest when we happen to be indoors, especially at night, because then we cannot see the lights dancing through the clouds, and the thunder comes out of nowhere. The thought that with all that thunder and strong winds, the thrones of both God and Jesus could come crashing down from heaven onto our little house and crush us all into the ground like red meat chutney, has given me many a sleepless night.

Another interesting thing: I once heard Pushpa and Khushal wondering why there are only two thrones in heaven. "Shouldn't there be three?" said Pushpa.

"Yeah, I meant to ask Mama the other day why there isn't a throne for the Holy Ghost in heaven? What does she sit on?" said Khushal. I cannot recall if we ever found the answer to their question. Did they ask Mother or the *Padre* sahib? I doubt. Children were not permitted to ask silly questions like that.

Where was I, oh yes; The breaking of wind by God is usually followed by hailstorms. I think it is either Narsi, or Rasmu from the village behind the trees, who has told Khushal that the hailstorms are actually ice pebbles that the angels use for playing the 'Pebble Games'. Since there are no stones and therefore no stone pebbles in heaven, the angels use ice pebbles. When they are playing the Pebble Games and they suddenly hear the loud thunder, the little angels jump up in shock, and run helter-skelter. In the process, they drop the pebbles. It is those pebbles, that come hurtling down as hailstorms, on to the earth.

The larger ones of those ice pebbles (Ole) can easily be the size of large apricots, with pointed ends. It may be harmless play to God and his angels but to us humans, those pebbles are a curse. They damage our fruit crops and let me tell you, those little things can hurt, especially on the end of your nose, ear lobes and back of your hands. Everyone with a long nose and/or big ears is advised, the moment they hear God breaking wind, they should get under some shelter.

Another bulb has just lit up in my head: I see all four children and Shankru in Dabi sitting on the veranda, waiting to be called in for morning prayers and breakfast, before Pushpa and Khushal leave for school. Shankru asks Pushpa, pointing to the mountains directly facing us in the east, "What's on the other side of those snow-clad Praying Mountains?" She says, "It is the land of our strong and rugged Tibetan neighbours, and beyond that, the Lake Mansrover, from whence comes our own river, Satluj, down there." She points to the river clearly visible from where we are sitting. "Beyond that," she continues with genuine disappointment in her voice, "is the magic land of China." "If only the Praying Mountains were not where God has put them," complains Khushal in frustration, "we could've seen, not only Tibet and China, but many other beautiful and wonderful lands far beyond." Khushal sounds like he knows what he is talking about. "God is a real spoilsport sometimes I think," says Pushpa. "Yeah! He didn't have to put those mountains there," add Khushal and Shankru. I agree with them. Anup, baby of the family is happily cooing at us in his rocking cradle. Pushpa warns us not to express our opinions about God within the hearing of Mama. With a finger to her lips, she cautions us in whispers, "You know, Mama does not like us being disrespectful towards God." We never say anything on the subject openly in case God or Mama hear us.

My father
Paul F Chaudhry
1900 -1947

My mother
Rup Devi Chaudhry
1908-1984

Chapter 2

The Cliff Hanger

Originally, there were two houses in Dabi: one large, two-storey square house, and a smaller two-room bungalow with a reasonably sized attic. A small Cow shed was attached to the north side of the bungalow. The foundations of both Dabi houses measured 7,020 feet above sea level. Rocks, rising at angles of between 85 and 90 degrees from the narrow ravine directly below, extended about 2,500–3,000 feet up, frighteningly close to the foundations of the two houses. In 1937, a landslide along its eastern boundary caused serious damage to the structure of the larger house. The family moved out into the smaller house, a hundred yards away to the north of the larger one. Sometime after that, the 'Dabi' house was demolished.

The forest that surrounded the small plot of land in Dabi on three sides, consisted of mainly tall pine and spruce trees, with a scattering of mountain oaks. There were also some rhododendrons, and smidgen of other varieties of trees for miles. To the front of the houses was the steep rocky cliff; sparsely wooded and generously covered over with a variety of shrubs and bushes to meet the needs of all life forms. Twelve months of the year, the snow-clad mountains facing the house in the east, looked down upon us with an icy-cold grimace. I cannot recall a time, when at some point between the latter part of December and mid-March, we did not have more than just one snowfall round the place. Not infrequently, the snowfall would easily be three to four feet deep.

I must have been nine years old when we recorded snow at six feet deep around our house. Lately though, the climate change and the introduction of 'civilisation' and 'progress' in those hills, has changed the scenery, the social structures, and even our culture beyond recognition. I would love for the 'There is No Global Warming' lobby to explain to me why, in the past twenty or so years, there has been little, or no snow fall on top of my Praying Mountains between the months of May and November?

Every spring, rhododendrons, laden with large crimson red flowers, made even the darker parts of the forest utterly desirable, at least to us kids. We loved to chew the juicy, sweet-and-sour petals of those flowers. Due to their close proximity to the festival, we also called rhododendron, the Easter flower. I recall us using them at Easter for decorating the front of our house and the church. The rhododendrons also helped to save the lives of many local children from severe dysentery during the summer months.

During the rhododendron season, we picked a few ripe and juicy flowers which Mama then dried in the shade. Once dry and crisp, she added them to equal measures of sugar and lightly roasted cumin seeds. With a pestle and mortar, the mixture was ground into powder. Parents were advised to administer the powder, in a three-finger pinch at a time, onto the child's tongue.

Mama had learned the recipe, I believe, from a Gurkha by the name of Chchanu. He, along with his wife and two sons, worked for our family before my time. He had been, in his words, 'a trusted house manager' and a 'good cook' of Rupi jee for many years, until a physical injury forced his untimely retirement.

When I was about eight years old, my friends let me into a secret. They had overheard some wise elders in the shopping village of Thanedhar say that anyone living a blameless life could see, from Dabi, the abode of the gods and the goddesses, and of the fairies in the white mountains. On another occasion, the same friends had heard the wise old men talking about those divine creatures. They said that the fairies, and even the ghosts had been known to stray uncomfortably close at times to where humans lived.

When we were little, we witnessed the goddesses and the fairies doing their evening dance for the gods on top of the snow mountain. "Some people don't believe us," said my sister, Pushpa. "We don't care," Khushal and I protested in unison, "we know they are real!" Khushal added that he had heard Mama say to some city folks once that the people in our mountains knew things that even the cleverest people in the outside world knew nothing about.

In our hills, people adhered strictly to the customs and traditions of their ancestors. One of those traditions forbade people from going unaccompanied into the woods. For there were ghosts that lived in the remote, thick woods. The ghosts didn't kill a person by chopping them up or by strangling and beating them up with lumps of wood or stone. No! "They played tricks on them," we were told. The most popular trick was, that when a person was lost in the woods and started to look around for a way out, the ghosts would lead the person round and round in circles. The person would be tricked into going deeper and deeper into the woods. Eventually, the person died of fear and fatigue, and the naughty ghosts took the soul away before God's angels could reach it.

Whenever we asked the grown-ups, "How do you

know what killed the person, since the person was already dead and couldn't have told anyone how they died?" The grown-ups would answer, "Because we know!" So, my friend Thisu and I decided, "When we are old enough to go deeper into the woods, then we will find out, if the grown-ups have been telling the truth."

Before my parents moved to Dabi during the third decade of the twentieth century, the larger house had been used exclusively by an American immigrant, a friend of Mr Satyanand Stokes. He was professor of something – no one ever mentioned the subject – in St John's College, in the city of Taj Mahal. Occasionally, the professor would be accompanied by small groups of friends and students from the college, escaping the searing heat of Agra. That was why the 'Dabi' was larger than a normal family house, in that part of the world.

One late afternoon, Nirmu, an elderly widow of indeterminable age, who lived half a mile away near the shopping village of Thanedhar, was talking with Mother about the American professor. "He was a shameless Angrez." (In India, all peoples of European descent with fair/pale skin, are referred to as 'Angrez'). She continued in a hush-hush voice and deeply embarrassed physical expressions, "he used to lie stark naked in the sun on the other side of that apricot tree, there." She underlined her disgust by stabbing her left index finger in the direction of the tree. "He pretended to be hidden from our view, but he knew we could see him. Passing by here, on our way to the forest every morning, we had to look the other way." She reinforced her sense of embarrassment by pulling down her *dhatu* over her face, looking away, as if he were still there lying naked under the tree.

Khushal and I, while seemingly engrossed in tending to the needs of our dozen or so week-old chicks, overheard every word of her comments, and were not convinced – not in the least – by her play on modesty. We tried to picture the scene, in purely childlike innocence, mind you. We knew a thing or two about the birds and the bees but had little or no idea of what they got up to when wc weren't looking.

In our lonely Dabi, even more lonely since the death of our father, Nirmu became a regular visitor and a trusted companion to our mother. She lived with her grandson in one of the servants' quarters attached to the old British Rest House in Thanedhar. She had adopted him when he was only a toddler. The grandson, Mushu, meaning 'mouse' in the local dialect, was about my age. Nirmu had moved into the area from some far away village and worked as a general cleaner at the Rest House. She had no immediate neighbours of the caste she belonged to in our small world. That made it impossible for her grandson to attract playmates from where they lived.

At our first meeting outside my house, the thought of Mushu's caste held me back from wanting to make friends with him. Mother argued that despite her low caste, Nirmu was much cleaner than some of the high caste people in our neck of the woods. "Can't you see for yourself how clean both are? Mushu always looks cleaner and smarter than the children of that Brahmin priest; you know the one I mean."

I let her think that she had convinced me. However, between the years of eight and thirteen, Mushu and I did spend some play time together. Despite her convictions to the contrary, Mother could not allow Nirmu and her grandson any further into the house than our veranda on the ground floor. According to the culture of India at the time, even that was too far over the line. Technically, we should not have allowed even the shadow of either of them to touch our house or our person. After the Independence of India, Gandhi and Nehru did make some serious and partially successful attempts to remove the stigma and practice of discrimination on the grounds of one's caste. Sadly, in the recent years, due to the resurgence of religious fervour in India, the controversies associated with caste and religion are threatening a comeback into the main society.

Houses all around us were generally small: 'two-up, two-down', and some 'two-room' bungalows. In order to keep the inside warm, the houses were built from locally quarried stone, in the double-wall method of construction. Every four to five feet up the wall, wooden beams in twos were placed side by side, all along the top of the walls. The beams were then joined by dovetail joints to bind the four corners of the house securely. Both inside and out, the walls were then filled in and plastered with a thick mixture of clay, some hay and *moonji* (a strong, stringy variety of grass). A final thin layer of plaster on the walls consisted of pure clay. The walls were finally decorated by splashing over with a weak mixture of a glossy clay, found in small deposits deep in the earth, in only half a dozen known sites in the woods.

Animals, such as cattle, sheep, and goats were housed on the ground floor. Cats and dogs, if any, usually shared the accommodation with humans on the first floor. The kitchen would normally be in the attic. This facilitated the escape of smoke from the open hearth through the gaps in the slated roof. It also helped to protect the cooking area and food from both the wild and the domestic creatures. The central heating system was supplied from the heat produced by the animals on the ground floor, reaching into the upper floor through the cracks between the floorboards. Combined with that, was the heat produced by the human inhabitants and domestic animals in the upstairs rooms, round the hearth and in beds. There were a minimum number of back-breaking low doors in the house and no more than one small window with wooden shutters in each room. That kept the cold winds out and the natural heat in.

Low doors and only one or two small windows in the walls proved highly useful during the Anglo-Nepalese war, which was started on 19 January 1814, by the colonial masters, in the hope of adding Nepal to their list of conquests. The local inhabitants' version of that war is obviously somewhat different from the version that the British historians would have written. The incursion of the British into Nepal was like poking a hornet's nest. Except, that the pain of the stings was borne wholly by the under-resourced Nepalese Army, and the poor people of Nepal. People on the north-western boarder of India (now known as Himachal Pradesh), close to Nepal, suffered the effects of the fallout.

There are many tales of heroism and ingenuity about both men and women, in the way they protected their homes and families from the tough Gurkha gorillas, at the time. Two of the many tales told to me by my two senior friends, Rasmu and Narsi, respectively, may help to illustrate the picture.

Rasmu was from Khlawn, the small village, less than half a mile away across the stream, hidden from our view by the tall pine trees. His story was that in a small village of five or six houses, not far from Dabi, a young mother was on her own with her two small children in the house. Everyone else was away at a wedding in the next village. Attending to chores around the house, she observed two men lurking in the nearby bushes. The woman rushed in and bolted the door from the inside. She filled a large pan with water, added a little cooking oil to it, and put the pan on the front burner. Through a narrow crack in the shutters of the only window in the room, she could see the two men crawling closer to the front door, each armed with a sword. Just as the water in the pan reached boiling point, she called out to them through the crack in the window. "I am all alone in the house with my two small babies. I am no threat to you. Come in and have something to eat and anything else you want from me. Then please leave me and my children alone." With that, she unbolted the door.

The men wasted no time on ceremonies. First one crawled in. Not wanting to miss out on the fun inside, his companion followed hastily. Before they had time to sit upright and adjust their eyes to the darkness on the inside of that little space, the woman took the pan of boiling mixture and poured it over the two of them. As they writhed in pain, she took the sword the first man had dropped on the floor and killed them both.

The second incident is equally as blood curdling but more dramatic than the first. This tale, as the one above, is un-researched but corroborated by more than one of my senior friends from the village behind the tall pine trees, was narrated to me by Narsi during one of our regular sittings in his sunny conservatory.

Narsi was a tailor from the same village as Rasmu. Some members of his family had worked for my parents from time to time in their previous lives, but since our father's death, they were all far better off than us. His family had recently purchased a small plot of woodland along the northern boundary of our land. About a furlong away from our place, he built a house on the sunniest spot in that shady part of our world. Compared to my shaded, cold veranda, and constant demands for chores from inside the kitchen, Narsi's place, with the afternoon sun hanging over it for much longer than it did over our place, was a cosey little haven in the bleak mid-winters of Dabi. Most winter weekend afternoons, I would escape to Narsi's place on some well-constructed pretext.

One icy, sunny afternoon in early March of 1953, I was sitting in Narsi's conservatory. As usual, he was busy sewing garments on his Singer machine for the forthcoming second or third wedding of one or the other of his relatives. The sun was dangling from a large patch of blue sky above the heads of tall pine trees and smiling in on us through a large, glazed window to my left. Narsi and I were engrossed in exchanging bits and pieces of local gossip. That, in a roundabout way, led to Narsi recalling another one of his battle stories between the Gurkhas and the locals, from the 'bad old days'. This one came from a village near Delatth, I think. Delatth is an insignificant tiny principality in Bushehar, halfway between our front door and the white mountains in the east. Narsi narrated the tale of the famous battle thus:

Long time ago, one fateful day, young lookouts from the village at the top of the hill reported seeing some Gurkhas hiding along the riverbank, more than a mile below. The steep rocky hill, leading up to the village, was sparsely covered with short grass and other low vegetation. The invaders had to stay put until darkness covered their approach up the hillside. After considering the report, the elders instructed every able-bodied man to cut down some smaller pine and spruce trees from around the village. The felled trees were then sawn into manageable sized logs. The women and children, in the meantime, were instructed to dig out every rope in the village and, if necessary, to make more ropes from *moonji* and any other suitable material they could lay their hands on. Everyone followed the instructions to the letter.

Once the logs and the ropes were ready, women and children shut themselves in their homes. The men busied themselves by placing the logs horizontally over the sloping land. Each log was then firmly secured to trees, bushes, and rocks by the ropes. Sounds of felling trees, and all other activities in the village above did not reach the ears of the invaders due to the noise of the fast-flowing river.

As soon as the daylight started to slip into the evening dusk, and shadows of impending darkness covered the hillside, the invaders began their ascent. When the village spies saw the Gurkhas halfway up the hill, they started cutting the ropes that secured the logs to the hillside. The invaders on their way up met the rolling logs and the accompanying debris, on their way down.

"The invaders were annihilated off the face of the earth. Not a single one of them survived," said Narsi, with a tinge of pride in his voice, as if he had been one of the villagers, cutting the ropes.

It was a triumph for the ingenuity of the villagers. According to Narsi, later endorsed by two other elders, that terrible battle became the last known encounter between the Gurkhas and the local people. I wanted to know what happened to the bodies of the dead Gurkhas. As far as Narsi could recall, they were all cremated 'respectfully' in the following two days.

I am glad to add that the brief, bitter past does not, in any way affect the present relations between us and the '*Bahadurs*' (braves) from Nepal. We take them for who they are, respected the world over for their honesty, hard work, and bravery.

As I was saying, our new home was 'safer', that is, until the monsoons of 1947. That year, the August monsoons rained non-stop for six days and six nights. We had started conjuring up pictures of Noah's boat sailing past our house any moment. On the fourth morning of the downpour, Mother and one of our helpers discovered a narrow crack in the earth, less than four feet from the front foundation of the house. The crack ran along the whole length of our 'new, safe' home. With her customary precision and clarity of purpose, Mother immediately arranged to temporarily evacuate the family to the home of a friend, half a mile away. The friend's house was large enough to accommodate our family, and it was built upon surer foundations, away from the edge of a precipice.

Every morning, Mother and Pushpa returned to the house to check on the cows and calves, the dogs, the cat, and the chickens. After attending to the essential chores around the place, they returned to join Khushal, Anup and I, in the safety of the friend's home for the night. The rains stopped two days after we moved out of our 'unsafe' house. A few days after that, Mother assured us that the crack along the front of the house had settled back, and therefore there was no imminent danger of us losing our second home down the rock face. I don't think we believed her. More significantly, neither do I recall the over-stretched family of our friends expressing any concerns for our safety. We duly returned home.

The day after our return to the still 'unsafe' home, we received the news that during our absence from Dabi, God or somebody had pulled the rug from under our feet. Our world had been reduced to rubble. Our mother's husband and our father were no more. He had been buried in Shimla cemetery four days earlier, they said. I don't know what the others thought but I knew he would come back home one day. For a whole year after that news, Mother continued to cook his favourite meals on the days of his regular visits from Theog.

part of Anup's house in Dabi

Chapter 3

Shameless Swingers and the Wily Hunters

One sure penalty for living in a house that clings to a rock face with the skin of its foundation teeth, is that no sane human wants to be your neighbour. Hence, we had no neighbours in Dabi. In daylight hours we had the company of two, sometimes three, individuals, usually from the village behind the pine trees, only because they worked for my parents, but after father's death, we could not afford the luxury of 'paid helpers'. During daytime, from the start of spring to the end of autumn, there was a regular trickle of people and animals from the villages behind the forest to the north and west of us.

Between the months of October and March each year, we would occasionally find ourselves welcoming complete strangers into our home for an unexpected sleepover. These were people, unfamiliar with the terrain, travelling east towards Rampore Bushair and beyond, in the direction of Tibet. At the point of late evenings, while there was still daylight in Thanedhar, they would continue on their way. Less than half a mile from Thanedhar, they turned the sharp right-hand bend in the road, about a furlong before reaching Dabi. Here, they would find themselves staring at the two-mile stretch of road, winding through the thick, dark forest before them.

Consequently, we would hear someone calling from the road above the house, requesting if we could see our way to offering a stranger shelter for the night. I can't recall us ever saying "no" to anyone. Untouched by 'modern civilisation', one thought nothing of providing a meal and a bed to a stranger for the night.

Village Khlawn, hidden behind the tall pine trees and across the stream from us, was about five hundred feet higher than Dabi. Whenever we needed, or wanted to interact with someone in the village, all we had to do was go to the upstairs window that opened in the direction of the village. Or go up onto the road, a mere hundred yards above the house, raise the volume of our voice, and have a hearty conversation, missing hardly a word.

The other living beings with whom we held regular conversations, were the domestic animals. Usually, a couple of cows in milk and their calves, one or two dogs, and never more than one cat. Occasionally, we would have a lamb or two being fattened for the winter supply of meat. Mother also kept plenty of hens, chicks, and cockerels, of course, for a regular supply of eggs and meat. All these were our permanent close companions.

On the wild side of life in Dabi, we had the monkeys, leopards, bears, foxes, wild cats, jackals, mongoose, rats, snakes, lizards, and some other members of the animal world that will remain nameless until I can find a charger for my last brain cell.

There were also birds of many varieties – some hunters, and some hunted. They enriched our lives with amazement, curiosity, entertainment, and frequent occasions to question God's love and sense of justice. I remember once being sent to bed on an empty stomach for daring to ask, "If God loves all the animals, then why does he allow leopards and lions to kill all the other animals? And ... and, if God loves all the birds, then why did he create the eagles and the kestrels that kill the smaller birds?"

Monkeys were the most troublesome visitors. They attacked every form of vegetation, as well as the sparsely planted fruit trees on our unfenced and unkempt plot of land. I was given to understand that during my father's time it was not necessary for us to find income from the land. He appeared to have provided reasonably well for his family in his short life.

Any significant information about my father's life came my way mainly via occasional references to him, or to our former way of life by some of his friends and acquaintances, and a small number of local men who believed that he had helped them in some way to better their lives. I cannot recall Mother ever speaking about my father to us, other than occasional passing comment about his extravagances. At other times, she expressed her frustrations with him in no more than a brief sentence or two for not having heeded her advice. Mother did not want him to take on the last venture, which she firmly believed to be the main cause of his absence from our lives, and our slide into frightening poverty. Nevertheless, she taught us many of the hymns, lyrics and *ghazals* that father had composed over the years. She appeared to take unspoken pride in his poetic and musical abilities, and indirectly expressed her admiration for his generous nature. Other than that, she said little or nothing about him, and all for good reason as I was to discover with the passing of time.

Monkeys required constant watching and chasing away from what we considered to be 'our land'. The monkeys had a different take on the matter. To them, it was, and is to this day, 'their land'. For they know they were there long before humans suddenly appeared on this earth. To be fair to my own race, monkeys ought to have shown some gratitude though; we did add significant varieties of fruits and vegetables to their boring diet of mushrooms, roots, and berries.

At night, they bedded in trees and in cracks and crannies in the rock face below us. At daybreak, they would swing their way in the direction of Dabi and leisurely walk onto our little plot to feast on our hard labour, our joys and our hopes. Everyone in Dabi spent much of their valuable time chasing the shameless and ungrateful swingers away, only for them to come back with reinforcements within minutes. Thus, the battle continued, hour after hour, day after day, week after week, and month after month, from April Fool's Day to the end of October each year.

After our father's absence from our lives, Khushal, Anup and I didn't always mind the presence of monkeys, all that much. Along with some other herbivores in the forests, the monkeys provided relief from the constant sense of isolation, and the drudgery of chores. They also added to our sadistic forms of entertainment. Chasing those troublesome 'ancestors' of ours into the trees, and then using them as targets for the slings and arrows that we had designed and crafted with our own hands from local materials, were among the highlights of our adventures. Fortunately for the monkeys, our projectiles hardly ever got close enough to do them any harm.

Another plus of having monkeys for neighbours, was that in moments of lethargy they forced us to get up and get out there. Kept us fit. The monkeys also provided us with the opportunity to stay outdoors and away from the house. Out there, we beat some old kerosene canister with sticks. Monkeys took little notice, but the din thus caused, prevented the constant barrage of orders to "do this" and to "fetch that" and "don't make that horrible noise all day" from reaching our ears.

From time to time, leopards made their presence known in Dabi, by trying to break into the cattle shed, the chicken coop, or the doghouse. On average, half a dozen times a year, we would be awakened in the middle of the night by some determined leopard trying to gain access to its dinner in one of the three places. The presence of a hungry leopard outside the house, in the middle of the night, or the early hours of the morning, could be worrying. Especially so when there was no man in the house. During the two years plus, between the death of our father and the homecoming of our eldest brother, there were only Mother, Pushpa, Khushal, little Anup and I in the house. Those were the scariest years of our lives.

One summer's afternoon, our dog Deeurhi was on her walkabouts in a nearby village. She grabbed a carpenter's lunch from his workbench. As she was running away with her prize, the carpenter threw a sharp tool after her, and nearly severed her hind leg from the rest of her body. She arrived home in a terrible state. Over the following days, Mother tried painstakingly to join the lower half of her leg back onto the upper half. We could not allow her four little pups anywhere near her. Fortunately, they were past the age of suckling. For the night-time, we built a makeshift shelter for her, immediately outside the door to the cow shed, wherein her puppies were housed for the night.

I must have been about nine or ten at the time. It was a warm, starry evening. A full moon was staring down onto our house from the clear blue skies, and the Banshiras were swinging away in the trees. Suddenly, Deeurhi's adopted brother in his doghouse went berserk. Mother said, "It must be the leopard come for our Deeurhi." She suggested that we children go downstairs to the window facing Deeurhi's shelter and make noises to scare the leopard away. We had hardly moved off from our seats when, out of the creepy stillness outside, we heard two screams from our convalescing bitch. First scream, as the leopard pounced upon her, and the second as it dragged her away, we guessed. Mother tried to console us by saying, "Thank God, the poor bitch is out of her misery."

That was my bitch that Mother's God had just put out of her misery, by offering her for the leopard's dinner. She was barely a month old when I had rescued her from outside a shop in Thanedhar. I shouted back angrily, "Shall we also thank God for leaving the little pups without their mother?"

"What do you mean?" Mother asked with a puzzled look in her brown eyes.

"Well!" I said, trying hard to hold my anger and tears back. "You are thanking God for letting the leopard take my dog; why not also thank him for depriving the puppies of their mother? And, while we are in the thanking mood, how about thanking the carpenter from nearly chopping my Deeurhi's leg off?" And I burst into uncontrollable sobs.

The all-round sense of grief and shock in the kitchen, helped to prevent her from coming back at me with another sermon about how I must never, ever speak disrespectfully of God. Or else!

Exactly ten nights after it had taken my Deeurhi, the leopard paid us another visit, close to midnight. We didn't have any time devices in our house, but we could tell the time within a few minutes, or maybe an hour or so either way, depending on the weather and time of the day or night. The leopard was pushing and scratching at the door to the cow shed. The pups were cooing and crying, assuming perhaps that the noises at the door were from their mother trying to get in. Their adopted uncle, Boris, was barking his head off from the safety of his enclosure, next door. The leopard concentrated on the softer targets: two cows, their two little calves, and the little pups.

First, we made some noises from within the comfort of our beds. Predictably, it took no notice. Eventually, we made our way to the window that overlooked the door to the cow shed. Fourteen-year-old Khushal, assuming the responsibility of 'the man of the house', pushed to the front of the queue. He opened one panel of the window a couple of inches wide, squeezed his mouth into the narrow opening, and shouted at the top of his voice. We all joined our voices to Khushal's, presented charivari with a selection of kitchen utensils, while Mother fiercely beat a cardboard box with a spoon. After a long minute, the leopard acknowledged our resolve against its persistence and moved away.

At other times, not far from the house, the leopards would lay in wait for hours, to get their evil teeth into one or the other of our animals, or a bird. We didn't always see them, but tended to infer their presence from various indicators, such as the urgency in the barking of a dog, suspicious clucking by the hens, or noises from the foxes, monkeys, and wild cats etc., in the vicinity.

I recall two occasions when I observed first-hand the hunting strategies and the wily tricks that the leopards employ to achieve their objective. The first one was on a September evening in 1952. We were all sitting outside on the veranda, enjoying the cool breeze at the end of a busy day in the fields. Our eldest brother, Rup Chand, or 'Rupbhai' as we called him, had inherited musical abilities from our parents, which, with the exception of Pushpa, were entirely absent in the rest of us. He played a few key instruments and his homemade flute. In the past forty years, people have become better off and 'civilised' and 'progressive'. The place has changed socially, culturally, economically, and in almost every other way possible. On a recent visit to my hills, I was more shocked than surprised to witness a very civilised and 'progressive' young man playing *dholak?* and flute at his own wedding.

On that night in September, two friends of Rupbhai, from Kotgarh, had dropped in for a sleepover. In our lonely Dabi, we loved having visitors. The visitors provided opportunity for exchange of gossip, a bit of a singsong, and a few games of cards, *Pachisi* or chess, lasting into the early hours of the morning.

On the evening I am referring to, Rupbhai was sitting in the corner of the veranda, reclining against the wall, playing the latest Bollywood film songs on his flute. The two guests and Pushpa were singing along and playing improvised drums. Mother and a young helper were in the kitchen preparing the evening meal. The two adult mongrels of mixed breed had been shut away for the night. Stretched out under Rupbhai's raised knees, was our latest pride and joy: a six-month-old jet-black Tibetan sheep dog, already as big as a fully grown mongrel. Suddenly, the pup flew out backwards into the air from under Rupbhai's knees. Before any of us could utter a sound, the dog was fifty yards away, past the chicken shed, hanging from the jaws of a leopard. Stunned by the speed and the nerve of the leopard, we remained frozen to the spot. By the time the event registered with us, it was too late to make rescue attempts. The leopard must have taken its time in working out its strategy for reaching the dog unnoticed.

The second example of the strategy and co-ordination that the leopards sometimes employ in preparation for a kill, comes from the summer of 1963. I was home from university on my summer break. We were the proud owners of two four-year-old mixed-breed dogs, at the time.

Evening shadows were touching the base of the eastern horizons. It was nearly time to be moving the dogs, birds, and ourselves indoors for the night. Mother and I were sitting on the veranda leisurely consuming some *chai-pani* (tea with light snacks). "Mama! Is that a leopard or a bush of dead fern down there next to the *Kamasharh* (Berberis/Thunburgii) bush?" I pointed to the spot.

Mama looked at the spot where my right index finger was pointing, and immediately confirmed my suspicions in hushed and concerned tones. Based upon the information we had about the leopards, we agreed to pretend that we were not at all aware of its presence. Probably too late, but no harm in hoping.

We hurriedly put our tea tumblers and snacks away. "You should know better than to point your finger at it. Please, go, find the dogs, and shut them securely in their shed. Don't forget to lock up the cow shed, and . . .", she whispered, "make sure there is sufficient water indoors to last the night." Mother then headed purposefully in the direction of the chicken shed. She picked up a large metal tray from the corner of the veranda and put a few handfuls of corn seeds into it from the bag. She stood near the entrance to the chicken coop, rattled the corns in the tray, and threw a handful into the inner enclosure. In seconds, all the birds were in. Mother shut the door behind them, as securely as possible. Living in those situations, one learns to be optimistic about everything in life.

In the meantime, I called the dogs down from the road.

Before I could get them into their shed, their ears perked up, noses up in the air – sniff, sniff. The beast saw them, rose tantalisingly to attract their attention. It succeeded. Against my frantic and urgent protestations and humble pleadings with the two usually very obedient animals, they charged towards it. They must have heard someone say that two large, healthy dogs can usually handle a leopard.

When the dogs were less than fifty yards from their target, the leopard turned round, and moved swiftly downhill. The two followed in pursuit. Unsuspectingly, from a small clump of bushes, less than twenty yards to the left of the first one, appeared another leopard, purposefully putting itself in the line of vision of both dogs. It caught the eye of the brown one.

As planned by the leopards, but not at all suspected by the dogs, the brown one turned its attention to the new apparition and headed straight for it. As soon as a safe distance separated the two dogs, the first leopard spun around ninety degrees, and with the element of surprise on its side, overpowered its pursuer within seconds. We stood there, hundred and fifty yards away, too scared and distressed to even scream and shout. On hearing the strangled cries of the black dog, the brown one turned on its tail, raced back home, rushed past us, straight into Mother's bedroom, and hid under the stairs until the following morning. The second leopard did not bother to pursue it. Mother and I offered our joint gratitude to God for the absence of human greed in the beasts and the birds of prey.

Bears, on the other hand are much slower than the leopards, at least physically. Like leopards, they are dangerous only when threatened or surprised by human presence. Bears came onto our land only after dark to forage for fruits and berries. During fruit season, we would often hear them chomping away under some tree, mainly apples and pears. They caused more damage to our precious fruit trees than was forgivable. But their favourite main course was corn on the cob. We heard and sensed their presence right through the summer months. We had heard of a few attacks on humans, but these were mainly attributed to human error, more than the ill intentions of the bear concerned.

One person from a nearby village, had been attacked twice, and each time he escaped with his life intact. In the first encounter, he suffered some grazes and a few deep bites to his left upper arm and left thigh, I remember! The second time, he got away unscathed. On both occasions, he was said to have beaten the beast away with a large, looped rope, which he always carried with him, slung over his shoulder, or dangled from the waist, in anticipation of odd jobs requiring the use of a sturdy rope.

Chapter 4

Dark Silence and the Tibetan Caravans

Most of the not-so-good and frightening experiences in the isolation of Dabi were caused by the wild creatures during the sinisterly dark and silent nights. Right through the waking hours of each day, we children carried clear images in our heads of what the nights in Dabi held in store for us – deep, dark silence, suddenly interrupted by howling and angry screams, usually accompanied by sounds of shuffles and whispers from outside our front door. I can't say with confidence what my siblings made of those noises. I would lie awake in bed, wondering if the ugly man from Kolkata (Calcutta) and his two friends in the shopping village of Thanedhar had come to carry out their frequently repeated threats: to break into our place, do bad things to us, slit our throats, finally, burn the house down with us inside it.

A normal night in Dabi was, like *hush-hush . . . Oh, no! It's the bloody monkeys again!* It was probably nothing more than a minor problem with their sleeping arrangements in the trees. Or some amorous young pretender caught in the forbidden attempts upon the harem of the alpha sheikh. Or perhaps it was some grumpy old ex-alpha, dreaming of the glories of bygone days. The most likely cause – as we silently cursed upon them the fires of hell – had to be some overly protective monkey mothers quarrelling over their precious brood. *Typical mothers!*

Before one could disentangle one's tired body and

haunted mind from the cursed distractions inflicted upon one's ears by the monkeys, there would be another scream. This time, it may be the ear-piercing cries of a jackal, or some other animal that physically shook the entire being of every member of the Paul family. It sounded like some leopard had got the poor thing. Everyone in Dabi was now wide awake. We didn't bother to turn the lights on. Talking in the dark was far better than in the dim light of a flickering, smelly kerosene lamp. The unsteady, lazy, flickering flames of a lamp, made the shadows on the walls move and skip all around the room, giving them shapes that reminded me of the scary images in the Book of the Revelation of St John. I could not fathom why God added that book to his Bible. That book must be singularly responsible for causing children all over the world more nightmares than all the ghost stories put together.

Middle-of-the-night conversation would often start with Mother mentioning her conversations she had during the day with one or the other of her friends from the local village. One night, it began with Mother expressing concern for Rupchand, her eldest. On the night in question, Rupchand was staying at his friend's place, three miles away to the west of Dabi. In the previous few weeks, not far from his friend's house, a leopard or 'something' had gone on a man-eating spree, across the Kumarsen river. Everybody in the district, who owned a gun, whether they could use it or not, had talked about becoming the hero.

There were many a weird story circulating about what this mysterious killer looked like, how big it was, and the various methods and strategies it employed to lure its victims. The latest tale we had heard from Nirmu, was that someone had seen eighteen-inch-long footprints on the outskirts of his village. The footprints looked like something between human feet and bear paws, with exceptionally long toes. She didn't say how many toes though. No one else in the entire neighbourhood had seen those footprints, but that did not stop the story from gathering credibility. A woman from one of the villages told us that she had it on good authority, that in order to lure and mesmerise its victims, this creature took on different personas. "That is why its victims make no sound when attacked by the creature," she said. The ensuing suffering of the families who had lost their loved ones to the man-eating leopard or invisible beast was heart breaking, even for little boys like me. Prayers and other offerings were being presented in temples and churches within the affected area. Our pleas and supplications posted to God for help seemed stuck somewhere in the heavenly postal system.

Mother sounded worried. The pitiful screams of the helpless jackal a few moments earlier, combined with the conspiratorial hush of the black night, made her words sound frightfully heavy. "Knowing Rupchand, he is likely to join a group of some young drunks in Kotgarh to try to kill the *bhirti* (man-eating leopard) He is easily led by his so-called friends."

I'd had plenty of practice seeing in the dark. I could tell Khushal was now half reclining against the wall nearest to his pillow. Pushpa was sitting up in bed, to my right. Everyone sounded scared, and helpless. I heard a deep sigh from Mother's lungs followed by a prolonged yawn of resignation. I was trying everything in my box of tricks to get back to sleep while the others were still awake. With all the noises and the dreadful pictures floating in the dark space inside my head, I did not want to be awake alone.

Mama and Pushpa were now talking about the latest victim of the bhirti, a young girl. She was the daughter of someone known to the older members of our family. In that part of the world everybody knew everybody else, of course.

Silence again. I am drifting in the direction of dreamland. Conversation starts again. Now, mother and Pushpa are talking about another *bhirti* in the same area, long before my time. I heard Mother's voice saying something like, "It was early evening. There was still plenty of daylight. She was only a yard from her front door when the *bhirti* attacked her. Her husband and the children still talk about that dreadful day." Mother mentioned the number of people that that one had killed . . . luckily for me, I was starting to drift in and out of sleepiness, and I missed most of the gruesome details of the narrative.

Mother changed the subject by relating a dream she had dreamt earlier that night. Whatever time of the night she woke up, she would relate to whosoever happened to be within her conversational range – whether they were awake or not, didn't seem to matter – what she considered to be her most significant dream of the preceding hours. We had heard two earlier versions of that particular one, on two previous nights.

On the night in question, it was still only a few minutes past midnight. The dream that night was about Papa riding on his favourite snow-white horse past the south-facing window of our bedroom. He was his usual carefree, jovial, happy-go-lucky self, singing his latest composition. He noticed my mother looking out of the window. He stopped, waved at her with, "The broadest smile I ever saw on his face," she said. He waved at her again and rode on. "I think he just wanted to tell me that he is fine, and that he knows that we too will be fine." We heard her sigh a deep, sad sigh. We knew she was fighting to hold back her need to cry out loud. To change the subject, she asked Pushpa to read a story from the book of Aesop's Tales.

Pushpa was already sitting up in bed. She lit the kerosene lamp and started to read. Not wanting to see the monsters from the Book of the Revelation dancing on our bedroom walls, I closed my eyes and soon dropped off to sleep.

I am awake, again . . . the room has returned to its pre-Aesop state . . . stifling darkness and soul-piercing silence. Everyone is breathing as if they are asleep, but I don't believe they are, any more than I am. I say my prayers for our safety through the night. I ask God, once again, not to come crashing down from his heaven in his big wooden throne. I tell him again about how, "Whenever I am feverishly delirious, I feel as if at any moment your ginormous throne is going to come crashing down through the skies onto our tiny little house." I stretch my right leg to check if Khushal is still with me at the other end of the bed. He is. Anup is merrily snoring next to Mama. I feel secure and soon drop off to sleep.

I had barely begun my journey back into the bosom of unconsciousness, when the mating calls of a *charaag* (wild cat), calling out for a date from somewhere behind our house, jolted me out of my comfort. Seconds later, I heard another *charaag* acknowledging its call from further down the cliff. "The lucky beggar has secured a date," I hissed through my teeth.

Writing this story in the spring of 2020 in Basildon a town in the south-east of England, my mind takes me back to Dabi. The computer screen is staring at me with puzzled curiosity from the top of the desk. I can virtually hear the mating calls of a *charaag*. It reminds me of the sounds that most sports fans will have heard on their television screens in recent years. It is the sound that escapes from the throats of certain female tennis players at the point when the ball leaves their racquet. I mean no offence. I am just stating a fact. As a result, I cannot watch the game of tennis when one or the other of those great players is on the court. Hearing their cries reminds me of the *charaag* and transports me back to the dark nights on that isolated patch of earth in the mountains far, far away.

Then, there were those two horrible birds! Their calling to each other all night, every night, right through the long summer months, was something I hated even more than the mating calls of a *charaag*. The birds were a brother and sister pair. The legend behind the two calling out for each other all night, was as follows:

Once upon a time in a faraway land, there was a king who was married to a beautiful queen. Their first child was a boy. While the boy was still only a toddler, the Queen gave birth to a girl. Not long after that, the Queen fell ill and died. The King didn't wait long to marry a princess from a neighbouring kingdom. This princess was not a nice person. When she fell pregnant with her first child, she reckoned that the King's children from his first wife would have to be got rid of if she wanted her child to inherit the throne. The cowardly, disgusting, henpecked king, without offering any resistance whatsoever to her wishes, sent his two children into exile.

The heartless coward! Spit! Spit! I would fume with fingers in my ears and my head buried deep under the duvet.

While in exile, the two became separated and spent the rest of their short lives searching for each other in vain. Eventually, they both died, and their souls migrated into the bodies of two birds. As they became capable of flying away on their own, they left their respective nests in search of each other. Their search continues to this day. The sister calls out, *Pock dada, pock.* (Wait brother, wait.) The brother responds in an elongated, deep-throated, *Pewoo ...! Pewoo ...!* (Come on ...! Come on ...!)

The constant calling out is irritating enough in its own right, but the legend behind their search for each other bestows upon the calls a haunting intensity, and that in turn makes the incessant calling for each other, sickeningly painful. I must have lost more sleep to that pair of siblings than a modern boy could possibly lose to all the late-night horror movies on the telly. And I did not have the benefit of a remote control to hand!

Like most things in life, our fears and frustrations of the night before, were often compensated by something the morning after. One of the compensations in Dabi was the two migratory seasons of the Tibetan caravans and their shepherding distant cousins from Kinnaur, during autumn and spring each year.

As summer cleared the way for the arrival of autumn, we would hear and see the Tibetan caravans of mules, ponies, and donkeys – often followed or preceded by their shepherds from Kinnaur – emerging from behind the mountain in Datnagar, twelve miles to the east of Dabi. For those who lived in and around Dabi, Datnagar was, and remains to this day, a major landmark along that road. It is here at Datnagar that the great river Satluj first becomes visible from the west. The river turns a sharp left-hand bend and continues on a gradual downhill journey on to the planes. The river is flanked on both its southern and northern banks by tall rocky hills.

Music from the bells dangling from the necks of the ponies and the mules, mingled with the early morning hush and haze, reached us on the wings of the easterly breeze. We could see the sun yawning and stretching out of the laps of gods from behind the Praying Mountains, eagerly accompanying our guests on their way to the west. The Tibetan caravans would generally be closely preceded or followed by the Kinnauras with their goats and sheep. The caravans were guided by the clouds of dust hovering low over them, as they journeyed farther and farther away from home, and closer to our Dabi. Mother often moaned about the caravan dust settling on her washing line.

We would hang around the front of the house so as not to miss any part of the journey of our guests from behind the mountains. We could see them all the way from Datnagar, to the stream in Khlawan – three hundred yards to the south of us. They usually arrived at the stream in the early hours of the evening and camped there for the night. Sometimes, they rested there for more than a day.

Khushal, Anup and I, usually accompanied by one of our young helpers, would skive off our chores and head to the top of the *Chcho ka Dhank* (Waterfall Cliff), about a hundred yards on our side of the stream. From there, we had a clear view of the campsite.

As soon as they reached the stream, they dismounted the horses and ponies. Next, the animals were unloaded, stripped, watered, and tied to makeshift stakes on the dry patches of earth on either side of the stream, for the night. Unfortunately for us, the Tibetan caravans seldom camped there on their way back home. The Kinnauras, on the other hand, appeared often to hang around the place for days before moving farther along the route.

Both the Tibetans and the Kinnauras found shelter on our side of the stream under the overhanging rocks along the road. Both groups made their beds, lit their fires, and got on with preparing meals for the night. We never noticed much conversation, nor any screaming and shouting at the children, either. They seemed disciplined in everything they did.

The physical stature of the Tibetans (they looked twice as big as our local men) and their rugged and unkempt appearance, we found very intimidating. In the daytime, whenever there were other folk in the vicinity, we would find excuses to get safely close to the camp. Those brief visits provided us with a closer look at their food habits, and other facets of their culture and social interactions. It also afforded us a chance to admire the fancy apparel of the 'better-offs'. We managed a few sideways looks at, what were to us, out-of-this-world garments. Their outer woollen garments were decorated with intricate silk and fine wool embroidery. Colours and designs of the embroidery appeared to signify the status of the wearer within the family or clan hierarchy. The horses and the ponies were often bedecked exactly to suit the status of each rider.

A significant majority were obviously quite poor, even poorer than most of us. We feared them more than the better offs, simply because they looked rougher and more rugged. The caravans, on their way to warmer climes beyond, passed by our place from the middle of September through to the end of October. Then from mid-March through to the end of April on their way back home to Tibet and Kinnaur.

The escape of the Dalai Lama into India, in March of

1959, was immediately preceded and followed not only by 'one way' caravans, but also by their increased frequency. Now, the free-spirited Tibetans that we children so feared only a few months before, were refugees in India, and working all around us. They were becoming an essential part of the road-building projects in many parts of the newly formed hill state of Himachal Pradesh. The Tibetans were also supplying a ready, willing, and honest workforce for the fast-expanding apple orchards and consequent development projects in our neck of the woods. Along with the labour force from Nepal, the Tibetans were a welcome addition to the 'progress' of the area. Their 'sing-as-you-work' culture became a welcome addition to the *lamans* of the natives.

Among the local male community, rumours about the out-of-this-world physical prowess possessed by the Tibetan men and women, was rife. We frequently heard tales about how some of their men were known to work all day, on just the *Sattu* (roasted barley flour) breakfast. 'Their women folk,' some said, 'can lift twice as much weight as the strongest of our men'. Our men were warned to stay away from any hanky-panky with the Tibetan women. They were rumoured to be able to kill a local man by simply wrapping their legs around his middle and squeezing the life out of him in seconds. My friends and I were disappointed that, despite numerous diligent searches, we never found a man in the woods with his life squeezed out of him.

Chapter 5

A Nameless Hermit

There is something ... no, it's someone up there, near that bangar (mountain oak). It's a sadhu (hermit). Have I seen him before . . .? What could he be doing up here at this time of the morning?

My mind raced back to when I first met him. It was ... let me think ... Mother and her helpers were cutting grass in the fields at the end of apple season. So, it must have been sometime in early October.

On that day, nearly five years before, I was sitting on a *maandri* (a knitted grass mat) in the shade of an apple tree near the house, babysitting my five-month-old brother, Anup. He was fast asleep beside me under his canopy. Mother and her helpers were working in the nearby fields, while at the same time, keeping an eye on us. To avoid boredom, I was playing the role of my elder brother's Assistant Transport Manager, with numerous lorries and many employees buzzing all around me. From fifty yards or so, directly above and behind us, I heard a loud sneeze. I looked up and noticed a *sadhu*, sitting cross-legged on a small grassy mound on the edge of the Shimla-Tibet Road. He was looking over the valley, towards the snow-clad Praying Mountains in the east, where the rivers Ganges and Satluj have their beginnings. Ganges, we were told, came out of the mouth of a holy cow from somewhere behind those mountains.

I called out, "*Babajee* (respectable form of addressing a hermit), come down and have some *chai-pani.*" I couldn't make out his response. In the meantime, I had been distracted by the unpleasant gurgling sounds coming from Anup's direction. He had brought the milk up, all over his right shoulder, and on to parts of his blanket. Mother had heard me inviting the *sadhu* down for some *chai-pani*. She hurriedly came over, closely followed by a busybody helper. Mother asked *if* and *how* I knew the *sadhu*? I pointed to the mess my little brother had made and said that I did not know the *sadhu*.

"Then why did you invite him down here?" she demanded to know.

My arms crossed, I stretched myself to my full three-foot plus height, took on the persona of a pious philanthropist, and said, "Because I thought he might be hungry or thirsty!"

Before Mother could repeat the 'dangers from strangers' litany, the subject of our conversation had made his way down from the road and was standing behind us. He apologised to my mother for causing her concern for the safety of her children. He stepped forward into our line of vision. In a soft, gentle voice he asked if she wouldn't mind him sitting down on the ground, a couple of yards to our right. Before Mother could respond, he sat down in Samadhi posture.

In the brief conversation that followed, Babajee said something about me and my little brother, which I did not comprehend at the time. I was more interested in his appearance. He had this freshly washed jet-black hair, oiled, and rolled up in a neat bun at the top of his head. He appeared quite different from all the other *sadhus* I had seen. He was exceptionally clean and well kempt. He refused our offer of *chai-pani*.

Later that evening, I heard Mother tell Papa, that she believed him to be an educated and well-informed young man from a good home. Mama and Papa wondered why someone like him would become a *sadhu* and expressed concern about my interest in *sadhus*. "I always make sure he doesn't invite any of them into the house," said Mother. Father agreed strongly. "They may look like it, but not all of them are real *sadhus*. Most are just work-shy vagrants," added Father.

Over the years, my 'weird' interest in *sadhus* did bring some benefits to the family, and to a good number of locals in general. Some of the *sadhus* passed on their knowledge of herbal cures and other titbits of wisdom to my mother, by way of 'thank you' for *my chai-pani*. My interest in *sadhus* has stayed with me all my life.

It was in September of 1974 in Kotgarh, that I discovered what the *sadhu* had said about me, under the apple tree, all those years ago. As Mother was saying goodbye to me, Mary and Shobha on our way to Manchester, she said to me, "What the *sadhu* had said, was that you will give me reasons to be proud of you, but eventually, will break my heart by making your home in some far away land, across the oceans." she added, "He foresaw, that you will be blessed with a long life, and will meet your end by a fall from the horseback, or a tumble from a roof top."

What worries me now, is that since my fall from a horse back at the age of fourteen, which I obviously survived, the thought of sitting on a horseback has never once entered my mind. To make matters worse, lately I have developed problems associated with vertigo. So, I am not going to be climbing on to any roof tops. Here's a thought ... I might live forever! An eternity of incontinence and dementia to look forward to? I must find an alternative to the horseback and the roof top before the misguided do-gooders stick a nappy on my backside for eternity. The picture of me on the 'Day of Judgement' (if ever there is one), with a nappy on my backside – need I say more? Exactly! I have no intention to keep breathing once I have stopped living. It will simply prolong my period of indignity and waste the resources that belong to the younger generation.

This, our second encounter, halfway up the Urhi Dharti (a narrow, steep ridge), took place on a bright sunny morning in July of 1950, nearly five years after the first chance meeting. This time, I noticed that Babajee was picking mushrooms a hundred yards up ahead.

I called out, "Namaste Babajee." *I don't think he's heard me.* I did a few throat-clearing noises and fake coughs to draw his attention. He straightened up, stared at me briefly and called out, "Hello *bhai*, how are you? Good to see you again."

I responded with enthusiasm and said how pleased I was to see him. I rushed up to my favourite, freezing cold boulder in the middle of the path. Sat down, and waited eagerly for him to join me in the shade of the trees.

Babajee put his wild mushrooms in a brown paper bag and came over to where I was. He put the bag on the ground in front of me, and sat down facing me on a lump wood that had lain across the path since before my time. Pointing to his mushroom bag, he said, "I like to take advantage of nature's generosity to meet the needs of my body and soul. This way I can be sure to eat fresh and stay healthy."

Babajee was wearing clean, fresh, saffron cotton *khaddar dhoti* wrapped around the lower half of his body, and a sleeveless top of the same colour and material. His hair was neatly tied in a bun on top of his head. His shiny black beard was brushed straight down over his chest. His teeth looked like sets of polished pearls. He looked very impressive. He had no sandals on, yet his feet were clean, and no cracked heels. He mentioned that he was acclimatising himself to the Himalayan environment before launching further into the mountains. He could smell the breath of *Paramatma* (the Supreme Soul) in these mountains and see the face of *Bhagvan* (personified God) in every innocent and contented face. "Do you understand what I am saying?" he asked. Yes, I did know what he was saying, but did not know how to put my response into words. I looked him in the eye and nodded my response.

He had heard about the death of my father. "Everyone in Thanedhar speaks highly of your *Pita jee* (respected father)," he said. He expressed hope that we were coping well. What did I think of my father being the only Indian in all the two hundred miles between Shimla and Tibet, who fought the British for the freedom of his motherland? "Are you proud of him? You should be!"

"No, my father wasn't the only one. Mr Stokes, the American gentleman who owns all this land", I pointed to the forests around us, "he was also a freedom fighter, even before my father. He actually met my father for the first time in Lahore Central jail."

I was also blessed, he believed, with an exceptionally courageous and intelligent mother.

"How do you know so much about my mother?" I said quite aggressively.

"No reason to feel threatened by my remarks, my brother. I am glad that you wish to protect the honour of your mother." He quickly changed the subject, and asked if the rumours about me talking to God had any truth in them?

"Where did you hear that? Why would I be talking to God?" I protested, feigning innocence.

He looked at me for long seconds, grinning. "What's wrong with talking to God?" He talked to God all the time, he said. He was talking to God while picking mushrooms, earlier. Did I think that people who talked to God were mad or something?

Not sure! I needed time to think. While uncomfortably working out my response, I watched him taking in the amazing scenery around us. Our surroundings were alive with the cacophony of sounds from the creatures of the forest: a howling jackal, the screeching monkeys as the villagers chased them away from their fruit crops, the chirping and humming of the birds and the bees. Through the whole in the canopy of pine trees above our heads, we could see scores of eagles, crows, kestrels and other highflyers. Added to all this splendour, were the sounds of songs and *lamans* of the women and men, tending to their animals deep in the woods to his left.

After a long silence, I decided to answer Babajee's question. "I do sometimes talk to God. I can't say that God has ever said more than a few words to me. Well, people say that God spoke only to his chosen prophets in olden times. He doesn't talk to people anymore." *I don't like the way he is looking at me. I bet he will laugh his head off behind my back.* To divert his attention away from my face, I changed the subject. I pointed to the nest of hornets up in the tree almost immediately above our heads and told him that if hornets decide to attack a person, the only safe place to hide is under water. I quickly moved on to tell him that I missed my father every waking moment of my life. I didn't believe that he had died in Shimla during the communal riots in the Punjab, in 1947. I said that I strongly felt in my heart that there had been some confusion in the chaotic circumstances during the riots, and the person they put in the coffin was not my father. I mentioned that I had been thinking of writing letters to God, asking him to find my father for me, and many other things I wanted to say to God. I must have sounded doolally. *Move on, quick* . . . "You know, I feel like I am alone all the time, until I can find my father. You know what I mean?"

He understood too well what I was saying, he assured me. I told Babajee we did not know much about working on the land, so some people from the local villages came and helped us with heavy jobs in the fields. There were times when Mother could not afford to pay them for their labour, but they still helped us. Everyone treated us with affection and respect, I said. All the women in the neighbouring villages were friendly and kind to our mother. "Yet, since the communal riots on the planes over the partition of India three years ago", I told him, "None of us in our house trusts the silence and deep darkness of the night.

I told him, how, every night after our evening meals and customary evening prayers, Mama led us outside into the dark night, to answer the call of nature, whether nature had called or not, in the outside open-air toilets. Being a left-hander, she held a large torchlight in her right hand, pointing directly in front of her, and in her left, a machete at the ready. During this particular exercise, we all talked simultaneously to let the undesirable animals or humans know of our strength in numbers. On return from our hurriedly answered calls, we bolted the door behind us with utmost haste. The door was further secured by placing one end of a *jhabbal* (a long, straight crowbar) halfway up in a groove on the inside panel, and the other end was firmly secured in a narrow gap between two floorboards on the bedroom floor.

Not used to being taken seriously by adults of my acquaintance, I was finding the undivided attention of Babajee quite flattering. I continued thinking aloud.

Since our father's disappearance, Mother had moved us all into her bedroom. Every night she placed a *datch (machette)* or a *brarha* (a lightweight axe) under her pillow. On the wall shelf above her bed, there was a small bottle that we were expressly instructed never to touch. She could reach it by stretching up her left arm. Every night, before settling into her bed, she carefully examined the small bottle. We suspected the purpose of both items. Occasionally, Pushpa, Khushal and I had spoken about it in whispers, but we never had the courage to ask Mother.

The purpose of those two items came to light in bits and pieces from the conversations we overheard between Mother and Nirmu. What we heard was that should someone attack us at night, Mama would administer the deadly poison in the bottle to us, in our sleep. That way we wouldn't have to witness and suffer the carnage. She was then going to "take one or two of the cowards out with my *datch* before they can lay their filthy hands on me or my children." We were scared, but since the return of our eldest brother, a few months previously, we had started to feel the darkness less frightening.

Babajee listened in silence. In the meantime, he had picked up a sizeable piece of white flint in his right hand and was using its pointed end to dig away the earth around a well-worn, small, rounded stone in the middle of the path in front of him. He kept throwing brief glances in my direction, yet, at the same time, carefully avoiding my eyes. I suspected that he was trying to feel my fears.

There was a fruit merchant from Calcutta, I told Babajee. He had been coming to our part of the world during the apple season for many years. I had seen him before, but since father's disappearance, he would follow me around whenever I happened to be shopping in Thanedhar. He would come up to me, bend his up-side-down ugly face and smelly mouth close to my ear and whisper, "My friends and I will break into your house one dark night, have some fun with your beautiful mother and sister in there, set the house on fire, and burn you all alive, inside ... ha! ha!" And then he would drift away, into the nearest shop.

I said "I can't tell Mama and my siblings about the ugly man. They have plenty of other things to worry about." I asked Babajee, "Why can't God keep that ugly man out of my way, and bring my papa back home?" He looked at me with, 'I wish I knew' expression in his eyes.

I stood up and went over to the oak tree. Hidden from Babajee's view, I emptied my full bladder. *Ooooh! What a relief!* Mission accomplished, and without a single drop down the front of the trousers, or on my toes, I returned to my seat. Suddenly, I felt overcome by exhaustion. I did not want to talk. A thick blanket of depressing silence was smothering us both. The warm and bright sun had somehow turned cold and shadowy grey. Our eyes darted about the scenes around us, anywhere but at the face of the other. What had only been a night-time preoccupation over the past three years, had suddenly overshadowed my daylight. I knew that I was awake, but what I wanted to know more than anything else, was, why was I feeling so strange? I did not like what I had just spoken with my lips, heard with my ears, and the pictures I had seen with my mind's eye. I dared not put into words what I thought of God, and how I wanted to have a real go at him.

The anger inside me started to push at the boundaries

of my soul. "I want to kill those cowards. Yes! I want to do to them what they want to do to us!" I hissed. I realised that I needed to hold back the rage. *Stay calm,* I counselled myself. But now, I felt afraid even of Babajee. I wondered if I should trust him. I felt uncomfortable and cold in his presence.

In a daze, Babajee dropped the flint, sharp end first. It landed on his foot, about an inch above the big toe. There was blood all over his foot. I tried to direct his attention to the bleeding foot, but my lips refused to move. My throat felt like all the dust clouds from the Tibetan caravans had blown into my mouth. The damp, cold stone I had been sitting on comfortably so far, suddenly turned into a lump of ice. Instead of attending to his injury, Babajee removed the strap of the water bottle from his left shoulder, and absentmindedly unscrewed the top with his right hand. He lifted the bottle to his mouth a few times without pouring a drop onto his tongue.

After much shifting about on our posteriors, he stretched out his left hand and silently offered me the bottle. I took it, poured a mouthful onto my dry, sandy tongue without touching the bottle to my lips, and handed it back to him. Only then, did I dare look at his face directly. His eyes were tearful. The eerie silence continued. Out of that deep silence, I heard a trembling voice, saying, "You are late to school, and it is all my fault."

Brief silence was followed by another trembling voice from within the deep space, "I don't want to go to school now. It's too late, anyway."

He looked at me with those sad, tearful eyes. "I don't know what your *Matajee* (mother) will have to say about all this, but I must take you to school now. I will apologise to your teachers for making you late. When I see your

Matajee again, I must also apologise to her."

By now the blood had begun to congeal all over his foot. "Before we can go anywhere, you need to see to that cut on your foot," I said grumpily.

He stood up. "Earlier, you said something about having to tell lies to all the grown-ups around you. Want to tell me more about why you have to do that?"

"Not now. Maybe next time. I am tired, and you need to see to your foot." I stood up, started walking up the hill. He followed. We moved in distressed silence in the direction of a small pond of fresh rainwater from two days before, a hundred yards up the narrow dirt path.

Chapter 6

Dhannu's Dilemma

Two days after our meeting on my way to school, Babajee appeared in Dabi just after midday. On seeing him, Dhannu put aside the pots he was washing, rinsed his hands, and came over to where Khushal and Anup were doting over a new addition to the family: a brown mongrel puppy. It was not like Mama to ignore any one of us walking out on a job, but in Dhannu's case, things had been different in the past few days. On seeing Babajee, I too abandoned my post at the firewood stack, and came over to welcome and to introduce him to the family. Mother was tending to a two-day-old calf on her favourite summer spot by her favourite rose bush next to her favourite apricot tree, in front of the chicken coop.

Before Babajee could start growling to Mother with his apologies, I told him that she had already been briefed about the whole incident by me. That was luckily the end of the matter. We could talk about other, more important, things.

During the previous two days, I had told Dhannu enough about my 'new friend' Babajee, to whet his appetite. Dhannu was one of the two young boys who Mother had engaged to help her tackle the spring and summer chores in and around the house. He had come into the world two years ahead of me, yet in size and appearance he hardly looked a day older. Small and tough, he carried a clever head on his shoulders. The utterly degrading caste system and backbreaking poverty had failed to wipe the smile from his handsome face.

A week earlier, swiping his shirtsleeve across the tip of his wet nose, Dhannu had asked me, "Does your Christian God answer your prayers when you ask him for something? Especially, you know ... like ... you know like when ... like I mean, when you need help, like, right on the spot?"

I crossed my arms, slightly leaned my head onto the right shoulder, pursed my lips, and stared at him thoughtfully, "You mean, like, real emergency?" I asked.

"Yes. That's what I said," Dhannu retorted impatiently.

I wanted to believe that my Christian God answered prayers – no question. But that would not be true, not always, I knew. We looked at Khushal for help. He didn't like talking about God. I did not want Dhannu to think that our Christian God was not up to the job, but I couldn't think of an honest answer, either. I shrugged my shoulders and returned to feeding the dog.

Now, from what I had told Dhannu about Babajee two days before, it was only natural that Dhannu should expect him to provide the answer to his dilemma.

Ten days earlier, Dhannu had gone five hundred yards below his village to fetch water from the spring by the stream. He placed his clay pitcher under the wooden spout that carried the water out from the belly of the earth, a couple of yards above. Once the pitcher was full, he placed his hands inside its neck, and tried to lift it up onto his shoulder. The upper half came away in his hands. The bottom half remained unmoved. Dhannu, quite naturally concluded, that the pitcher must have had a hairline crack all the way round the joint of its belly before he filled it with water. He carefully carried the two halves back home, confident that his father would accept his explanation.

His father took one look at the two pieces dangling from Dhannu's hands. He told Dhannu to put them on the ground. "Gently," he whispered. Then, he pointed to the axe that stood against the side wall of their one-up-one-down house and asked Dhannu to bring it over. He carefully removed the blade from the handle and stood there indecisively for a few brief seconds. He then put both the handle and the axe down on the floor, straightened up slowly and deliberately. He picked up his walking stick from the veranda. All this time, Dhannu and his two younger sisters watched the proceedings with apprehension.

Before Dhannu could move, his father let into him with the stick. The whole village heard the screams, but none came to the rescue. When he was done, "That should teach you how to look after earthenware, in future," his father admonished, proudly.

After two days sick leave, Dhannu arrived for work with a slight limp. In response to our inquiries, he described his torture in detail, and we saw the full extent of his injuries. Despite his reluctance to let my mother see him unclothed, she insisted on washing him down with warm water, soap, and some antiseptics, which she always kept handy. My little brother Anup and I watched the play intently, adding to poor Dhannu's embarrassment.

After a thorough clean-up of a body that was unaccustomed to water being splashed all over it, except at special occasions, or during monsoon rains, Mother applied the green, bitter juice of crushed *kubush* leaves to the bruises, all over his emaciated body. On half-a-dozen deeper bruises, Mama applied *Shilajeet* paste with the tip of her finger. *Shilajeet* is a kind of hard resin, that, in popular myth, oozes from the cracks in the rocks in certain parts of Tibet. Some say that it is Eagle's excretions that have hardened between the rocks over many years. The paste burns and bites a bit (more than a bit, if truth be told) for a few short minutes, but is a highly effective healer. Through the long, painful ordeal, Dhannu flinched a little, but never uttered a cry.

In order to keep Dhannu away from his father for the next couple of weeks, Mother made up some excuses, and I'm sure, told a few truthful lies to his father. After a week's rest and TLC, Dhannu went back to doing the chores that he believed he could manage without too much discomfort.

Writing about Dhannu has brought to mind some fond memories of our favourite pastimes in summer months. Possible only during school holidays or weekends.

There is one that is constantly popping up in my head, I might as well put it on paper now, before it sinks into the depths of my brain cell.

During the summer months, Dhannu, Khushal and I, joined by some boys and girls from nearby villages, spent many happy hours by the stream in Khlawan. At the stream, we made paper boats out of glossy pages acquired from old glossy magazines. We also made boats out of dry bark of a special variety of spruce, called *cheel*.

Boats were carried on the fast-flowing waters, speeding down the stream, ducking and diving between the rocks for many yards before meeting with an inevitably violent end at the hands of the 'owners-turned-pirates'.

Another of our water sports – again, possible only during summer months – required a group of at least half-a-dozen youngsters, reasonably able bodied and willing to take orders from Khushal.

For this, we cleared as much mud and silt from one of the wider beds of the stream near the road, and created a pond about two yards in diameter and about a yard or so deep at the center. Job done, we took a break and hastily devoured our meagre picnic lunches, complemented by fresh watercress from the stream, some seasonal fruits, and wild berries. All washed down with a drink of fresh water from the nearby spring.

After the picnic, came the best part of the day. We took our clothes off and dived in. Nothing could have prevented us from enjoying that rare experience of being shoulder deep in freezing cold water. We swam, we dived, we bathed, we raced our boats, and performed many a rescue mission in the murky oceans of our little stream.

Round one o'clock in the afternoon, sun dipping behind the trees, play time over, our cattle ready for home. We filled Dhannu's boat-shaped cotton cap (waterproofed by years of oil, sweat and dust caked into the material) with water and carried it all the way back to the one and only mulberry tree in sight, on the north side of the house. Once there, we poured the water into a deep dimple on top of a rock on the edge of a terraced field. Round the water, we scattered some grains of wheat, barley, and any other seeds we could lay our hands on. We then withdrew back to the mulberry tree. From there, we could safely spy on the birds coming down onto the rock for a quick snack and drink. Occasionally, the larger birds would swoop down, chase the smaller ones away, and after a quick *chai-pani* they would spoil the rest by taking a quick bath in it. We were disappointed to see the birds being nasty and spiteful, like so many humans.

I can't think why none of us Dabi brothers had a cap. Too late now to ask Mother. We were given Mother's knitted mufflers instead. Apart from the possibility of strangling someone (one can but dream), mufflers didn't provide half the fun that a dirty, old cotton cap did.

The cap wasn't just for carrying the water; one could also pluck a lizard off the ground between the tips of one's fingers, place it on the head, and quickly cover it with the cap, waterproof or not. While under the cap, the lizard picked the nits and lice clean off the head of its captor in less than five minutes. You couldn't do that with a muffler!

I better get back to Babajee's visit to Dabi. On that warm and sunny afternoon, we sipped and slurped our concoction, which in the outside world would easily pass for anything but tea, while Mama and Babajee engaged in peripheral social chit-chat.

With Mother's permission, Khushal fetched the largest and the healthiest looking cucumber from halfway up the pear tree, right next to where Babajee was sitting on the edge of the wall. I provided some salt and ground black pepper from the kitchen cupboard. The higher they climbed the more abundant and larger the cucumbers grew. Nature's generosity and our mother's ingenuity made it possible for us to always have something growing out of the earth, to share with the many weary travelers and kind locals that passed by our lonely place. The few fruit trees on our plot of land seemed generous beyond belief.

After chomping through the cucumber slices, I asked Babajee to follow me to our chicken shed. Dhannu joined us at the new extension to the old chicken shed that mother, Khushal and I had built ourselves, with some professional help from our trusted carpenter, Jhoppa. Extra space helped to separate the brooding mums and their chicks from the rest of the clan. The three hens had hatched sixteen chicks between them. Babajee partially opened the door of the nursery section and picked a chicken in each hand. He was like a little boy holding those chicks in his hands, talking to them, and laughing and cooing. He said he had never imagined that chicks could be so beautiful. Looking at us, he cooed, "You are so fortunate to experience Bhagvan and his *leela* (pleasures) so close at hand."

Dhannu took the last remark as his cue to ask Babajee the big question. Babajee looked at him a little bemused. "Let me put these back," he said to Dhannu. As he was putting the chicks back inside the coop, one of the broody mums reached out and nipped the back of his hand twice in the same spot. He dropped the chicks inside and instinctively jumped back from the enclosure. Nursing his hand, he looked at Dhannu and then back at me. The question in his eyes read, *do you know what Dhannu is talking about?*

I suggested to Dhannu that he tell Babajee the reason for asking the question. Dhannu put his left arm over the back of my shoulders, right hand in his shirt pocket, gently leaning against me, he said, "Go on then, you tell him. You're better at explaining things."

I told Babajee every detail about how Dhannu had suffered at the hands of his father, and how Dhannu had called out for help from a whole army of gods. "And just like the grownups in Dhannu's village, none of the gods turned up to help him," I added angrily.

"I am so very sorry to hear about what your father did to you," replied Babajee, genuinely moved by the horror.

"Dhannu wants to know if you know of a god he could call upon, should he need help again. I want to know as well. I don't think our Christian God does much about helping people in really bad situations."

"Does he not? How do you know?"

I did not like the way he directed his question into my eyes. "You know what I mean," I said, making no attempt at disguising my annoyance.

"I think I know what you mean. But I don't know a god who answers our prayers, the way we want them answered, not often." He looked directly at Dhannu, and in his usual soft and gentle voice said, "I so wish I could help you, my little brother. I am even more useless than the gods you called upon. I don't know the answer. The only thing I know, is, that your father had no right to beat you at all, let alone with his walking stick." His eyes were welling up. With a nod in my direction, he said to Dhannu, "Like your friend here, don't stop asking until you get the answer."

He has not answered our question, I am sure, but why do I feel comforted, as if he has? I feel so peaceful, suddenly. There's something weird about this!

Some years later, when I mentioned it to my parish priest, whom I considered to be intelligent and rational, he answered by saying, that the fact that Dhannu and I had felt comforted by Babajee's words was clear evidence that God had used that *sadhu* to answer Dhannu's prayers.

"But that did not prevent Dhannu's father from nearly disabling him for life. And why does God never do anything himself? Why does God not deal with our prayers directly himself?" I asked the padre.

He looked at me with genuine pity in his eyes. "Nihal, you have much to learn. You must not question God."

Here we go again! Was I questioning God? Let me try another angle. "You know what I think? I think that the God we talk about as our 'Loving Father', is not the real God; I mean that it can't be the real God, because this God can never do anything himself. He always needs the help of some delivery man, and even then, the help will not necessarily be when and where the person needs it. Or the answer won't even be what the person has prayed for. In other words, this God is going to do what he is going to do, and only when he can find someone to do it for him. Or he may choose not to do anything at all. What is the point of praying to our God?"

I expected an honest and intelligent answer. Instead, the padre replied, "I cannot for the life of me imagine why someone like you should be thinking of going into the ministry."

Back in Dabi, the shadows were swiftly moving on towards the eastern horizon. It was time for Babajee to leave. He thanked us boys for what he described as a very educational companionship, and thanked Mother for her kindness and generosity in trusting and accepting him as a guest of her family. He walked over to the little calf that she had been attending to when Babajee first arrived. While he was bestowing his affections upon the little blighter, it peed on his foot, and to celebrate the achievement it bounded off, laughing all the way to the cow shed to brag to its mother, I guess.

Mother apologised for the calf's misdemeanour. The rest of us simply sniggered and expressed our embarrassment in all sorts of childish ways – Khushal dropped the poor little pup on the ground. The pup's adopted uncle made such a song and dance over the squeaking pup, we could hardly hear ourselves speak. Dhannu released an obnoxious stink bomb. To save us from further embarrassment, I hurriedly fetched Babajee a jug of water for him to wash his foot.

Away from Babajee's hearing, I asked Mother if Dhannu and I could accompany him to the shops in Thanedhar. Khushal wondered if he too could join us.

Mother reminded him firmly that he had his chores to finish. "Why does he …" looking at me with disdain, "…always get what he wants, while I am required to do all the work around this place?"

"Nihal has his chores and you have yours. Stop winging," said Mother. And that was that. We were not permitted to backchat or argue with our elders. Mother was always right, of course; she said so. Khushal expressed his frustration and disappointment by uttering the unutterable under his breath, *'Hitler!'* Since the start of the WWII, every cruel person we knew had been christened, *'Hitler'*.

Mother called me into the kitchen on some pretext. Once inside, she wanted to know if the *sadhu* had ever touched me inappropriately. To which my honest answer was, "No! Never!" Had he ever made any suggestions or used language that one should not use in the presence of a child? Again, the honest answer was an emphatic "No!"

"Why are you asking me silly questions? You know he is a holy man. He even talks to God. He is just like our prophets in the Bible."

"All right, all right! Enough of that. You may go with him but be back before sunset." Mother counted the money and handed it to me, emphasising that I must double-check the change before leaving the shop.

I picked up my shoulder bag. Dhannu and I followed Babajee up the narrow dirt path, in thoughtful silence. Once we hit the road behind the house, Babajee stopped, turned round to face us, his smiley eyes squinting. He said in a soft voice, barely audible, "I wish I were you. I cannot think of anything I would have wanted to do more when I was your age, than what you boys are doing now." He fixed his gaze at the top of the Praying Mountains. After a brief silence he turned to us, "Be proud of yourselves, and don't be afraid of speaking with God." After another brief pause, "You know something? I am proud to know you boys."

I was glad he included Dhannu in his compliments. Had it been 'God' himself telling me that he had booked a place for me in heaven, it would not have meant half as much as those words of Babajee meant at the time. We moved on in the direction of Thanedhar.

Chapter 7

The Truthful Lies

A few steps up the road I asked Babajee where his home was and why he had become a sadhu? My picture memory tells me: we stopped in the middle of the road. Babajee said, "My birthplace is Lucknow, a very significant city in the state of Utter Pradesh." We moved on, again very slowly. He emphasised 'birthplace' as against 'home'. With a smile that lit up his holy face, he spread his arms out, "Now the whole world is my home."

He was the eldest of three siblings. He had studied law at the University of Allahabad, he said. After completing his top degrees, he followed in the footsteps of his father by joining the family firm in a city, couple of hundred miles away from Allahabad. The firm was established by his grandfather many years before. A few years in, he became disillusioned with the society he was expected to relate to. I can't quote him, but I think he felt that the law courts were interested more in the quality of presentation of a case than in the truth. He also told us something about how he escaped being tied down in an arranged marriage to the daughter of a rich merchant, and well-known criminal, in the state of Utter Pradesh. Sorry, I am not sure if I am making some of this up ...

He confided in his mother, he told us, for she was herself unhappy about the way her husband and her younger son amassed wealth. One night, with his mother's blessings and co-operation, he left home under cover of darkness, taking with him nothing but the clothes he was wearing and the train and bus fare to Hardwar, a popular place of pilgrimage for Hindus. He had now been on the road for over seven years, "And these have been the happiest years of my life so far," he said, with a real sense of achievement. He tried to visit his parents once every two years. For it was they who brought him into this world, loved and cared for him for all those wonderful years when he was with them. "I honour them, for they are the channels of my manifestation into human form," – or words to that effect.

Halfway through his next sentence, the ground beneath our feet started to vibrate, like thousands of hammers aggressively pounding the earth in rhythm. From previous experiences, Dhannu and I knew what it was all about. Our eyes met, *let's get out of here.* With practiced ease, we clawed ten/fifteen feet up the hill behind us. Only when we were safely out of reach of the approaching danger, did we realise that our honoured guest was still standing smack in the middle of the path of certain death, looking confused.

"Babajee, come, come. Come up here, quick!" we shouted frantically.

"Why?" He looked up at us with big question marks in his eyes.

Before the answer to his question could find its way from our lips to his ears, he heard, and then saw, with his own eyes – now bulging with deathly fear – the answer to his question. He scrambled up before the first of the fifty killers, with their teeth bared and their legs kicking in all directions, reached the spot where he had been standing less than ten seconds before.

Once the stampeding mules were at a safe distance past us, we scrambled back down onto the road. I realised for the first time, the benefit of not having the movement of one's feet restricted by shoes. I mentioned my revelation to Babajee. He patted me on the head and we enjoyed a long, loud fit of giggles.

"Why are mules and horses so frisky on their way to and from water?" asked Dhannu.

"No idea," I replied, truthfully.

We moved on towards Thanedhar. Halfway up the road, we reached the *bawrhy* (a small waterhole) by the roadside. We stopped to admire the 360-degree views of nature. Babajee whispered ecstatically, *"Bhagvan ki leela!"* (God's playground). He turned towards me, catching my eye, "What were we talking about when the mules nearly trampled us into the dust? Oh yes! You were telling me about your school."

"No, it was you, not Nihal, telling us about why you became a Sant (holy man!)," corrected Dhannu.

"Oh yes! Well, there is not much more to my story. I may be a *sadhu*, but please don't call me a Sant." He wanted to be seen as someone who liked to be out and about with God in His beautiful world. He just wanted to live a simple life. His father and his elder sister were not happy with his lifestyle, but they still loved him. His mother said nothing, but that she missed him. His brother didn't want to have anything to do with him. "According to my brother, I am a disgrace to the family." He laughed.

Standing on the edge of the road, he reclined back against the large trunk of a dead pine. He poured a few mouthfuls of water into his mouth from the water bottle and offered it to Dhannu who looked at him in horror, trying to refuse in halting speech. Trying to tell him that he couldn't drink from the same bottle as Babajee, because he … but he couldn't come up with the right words.

Dhannu was a low caste boy. I did not want him to degrade himself before a relative stranger. Perhaps it was my Christian conscience? Or my family culture? Whichever! I interrupted Dhannu mid-sentence by diverting Babajee's attention to a group of vultures, hovering half a mile above our heads. I took the bottle from his hand and gave it to Dhannu. I gestured forcefully for him to take a sip from it. Dhannu reluctantly poured some water onto his tongue. With trembling hands, he handed the bottle back to me. I poured a mouthful onto my tongue and passed it back to Babajee.

"Babajee, do you remember, last Thursday you asked me why sometimes I did not like God?"

"Yes, I do remember, but you didn't want to answer my question, then."

"Well, they all say different things about God. Uncle Saddiqui – he is a Musalmaan – he says that his Allah does not like the Jews and the Christians much, and he simply hates the rest of the humans. He says that only Musalmaans are allowed into heaven. And then, in the Old Testament, the God of the Israelis – they call him Yahova, but he also has other names, I can't think what, just now – he only liked the Israelis. He told the children of Abraham they could take the lands and homes of other people and slaughter anyone who dared to get in their way. And then, not so long ago, a visiting preacher in our church was saying that our Christian God will not let anyone, other than us Christians, into his heaven. That's not fair. I don't like any of these gods."

"Are you sure that is what the Holy books say?" He had not read the Muslims' Holy book, nor the Holy book of the Israelis, but he had read the New Testament many times in the past few years, he said.

I told him that a visiting Christian I had met the year

before told me that in one of the books, in the Old Testament, he remembered reading that one dark night, a long time ago, one of the great Generals of the Armies of the Israelis, after having been on the battlefield all day, was sleeping in his tent. He must have been tired. Anyway, Yahova comes into his tent and wakes him up, because he wants to know what had happened in the battle that day. The general gives his report. This Yahova God is ecstatic that the general had won the battle. But then he asks the general if he had killed everyone, including all the animals, and burned down the entire town? The general says, "No, I didn't kill the women and children and the animals." He did not think that was necessary. Hearing that, Yahova gets really angry. He says to the general that he should have obeyed the law, which clearly says, that when you defeat your enemy, you kill their women, their children, their animals; the whole lot of them, and burn the place down.

So, the general gets out of his bed, takes his soldiers with him in the middle of the night, and kills every living thing and burns the town to ashes. They return and go back to bed.

"That makes me sick," shouted Dhannu angrily, absolutely disgusted. "How can you kill children and animals? What harm could have they done to this horrible God?"

Babajee looked at me thoughtfully but said nothing. He took out three apples that Mother had given him, out of his shoulder bag, gave one each to Dhannu and me, and dug his teeth into the third one himself. We ate the apples in silence, while leisurely studying the flight of scores of buzzards and crows above our heads. After we had swallowed the last remains of our apples in thoughtful silence, Babajee said, "You remember when we met on your way to school the other day? You said God will send you to hell because you have to make up lies to protect yourself from your mother and the teachers?"

I couldn't think how to respond to his question. After a brief silence, he said, "Nihal, what I think is, that no one will ever punish you for the kind of lies you have told me about. If there is a God," he added, "then he will bless you for your honesty, and not punish you for what you think are your lies." I wanted to believe him. I did feel some relief but wasn't 100 per cent sure about God being so overly generous. He must have read my mind. With a healthy smirk dancing all over his face, he added, "Don't believe all the bad things the holy men say about God. Bhagvan himself is not bad, it's his ignorant followers who make him look bad."

This was completely different from anything I had ever heard from the mouth of an adult, before. Especially from people who called themselves the servants and children of God and were praying to him all the time.

"Let me tell you a story," he said, and squatted down on the ground. When he was at the University of Delhi, he often attended a church near the Houses of Parliament, he told us. The story was narrated by the padre there in one of his sermons, and the story went like this:

A mother and father go to church every Sunday with their son, Suneel. They want him to grow up to be a good Christian. They are proud of their padre, whom they believe to be a great preacher. One Sunday, as the parents are saying, "Bye, Padre sahib, see you next Sunday, Padre sahib." The padre asks Suneel if he knew what was in the deep cellar of the church? Suneel had heard a few passing, hush-hush references from some other children about a cellar beneath the church. Everyone had been warned never to go into the cellar or to speak about it to anyone.

Suneel, said, "No, I don't know."

"Would you like to take a look?" asks the padre, temptingly.

"No. Thank you. I don't want go there," Suneel says sheepishly.

"I am sure, Padre sahib will go with you, Suneel. You can trust him, I am sure," says the mother encouragingly, looking at the padre in a way that embarrasses little Suneel.

Padre takes eight-year-old Suneel gently by the hand and turns towards the secret entrance that leads to the cellar below. At the back of the church, in a dark, dingy, dank corner under the stairs to the bell tower, is a small trapdoor in the wall, decorated profusely with cobwebs. Padre opens the door, and they step on to a narrow spiral staircase. A few steps down, Suneel's feeling of discomfort starts to upgrade to suspicion and fear. He can barely see his hands in front of him. The heat rising from the cellar becomes more stifling with each step. Suneel is now filled with terror and foreboding.

Eventually, sweating, and his skin about to peel off his body, they arrive at the bottom of the stairs, at the end of which, is a large iron gate. Beyond the gate is an inferno, the like of which Suneel had never seen, not even in the films in the cinema hall. There is screaming, swearing, pleading and finger pointing among the crowds in the fire. Poor Suneel is terrified. There is an enormous male figure, dressed in a red leotard, walking through the flames. He has two huge horns sticking up from his enormous forehead. He has a large pitchfork in his hands, which he uses to throw a stream of new entrants onto the flames. He uses the same fork to prevent anyone trying to find their way up Suneel's spiral stairs, and out of the fiery furnace.

"That is Satan." Padre points to the male figure. "The gate," explains the padre, "is to prevent those on the other side from coming out and up the steps, into the church."

Suneel raises his head up and opens his mouth to scream, when he hears his mother's voice in his head, "Good Christian children do not complain, and they certainly do not question the judgement of their padre." Against his better judgement, Suneel chooses to keep his counsel. *With a head that big, Satan must be very clever. He will know I've done nothing for him to throw me into that fire,* Suneel comforts himself.

"Suneel, this is hell," says the padre, in his usual pious tones, "where all the sinners and unbelievers are sent, when they die."

"Will my mummy and daddy be sent here when they die?" Suneel cries out loud, tears streaming down his red-hot cheeks. "God won't send them here, will he?"

"No! Your mummy and daddy are good Christians. God sends only the sinners into this place. This is where God will send you if you are a naughty boy." Having made his point, the padre leads Suneel back up into the main church building where his parents are waiting just inside the front door.

Mummy thanks the padre and tells Suneel to thank him for his kindness. Suneel wishes his mum didn't look at the padre in that way. He hated her for embarrassing him and his daddy. They leave the church and walk all the way home, as usual. On the way, he hears his mummy saying wonderful things about their padre sahib, while daddy agrees in infrequent 'grunts'. Just outside the front door to their house, they stop. Suneel's mummy, a tall woman, bends down, and with her lips close to Suneel's ear asks, "What did you think of our Padre sahib? Isn't he a wonderful man, Suneel?" Suneel answers, "If you say so." And walks away in disgust.

Thoughtful brief silence, again, which felt much longer than it was. Dhannu and I tried to fathom the moral behind the parable – *I hate long silences in conversations.* We stared silently into the distant glories of *Bhagvan ki leela.* Waves of shadows, formed by the forested hills behind us, were lazily creeping out from the bottom of the Dabi Cliff, in the direction of the white mountains. We were embraced by soothing sounds and smells that have no name.

Babajee suggested we better move on and do our shopping. We moved on in the direction of Thanedhar. When we reached the Rest House, half a furlong short of the first shop on Thanedhar high street, we stopped to watch the evening sun on its way to the western horizons. Babajee said, "On the way to school the other day you told me some lies you had made up in the past, you said. Remember? Do you have any more you want to tell me about?"

I considered whether I really wanted him to know more than I had already revealed of the dark side of my character. I needed to think. To buy time, I fidgeted in my jacket pockets where I came upon a small lump of sticky *jagari* from, maybe the week before, covered in dust and fluff. I threw that into the bushes across the road. "Rat's love jaggery," I recalled Nirmu telling Mushu once.

Can I trust him? I wondered. Then, I noticed a smile lurking at the far corner of his mouth. "I am listening," he said.

"Ah . . . ere . . . umm . . . well, I tell lies only to protect myself."

"You told me the other day, but I wasn't quite sure what you meant by, 'to protect myself'." He sounded both curious and bemused, at the same time.

Should I tell him about that one? Why not? I said that, for example, some months back, over a period of five Wednesdays, I had been watching a man and a woman from the village across the stream doing naughty things in the woods, not far from where he and I first met on my way to school. When I got to the rocks under the three oaks, the two of them were taking their clothes off. Had I kept coming down the path, they would have seen me looking at them.

"So? It is their fault if they allow themselves to be seen by passers-by! How does that make you the guilty one?" He sounded incredulous.

I explained that the reason why it would have been me in trouble, was that I had taken the longer route, because I didn't like the narrow, dark gully on the shorter route that everyone else uses. They would have concluded that I had taken the longer route specially to watch them. I would have had a good hiding from the man, or he might have even killed me to protect their secret. For those five Wednesdays, I had to hide behind the trees until they were finished and moved away from the spot. At home, I made up all sorts of stories to cover up for being late back from school.

Babajee smiled. "That is not fair. Why didn't you tell your Matajee the truth?"

Tell my mother about what I saw up there? He doesn't mean it, surely? Dhannu and I looked at each other. I saw my thoughts reflected in Dhannu's eyes. We were tickled by his innocence. "No way! I couldn't tell Mother the truth, how could I? I just had to make up stories to explain my delay over those five Wednesdays, that's all," I added.

"Like what?"

Like, once I told Mamajee that halfway down my way, I saw a leopard sitting in the bushes, not far from my path. So, I sat up there behind those trees until the leopard moved away.

"And did Matajee believe you?"

"She must have, or I would have ended up with a sore bottom from a healthy smacking."

"Another time, I told Mama that my way home from school had been barred by the dog of Mrs Prem Chand Stokes, in Barubag."

"That bastard will kill someone one day, I'm telling you!" added Dhannu.

"Pushpa, Khushal and I tell lies because sometimes Mama doesn't accept the truth. There are too many times when telling the truth only gets us into more trouble. In our situation, telling the truth is not always the best policy."

"I don't know why," he said, "but, like I said to you earlier, your lies don't sound like lies to me. This is really strange." He kept staring from one face to the other with a puzzled look twirling in his eyes.

Suddenly, a bulb lit up in my head. I said with the confidence of a good Christian boy, "My lies are truths that didn't necessarily happen when I said that they had happened, but some of them have happened either to me or to someone else somewhere, and others will happen in the future. So, they couldn't be lies."

Babajee looked like he was enjoying my stories. "I don't know what to say. I could listen to your stories for the rest of the evening." He laughed. "How about you tell me one more, before we go our separate ways?" As an afterthought he asked me if I was comfortable talking about the subject in Dhannu's presence.

"I keep no secrets from Dhannu," I assured him. Dhannu nodded back in agreement.

He stood up from the Rest House wall. "I am afraid your lie will have to wait for another time. You better go and do your shopping. No point in being told off again for being late getting back home. Who knows, you might run into a real leopard this time." He gently swatted me on the back of my head and started walking briskly in the direction of the shops. Dhannu and I followed.

When we reached the first shop, Babajee asked us if we were all right. "All you boys in Dabi are very brave, and I am privileged to have met you."

He blessed us both and bade us farewell. As he turned to go, Dhannu asked, "When will we see you again?"

He turned round, "I don't know." He smiled, and off he went. We waited for him to look back, wave a goodbye, say something in parting. Nothing! He just walked on. Didn't look back. Not even a quick glance.

Seconds before the sun went to bed for the night, we arrived home safely, wondering if we would ever see our holy Babajee again.

Chapter 8

The Sunday School Fiasco

On a warm and sultry afternoon in July of that year, I had been confined to bed for two weeks. On the veranda immediately outside my bedroom door, Mama was talking to one of her regular visitors from the village of Shathla. They must have assumed I was asleep. I overheard the entire conversation. Mother sounded deeply concerned about my condition.

"I'm not sure what exactly our Nihal is suffering from. He's getting weaker by the day."

"Surely, you of all the people must know what's wrong with your poor boy."

"I wish I did. I am not a doctor. I only use my common sense, and a few tricks I've picked up from Nihal's s*adhu* friends. To make matters worse, apart from some barley porridge, there is nothing in the house I can give him in his condition. Even most of the porridge he brings straight up."

I heard Mother say that her own tried-and-tested remedies were having no visible effect on my condition. The hospital (three miles away in Kotgarh) had neither a doctor nor any medicines to speak of.

Before completing my eleventh year on this earth, I had had three near misses with death. Twice, due to dysentery, and once, when a 'real' mummy leopard checked me out at close quarters. Luckily for me, the leopard wisely decided to look for something with more flesh on its bones. Now, talking to her friend, Mother sounded pessimistic about me reaching my thirteenth birthday. All this led me to the inevitable conclusion, that I was not long for this world. My first reaction was fear of death. Thought of death started me thinking about where I will go after dying. *I may not be going to heaven, for all the questions I've been asking God and annoying him and so many good people. All the lies I have told over the years, and the sinful thoughts I have allowed my heart to entertain lately.* A deep, dark cloud of gloom plonked itself over my already miserable existence.

I started preparing myself to die. I had seen enough dead bodies being taken to the various cremation spots and churchyards to know the exact posture of a dead body. I turned over onto my back, stretched out my body, legs together, arms straight down on either side of my body, and my eyes shut. I pleaded with God to please let my soul into heaven.

My mind whirled around at great speed, surveying my entire life of twelve years and some months, on this earth. It stopped over a picture in which I saw my favourite holy man, Babajee, accompanied by Dhannu and Hubau, standing behind my house on the edge of the road. I heard Babajee say, "There is no sin in asking God questions. Sin is in not wanting to know or to understand things as they really are." He added, "Don't be afraid to talk to God. I talk to God all the time." *Could Babajee have been wrong?*

I tossed and turned, full of fear, not knowing what to think or do. At some point, I must have dropped off into fear-induced sleep. When I came to, I felt calm and defiant, and physically not as weak as I had been only an hour or so before. I had accepted the inevitable; I was going to die, but now I was not afraid of dying. I was not afraid of God either. I knew that Babajee was right. *God will not punish me for speaking to him, I am sure.*

Mentally, I entered into what I believed to be my

'conversation with God' mode:

Thank you, God! No, I am not afraid anymore. Or am I? I'm not sure! Can I ask you a few questions before I die? Stop me if you don't like my question. Please stop me, before I make you angry!

Suddenly, I heard this deep, resounding laughter from far away. Sounded like God was laughing. *"If your padre says that I am the Loving Father of all Creation, ask him, how then can I send you, or anyone else, to a place like hell?"* said the voice.

"That's what the Bible says. You send more people into hell than into heaven," I retorted. While God was still laughing, I dropped off into deep sleep, again. I can't say how long I remained in that state, but when I woke up, I heard myself talking to God at the point where I had snoozed off.

Now, where shall I start? Umm... That'll do. I am thinking about that Sunday in June of the year before. I did not understand why you had to be so cruel to those two little girls and their mother. The girls can't have been more than five and three years old, respectively, at the time. Their mother was made to stand in front of the whole congregation, inside the church. She was asked to confess her sins and to ask for forgiveness from you and the whole worldwide Church. If she didn't do that, she was told, she would be boycotted by the whole Church, and you would send her to hell. My friends and I did not like the way that family was treated. The little girls are our friends. All that humiliation, just to please you. I can't understand your love and your sense of justice.

I know that you know everything, but may I please tell you things in my own words? You remember the great preacher we had in our church last month? He said that you had called him all the way from Bambai to preach in our hills. That's an awful long way to call someone to preach one scary sermon in our beautiful church. Did you really call him all the way from Bambai, or did he make up the story to get away from the heat on the planes? Never mind if you don't want to answer that. The preacher said that you will punish all the sinners in hell, where there is non-stop weeping and gnashing of teeth. Phew! We were glad he was there only that one Sunday.

Oh, I also wanted to talk to you about the trouble I had with my Sunday School teacher and our Padre saab, last year. You remember the Sunday in March I am referring to? The day started with a particularly beautiful, bright morning. The usual piercingly cold and fresh breeze from the mountains whistled through the pine trees all the way to our Dabi. As always, the breeze crept up under our skimpy pajama legs, and right into our bones.

Sunday morning routine was the same as ever. Out of bed before sunrise, wash down in the draughty bathroom outdoors. Then morning prayers, followed by breakfast, followed by the regular chores in and around the house. Oh, and check the chicken-shed door, spread the dry pine needles in the cow shed. See to the fodder, hay, water, rock salt for the cattle outside to last the day. Hubau and Dhannu were instructed to secure the two dogs to the stake outside the chicken coop. Keep an eye out for the monkeys ..." etcetera, etcetera. All concluded by ten o'clock.

We calculate time in Dabi from the position of the sun in the sky, or shadows on the landscape. As you know, on our way to church, three miles away in Kotgarh, we always leave at 10.00 a.m. precisely. Khushal, Anup and I follow Mother in single file, a hundred yards up the narrow dirt path, onto the road behind the house. As usual, every few yards we run into someone we know.

After a brief conversation with each one, on we go. Have you noticed how so many of our neighbours greet Mama with such respect? I mean, we are so poor now, but everyone, even the rich folks, always say, 'Namaste Bui jee', 'Namaste Rupi bua', 'Namaste Mashtrani jee'. Thank you, God, I feel so proud of my mama.

On that Sunday, as always, we arrived a few minutes after eleven o'clock. There was the usual chit-chat with people we hadn't seen since the previous Sunday. Eventually, we all filed in for the start of the 11.00 a.m. Service, a few minutes late, as usual.

Hymn before the sermon, is a signal for those between the ages of eight and fourteen, to file out of the church building in an orderly fashion to the Sunday School. We leave the grown-ups inside, in peace, to listen to Padre Saab's boring, long sermons. I know what the sermons are like, from what we pick up from listening to the grown-ups, over their *chai-pani* on the lawn outside Padre Saab's big house. And also, because, on the odd occasion when the Sunday School teacher is unwell or out of station, we are also sentenced to sit through the whole Service.

From the middle of March to halfway into autumn, the Sunday School sessions are held outdoors, except in inclement weather. The Sunday I am talking about, we settled our posteriors on the ground at the far end of the school volley ball courts. We heard *Mashi's* (master jee) usual instructions: "Come on . . . all of you ... sit down and behave yourselves." Followed by, "Let us pray ... come on ... sit properly ... You, yes you! Cross your legs!" Shouted Mashi, more out of habit than anything else. "Put your hands together and shut your eyes. If I catch anyone with their eyes open during prayers, they will not be allowed *chai-pani* after the Service."

"Mashi, how will you know if anyone has their eyes open, sir? I mean, with your own eyes shut, how will you see?" asked Mohan, with all the innocence of an eleven-year-old. Back came the reply, "Shut up." Followed by a smile dripping with embarrassment.

After Mashi had said a long prayer, we all joined him dutifully, wearily clapping our lips under our cold noses, making noises that sounded like, The Lord's Prayer. *"Ai hamare pita, tu jo swarg main hai, tera naam pavitra maana jai, tera rajya ai ... Amen."* All said in perfect harmony.

Putting my hand up, I said timidly, "Mashi."

"And what's wrong now, question master?" he asked calmly, while busily fiddling with the loose bandage on his left thumb.

"Mashi, when we say, 'Our Father' in the Lord's Prayer, does it mean that God is 'Father' only of us Christians, or does it mean that—"

"Stand up." he shouted angrily. The command hit me right in the solar plexus. I could not understand what was wrong about my question, but I sure wished I hadn't asked it. I realised, regretfully, that once again I was in deep shit. He hissed, "There ... right next to the nettles. God's nettles." pointing with his weatherworn, overworked, grubby finger. His rugged face – too-old-for-his-age – looked offended.

I stood up, feeling angry, fearful, and confused. Walked over to the clump of nettles near the edge of the playground. Mashi carried on with the day's lesson. My peers glanced sideways at me. They knew that I had done something wrong, and being good Christians, they expected to see me punished for whatever it was. Can you believe that God? I was asking Mashi a simple question about you, not questioning you! You weren't even there!

Well! As you know, merciful Father . . . *Oh . . . I am so tired and hungry . . .* just because I ask questions, and sometimes I say a bit more than they think I should, doesn't mean that I don't respect you. Only a few months ago, I heard uncle Bduraman's first wife – she is a Musalmaan – advising Mama to have me exorcised. Why can't you tell them to listen to us children, sometime? Hear me out, that's all I ask! You know, generally I am always helping everyone. I am simply trying to survive and stand up for myself. God, I hope you see that.

Oh, I am hungry. I don't know where Mama has gone to. Please wait a moment God. I just need to have a break ... *Oh. That's better. Where was I? Oh yes.* For example, no one within my family and friends knows how, after Papajee's death, I suffered bullying by that ugly man in Thanedhar, and from those two boys from Bhutti, every day for three years. You know how horrible that man was to me, and the way those two schoolmates lay in wait for me, on my way back from school, every afternoon! They said things to me that I can't even tell you. More than once, they nearly twisted my ear off the side of my skull. Why? Just so they could make me beg them for mercy, which I never did. What do you think of that, then?

You never once offered me help. I had to fight them on my own. Did you see, the day I went for those two bullies with my datch (machete)? Had they not run away I would have killed at least one of them, and they knew that. They never touched me again. May I ask you – if I had killed one, or both of them, would you have sent me to hell? And would that be fair? Were you happy for them to keep bullying me for the rest of my days? Sorry, I didn't mean to be rude. Please forgive me.

See, this is what happens, when you don't say a word; I waffle on completely off track. Let's get back to Sunday

School.

Standing six feet outside the 'semi-circle' by the nettles, under the clear blue skies and the warm sun, I slowly slipped into a state of daydreaming. In my angry heart and head, I invented an enormous, gigantic weapon to shoot you down from your heaven! I wanted to put an end to the cause of all the miseries and lies and confusions and injustices and . . . and . . . I felt dizzy and keeled over onto the dusty, hard, rough earth. The whole of my left side hit against the rubble on the ground. I came to, I think, quite quickly. The pain was as intense as any I'd ever known. I stood up, swatted the dust off my clothes. The sight of a red smudge on the sleeve of my *best* and *only hand-me-down*-jacket of Khushal, was more than I was willing to take. Without so much as a "May I go to the loo, sir?" I marched off to the church, a hundred yards up the steps. I planted my two bare feet firmly on the large slab of blue stone, about three feet in front of the main door.

I heard a few muffled prayers, followed by a familiar-sounding hymn. Two minutes after that, the door swung open. The congregation trickled out in ones and twos, adjusting their eyes to the bright sunshine. They seemed to willy-nilly guide their feet into the shoes outside the front door, while busily making conversation with the nearest person. Not wearing shoes inside the church must have something to do with you telling Moses to take off his shoes as a sign of respect for you. Am I right? Why do I keep asking you questions? You never answer me.

As they moved away from the front door, a small number were still in contemplative silence. Others were busily looking around to join in some saucy gossip. Midst one particular group of three women – all related to each other by marriage – there were clear signs of discomfort or anger forming into dark clouds, ready for a full-blown session of lightning and thunder. I guessed that from what I knew had happened between the ladies about six months before. I stayed put on the blue slab and waited for my moment of revenge. I was certain of a triumphant return to my pack in the school playground.

By the time Padre saab came out of the church, all except two of his flock had shuffled off to the vicarage veranda for the post-Service ritual of *chai-pani*. Without any formalities, I told him the whole episode of my innocent attempt to find an answer to something that had been bugging me for some time, and the unjust reaction I had received from my Sunday School teacher. I drew his attention to the fresh cut above my ear, and the smudge of blood on my 'best and only jacket'. All in one single breath. Padre saab turned his pious mask in the direction of the two sheep who were waiting to talk to him. "Children of today! They are becoming *sooo* ungodly," he prophesied. "How many times do you have to be told, it is sinful to question God and the teachings of the Bible." Luckily for me, the *chai-pani* ritual saved me from the embarrassment of the whole flock of his older sheep staring at me in derision, or whatever.

Sorry, God, I'm feeling tired again. Do you mind if I have a break? *I don't know where I am going with this.*

A brief snooze later: Sorry God, for dozing off. I am OK now. *Where was I? . . . Oh, yes!* Standing outside the church door, my eyes welled up. I felt drops of fluid trickle down the front of my trousers – it wasn't from my eyes. I could feel the heat of hell fire all around me. I needed to find a bush, but my feet would not move. Will you send me to hell for what happened on that day? Surely, you can't! You, of all the people should know that I had done nothing wrong!

I have been meaning to ask you for some time now. Why are you like my elders, so touchy about your power and authority ... and ... and may I ask you, are you, Yahova and Allah and the millions of Hindu gods one and the same? I really would like to know. Please, don't make me wait for the rest of my life for an answer!

Before God could answer, I felt a gentle pat on my left shoulder. "Hi, *beta* (son). How are you feeling now? You've been talking in your sleep, again." Mother opened the south-facing window – the same one through which she had seen Papa, riding past on his white horse, in her dreams – to let some light and fresh air in. "Wow! You are looking so much better than you did this morning. Tell you what: if you finish this porridge, I will give you a special treat for tea this evening – your favourite, spinach and zarga *pakorhas*, just the way you like them, hot and crispy." Mother helped me to sit up in bed, put the pillow against the wall behind my head. She cradled the porridge bowl in my hands. "Here, eat it all up. I'll go and feed the chickens and bring the cows in."

Chapter 9

Rhoga Khad

I survived my illness, celebrated my fourteenth birthday, and was now ploughing through my fifteenth year on this earth. Like any other normal morning in Dabi, after a long list of chores and a hurriedly swallowed breakfast, I was unhappily dragging my anxious self in the direction of school.

For the second consecutive week, I had not done my math's homework. I had lost my one and only exercise book, which had in it the homework for math, Hindi, English, science, history, geography, geometry, and the most useless and utterly pointless subject – algebra.

Our new math's and science teacher did not take kindly to his pupils not doing as they were told. He had only been in the job for six months and had already earned the title of 'the most despised teacher' in the entire school. At fourteen years, nine months, and some days old, I was not prepared to be hit by anyone. No other teacher had ever hit me, except once in primary school when our head teacher had a fit of temper for whatever reason. He thrashed everyone and everything in his class on that day. I was determined that if the science teacher ever hit me again, I would hit him back. But the pleasure thus derived, would not have been enough to make up for the fallout. Our grown-ups – if only they were – always took the teacher's side, no matter what! So, go to school and get into serious trouble? Or stay away and face the consequences of truancy. I took the softer option.

Halfway along the three-mile stretch between school

and home, I stopped at my 'truancy station'. It was a beautiful spot on the side of Rhoga Hill, with plenty of sunny and shady spots under the pine trees to choose from. The small area of flat earth was sheltered by thorny bushes from any prying eyes on the road below.

Sitting there, on a flat piece of blue granite slab, I had about five hundred feet of sheer rock face, dropping into the stream of Rhoga on my left. On the far side of the stream, was the dreaded dark and damp pine forest that led all the way to the graveyard and the school's upper playgrounds, a mile and a half away. Through gaps between the trees, I could see two short stretches of the road where, later in the afternoon, I would see my schoolmates on their way back from school. That would be my cue to return home from the school that I would not have been to.

Immediately behind me, the rocky hill rose steeply a couple of thousand feet and disappeared into the skies above. Facing me in the north-west, the panoramic view of small farms, apple orchards and tiny villages, dipped sharply to the river Satluj, five miles below. Across the river, the land climbed sharply up into the tall, rocky hills of the district of Kullu. In hindsight, it was educationally and religiously more beneficial than the stifling environment of my classroom and the Sunday School. Don't let your children read this!

Now, all I had to do, was to find something to keep my mind off school, and the possible consequences of not being where I was meant to be. Daydreaming about a couple of girls at school seemed the best thing to do. *But Jesus says that thinking naughty thoughts was as good as doing those naughty things in real life. I better think of something else,* I moaned with disappointment and frustration.

Trying another conversation with God didn't appeal to me at that moment. I had written one or two letters to him, when I was about nine or ten. I had secured them to the trees in the darkest parts of the woods. I checked each letter the day after. The letters had gone. It took me a couple of years to work out that the letters must have been eaten by goats or cows in those woods. In more recent times, I had written a few long letters, but without the use of pen and paper.

Thoughts of the consequences of skiving off school again, only helped to further re-enforce the sense of isolation in that empty space. I was wondering about what to do with my day when I heard a girl's voice from a few feet away to my right say, "Is my friend Nihal talking to himself, again?"

"You silly girl! What did you do that for? Scared the life out of me."

"What are you doing out here? Why are you not in school?" she asked cheekily.

"I may ask you the same question . . . what are you doing here? Why are you not at home, doing that son-of-a-pig's biddings?" I reacted sharply.

The surprise visitor was my friend Shakuntala (not her real name) from a village up the hill. Our friendship had started in primary school in Barubag. Despite no literacy at home and no support from her mother and stepfather, Shakuntala had maintained her position near the top of the class throughout. A few months short of completing her primary education, her mother took her out of school. After that, when I moved to the high school in Kotgarh, the following academic year, we had run into each other a couple of times round my 'truancy station', which fell on the way to her aunt's place about a mile down the hill, across two shallow streams.

Shakuntala came up close, put her bundle of 'all sorts' tied up in an old shirt, on the ground. She sat down next to me, put her arm round my back, leaned against my shoulder and said softly, "You are the only friend I have in this whole wretched world," and broke down in tears and sobs. I guessed the reason and decided to allow her time to have a good cry. Having been familiar with her tragic life, ever since we were both about seven, I felt my eyes welling up. I so wanted to put my arms around her, to hold her in a tight hug, but due to the fear of 'sin', I dared not. I sat there in angry silence, asking God, how he could sit up there in his wonderful heaven, surrounded by his son and all the angels, the saints, and all his heavenly ugly creatures, and watch this beautiful, innocent girl suffer.

Can't have been more than ten minutes – felt like hours – when she stopped sobbing, dried her tears on her shirt sleeves, blew her nose hard on to the ground and wiped her fingers on a piece of crushed newspaper she had tucked away in the pocket of her waistcoat. She asked if I had something to eat. In silence, I took the 'rich man's' lunch from my school bag: a two-egg omelette wrapped between two *rotis* and a large, ripe golden apple. I broke the lunch roll into two equal halves. We ate in silence. After lunch, I broke the apple in two halves. We munched away at the apple. The silence continued. From time to time, we looked at each other; each hoping for the other to break that uncomfortable silence. Finally, our early lunch over, Shakuntala said, "This is the best meal of my life. You are so lucky." After hiding our meagre belongings securely under the bushes, we ran all the way to the stream, two hundred yards down the hill. Drank as much water as our bodies could accommodate, and ran back to the truancy station, hoping that no one had seen us.

Safely back, Shakuntala told me that she had run away from home that morning, for the last time, determined never to return to that hellhole. Her stepfather wouldn't leave her alone, and her mother didn't see anything wrong with him occasionally having a 'bit of fun with you', as her mother put it. If Shakuntala didn't do as desired by the old man, he would slap her about, and her mother would then starve her the whole day. They forced her to work on an empty stomach. She was warned to keep her mouth shut, or things could get far worse. She was nine years of age when she first ran away from home, but with nowhere to go, she never stayed out for more than a few hours each time. Not knowing what to say to comfort her, or what to do to help her, was burning my inside with frustration and rage.

"You are always kind to me. You mind if I sit closer to you?" We were both squatting on the ground. She moved closer, put her arms round my right leg, rested her head on my knee, and within minutes, she was fast asleep. I sat still for nearly one-half hour.

Shakuntala woke up, pulled away from my leg sharply, sat upright, and before I could react, she asked, as if continuing a conversation, "Do you remember telling me about the Chinese preacher in your church a few months ago? You know the one, who said that he was from Amreeka?"

I was still rummaging around in my head for something kind and helpful to say, finding nothing, I sat in glum silence.

"Did you hear me?" She poked me in the ribs.

"Yeah! I heard you alright," I said irritably. "He read the whole chapter from the Bible from memory. He was going on about God and this man, called Job, being great friends and all that."

I turned to face Shakuntala, took her hand in my hands, "How could that be? I mean, God and Satan had ganged up against that poor man and his entire family. God did all that, just to please the Satan! Makes no sense to me!"

"I don't know. I spend half my life praying to your god and all my gods. None of them are there when I am being abused and starved by that filthy, evil son-of-a-pig and my witchy mother."

"I don't know, either! Our Padre saab says that God knows all our needs, even before we ask. All we have to do is, 'be faithful in prayer', he says. Well, if God knows about you, even before that bastard son-of-a-pig molests you, and before you are being starved, then why doesn't he do something about protecting you and feeding you? Jesus fed five thousand grown-ups out of five loaves and two fishes! And they had only missed just one meal of the day. Oh, how I wish Jesus or someone like him were around. No way would he let you go through all this horrible suffering."

"I love your stories about Jesus. I remember you telling me about how he loved everyone so much. Did he say something like, 'ask anything you want, and my father in heaven will give it to you?' Well, I've not asked for much. I don't know if his father will ever give me what little I want." She took my hand between her hands, squeezed it gently and looking into my eyes said, "I love you so much. I wish I could live with you." She placed my hand on her cheek and held it there for what felt like eternity . . . eternity of a few seconds.

"You know, if it was at all possible, I would take you to my home and keep you safe with me. Even if my Mama allowed us to live in our home, that son-of-a-pig will not let that happen. Things could get a lot worse for both of us. He might kill us both and kill my Mama as well."

She looked at me with tearful eyes. "How could things ever get any worse for me than they've always been?" She let go of my hand. "Do you think I am a dirty girl or something?" Before I could answer, she stood up and made some excuses about being late to visit her aunt across the stream. "Hope to see you again, soon. Please don't stop being my friend because of what I said to you." And she whizzed off. I didn't know what she was talking about!

Sitting there, I tried to convince myself that there really was nothing objectionable in the way Shakuntala and I felt about each other. In my heart I was hoping that God being God, would understand that Shakuntala desperately needed to feel loved, and I wanted to make her feel loved. I wondered why it was sinful to love a friend, just because she was a girl. I was struggling to put my feelings into words that would be acceptable to God.

Through this deep discussion between me and my other self, I could hear the rustling of slow movement of animals approaching me from my right. I withdrew from the internal discussion and looked up to see who or what it was. It was Budu with his animals. They were only a few yards away from me. With a mixture of mischief and suspicion writ large on his cheeky face, he asked "Do you know that girl? What was she doing here at this time of the day? . . . What were you two up to?"

I answered, "None of your bloody business. If you must know, she was telling me about her sad life." I answered in an angry voice.

He winked mischievously. "Wait till your mother finds out."

Old Budu was from a village, higher up the hill. He was

out there with his three cows, two goats and an ox, grazing over the few green dimples between the rocks and trees. His other ox had slipped off the side of a cliff on the wooded side across the stream a month ago. Budu ambled over to where I was, cleared a small patch of earth with his bare hands, put some dry pine needles down, and sat on them in his ancient and holey pajama bottoms. He pulled his *datch* up from the back of his neck, where it had been resting between an ancient, dirty shirt and his bare back. All the locals carried a *datch* (a bow-headed machete) or a *brarha* (lightweight, wide-bladed axe), for lopping green branches for the animals, and firewood for home, while out and about in the woods.

In emergencies, the *brarha* and the *datch* also served as useful weapons against attacks by leopards and bears. Not that that was a common occurrence, but it did happen often enough to expect one to be prepared when encroaching upon the territory of the beasts. When not on active duty, *datch* functioned as an adequate substitute for a tobacco pipe.

Budu took a small piece of soft charcoal from his tobacco pouch, carefully smoothed off the edges on a stone, and placed it an inch or so in, at the wider end of the trumpet-shaped hollow handle of the *datch*. He then held the *datch* between his knees, handle pointing straight up. Now, with both his hands free, he drew a large pinch of home-grown dry tobacco leaves from his pouch, placed it in the palm of his left hand, rubbed it with his right thumb in a circular motion. He gathered the softened leaves into a ball, placed it on top of the charcoal inside the handle, and pushed it in firmly with his thumb. He clapped off the powdery remnants from the palm of his hand. Cupping his hands over the tobacco inside the handle of the *datch*, he gently blew onto it a few times to moisten it. One more press with the thumb. "That should do it." He smiled up at me.

Next, he took small bits of dry, white strips of what looked like silk fabric. The strips were obtained from the underside of large, green leaves that grew between the joints of rocks all around us. He folded the strips tightly, placed them on a piece of flint and held the flint and the rolled-up strips firmly between the thumb and index finger of his left hand. Then, he sharply struck the edge of the flint with a two-finger iron knuckleduster a couple of times. Sparks thus produced, were enough to get the strips smoldering gently. He rolled the strips and placed them on top of the tobacco. Holding them there lightly under his two fingers, he wrapped his dirty handkerchief over the small hole at the narrow, tapered end of the handle; reclined against the rock behind him and made every drag an act of sheer pleasure. I could see all the worries and stresses, caused by his crippling poverty, ride away on the puffs of smoke, into the wide-open spaces above.

Halfway through, he offered the *datch* to me. I wanted to say 'no' but didn't have the heart to disappoint that lovely man. I took the datch, took a long, hard drag, and nearly died coughing, spitting, spluttering, and choking. My mind played out a scene from six months back, when I had been suspected by Mother of having smoked a cigarette. I had not smoked, scout's honour. I had picked up the tobacco stink from other smokers nearby. On that occasion, I was made to chew and swallow a large, red, hot chili as my reward for the sin I had not even committed. For the next two days, the red chili burned me at both ends, and in the middle too. I scrolled the picture to the bottom of the page, and after getting my breath back, tried my luck again. This time, I savoured the gentle puffs of aromatic home-grown tobacco from Budu's *datch*.

In between puffing, coughing, and blowing clouds of smoke, Budu brought me up to date on the village gossip about who was marrying whom, who had added to the human population since we last met some weeks before, who is leaving whom and moving in with whom. Couple of our common acquaintances in the nearby villages had married their second and third wives. He also told me, with tongue in cheek, about the affair his younger brother was carrying on with their next door's wife. He added a few saucy 'truthful lies', I suspect, to spice up the second tale. Until the middle of the twentieth century, one man having two or three wives – usually sisters, or a woman marrying two or three brothers was not entirely uncommon in our neck of the woods. This was one sure way of keeping the small piece of land and home under one ownership. Since then, with education and money more easily accessible, the culture has changed. Since a decade or two before the middle of the twentieth century, it is one man, one wife … one woman, one husband. There may be exceptions that I am not aware of.

Halfway through his tales, Budu reached out to his right, and with electrifying speed grabbed a *lhulti* (small lizard) off the ground, between his thumb and two fingers. He took his cap off in one hand, placed the *lhulti* on his head, and quickly put the cap back on. He turned to me, pointing to the lizard under his cap, "This will clear my head of all the lice and fleas in seconds." With that, he returned to the rest of his story about his plans for acquiring a share of his late uncle's piece of land in the next village. After two long minutes, he sneaked his fingers under the cap, grabbed the *lhulti* and dropped it back on the ground.

He reclined against the rock behind him and took out a large red apple from his tatty cotton bag, cut it in two, and gave one half to me. Before the last bits of that juicy apple had cleared our gullets, we noticed signs of excitement and commotion among a small gathering of monkeys a few yards away to our right. The two big males were under a tree, staring suspiciously at something in front of them on the ground. Other members of the family had taken to the trees, from where they continued to chatter and point with their eyes to 'the thing' on the ground below. We guessed the cause of the excitement and made our way towards the scene. As we approached the spot, the two males scampered up the tree and calmly settled up there to watch the show below. As we had suspected, under the tree was a cobra, curled up and ready to attack. Its hissing and darting tongue should have been warning enough for any sensible creature to stay away and mind their own business.

"It looks ready to attack," I cautioned.

Not taking his eyes off the snake, Budu pointed to a broken branch of pine tree six feet away, "Get that *shanta*." I fetched the *shanta*. He handed his cap over to me, suggesting that I wrap it round one end of the *shanta*, with the help of a long spindly piece of ivy, growing within my reach. I followed his instructions, handed the contraption over, and stood behind him for self-preservation. Pointing the capped end of the *shanta* directly at the snake, Budu cautiously moved it forward. I could see the cobra's eyes fixed on the cap. Once within striking distance, the snake's head darted forward. Budu swung his *datch* and slashed the head right off from the snake's body. The head landed dangerously close to my bare feet. I crushed it under the lump of rock I was holding at the ready, just in case.

The whole operation was over within seconds and left me shaken. Budu, on the other hand, looked at me as if to say, 'That's what I do for living'. He stretched the body of the snake in a straight line, measured it with his *datch.* The snake was a little over four feet, head and all. We returned to our spot. Budu had another smoke; this time I declined to share in the pleasure. By now, his animals were grazing their way homeward, up the hill. He stood, shook off the dust from his holey trousers, picked up his bag and the *datch,* and with a "Hope to see you again!" he followed the animals in the direction of his village.

I stretched out on one of the few flat, shady surfaces in sight, and soon snoozed off into heaven. I expected to be stopped by St Peter at the pearly gates, which were disappointingly simple. There were no pearls or anything else fancy about them. The gates were open and unattended. I walked through, like I had been there before. Far, far away, yet clearly visible, an old man was levitating in empty space, and on his right hand levitated a bearded young man. I thought I had seen the young man somewhere before but couldn't think where? Floating around them, were some strange and weird creatures. Some had huge wings. Some had hundreds of eyes all over their bodies. Most had more fingers on one hand than I had on my two. They wore long, shiny, white hair in ponytails. The one nearest to me had the body of an angel with a lamb on its shoulders, and a large eye in the center of its forehead.

The old man, I guessed to be God, was staring at me with an angry contorted face. He looked grumpy, miserable – almost ugly. I expected to see a face brighter than the midday sun. The young man next to God, had more of a kind face and a forgiving smile. A very tall, ugly angel standing before them, was addressing them with overly exaggerated gestures. I could not hear his words, but he kept pointing in my direction with his right hand in an aggressive and accusatory manner.

The angel shouted in my direction angrily. I wanted to hear what he was saying, but it was too late. I was already back in Rhoga. Fear froze me to the ground upon which I lay. No matter how hard I tried, I could not move. When eventually I managed to sit up, I realised that the shouting sounds were coming from my schoolmates across the stream on their way back from school.

I was hearing the rustle of gentle breeze through the pine trees, the singing of many birds, each species competing with all the others. I was smelling the invigorating scent of pine forest, and seeing the monkeys frolicking in the trees. The pleasures simply refused to register on the choppy seas of my mind.

It was time to be heading back home from the school that I had not been to. At home, multiple chores were eagerly awaiting my return.

"Sorry God, got to go. In the meantime, please don't be angry with me."

Chapter 10

Will He Ever Come Back?

On Sunday 4 September 1955, I was fifteen years, one month and twenty-nine days old. Mama and Anup were suffering from a potent flu virus. On that bright and sunny morning, I went to church all by myself without any of the usual: 'don't do that', 'stop asking questions', and 'look where you're going', from Mother.

At the end of the Service, my friends and I joined the grown-ups for *chai-pani* outside the Padre's house. Despite the culture of caution concerning physical closeness, our parents did permit us freedom, within strict limits, for social interaction. Time for home, and the mother of one of my two female friends (first cousins) wondered if I would like to go home via their place, a mile and a half up the hill. I wasn't going to say 'no' to the opportunity of spending some more time with friends on the sunnier side of the earth. On my direct route home, I would have been into a mile-and-a-half-long trek of thick, dark woods within less than five minutes from the church.

We leisurely followed the two sets of my friends' parents up the hill. When we reached within a few yards of their home, one of my friends suggested that I should stay at their place for a sleepover. With the usual sparkle in her eyes, she said affectionately, "We'll have a few card games and you can tell us your stories." I looked at her, broody-eyed. While I was struggling to make up my mind, her mother poured a whole bucket load of cold water over my head. She pointed out that we had no means of asking for my mother's permission for a sleep over. There were no facilities of telephone or telepathy at their place. We hurriedly said and gestured our goodbyes. They turned right for home and I, grudgingly, carried on another two hundred yards up the road.

On hitting the Shimla-Tibet Road, instead of turning left and continuing on my journey home, something urged me to cross the road. I did, and ran into a 'grumpy' little classmate from the nearby village standing outside the one and only shop for miles around. "Oh, it's you. What brings you here on a Sunday afternoon?" he asked grumpily.

"I missed you. Why are you looking at me like that?"

"Like what?"

"Like a constipated monkey."

"How do you know what a constipated monkey looks like?" he asked angrily.

"I am looking at one, right now," I countered immediately feeling guilty for having over-stepped the mark. "Sorry, *yaar (mate)*. I didn't mean that." He ignored my apology and walked away. I went into the shop, used my life savings to buy some roasted-in-shell monkey nuts. Put half away in my shoulder bag for Mama, Anup and Hubau; the other half in my jacket pocket, and headed home. By the time I emerged from the mile-long densely wooded forest, I had managed to chew through my share of the nuts. For the next mile and a half, the gently sloping 'jeepable' road in front of me, was hemmed in on both sides by apple orchards and tiny villages. God was teasingly dangling the sun over the western horizon from my left.

Soon, I was between Upper and Lower Pamlai villages, I didn't want to go home. I wanted to be somewhere where the sun was still sunshine, there were other houses around my house; neighbours talking, laughing, gossiping, children playing outdoors, and whatever else people in villages do of an evening. I wanted people, other than the same three in Dabi. I called out to a couple of my school friends in the village. They were not home.

My unwilling steps moved resentfully homeward. *Wish I had uncles, aunties, and cousins to visit.* I wanted to go back to my friends. Or, anywhere, but Dabi. Few yards down the road, I heard someone calling out my name, a short distance behind me. I turned to face the voice and saw a blurred roly-poly, five-foot-six male figure against the setting sun. He was wearing a *dhoti* (single piece of cotton material wrapped round the lower part of one's body) and a long shirt, shawl over his shoulders, and a full head of long and wavy, white hair.

I said a hesitating "*Namaste*" not sure who I was addressing. As he approached closer, a big smile lit up his round, brown face, exposing a perfect set of pearly white teeth.

"Yes, it is Nihal. Lovely to see you, son. Do you remember me?" Without waiting for my answer, he continued, "We first met in Thanedhar, two summers ago. Remember?" His friends in Barubag had invited him back again this year, he said, to spend part of his summer vacation with them.

"Yes sir, I remember you. You are Professor Ba ... Ba ... Banerjee? I am glad to meet you, again, sir." We shook hands.

"I see you've been crying. Is something wrong?" He looked at me with genuine concern.

I was fine, I assured him. "Oh, you mean my tears. It was just a whiff of breeze back there. Blew some dust into my eyes." I lied. His smiley eyes said – *I don't believe you.*

He remembered the names of everyone in Dabi, which

flattered me no end. "Had things improved at all since his last visit two years ago?" he enquired.

"Not as much as one would want, but we have had a few more boxes of apples each year, and both our cows are in milk. We have a dozen more hens laying eggs. Things are starting to look up. My brother Khushal has joined the army, since your last visit. Rupbhai has found a job in our school, and he still does private tuitions during winter months," I rattled on proudly, as we moved Dabiward.

He told me briefly about various developments within his family. By this time, we had arrived behind my house. I invited him for a quick *chai-pani.* He declined and asked me if I had put any of my stories to pen and paper. I said I had recently written a story.

"Any chance of me taking a look at your story?" he asked, politely.

"Can you join us for some *chai-pani* tomorrow afternoon? I would love to read my story to you!" I said, with excited anticipation. He accepted my invitation, and on that note, we said, "See you tomorrow." He carried on to the stream and I ran the hundred yards down to my house.

I told Mother all about my meeting with Professor Banerjee. "I hope you don't mind ... I've invited him for some *chai-pani* tomorrow afternoon." Surprise, surprise. Apart from a brief, *what is wrong with you?* stare, Mama did not mind!

The next day, after *chai-pani*, Hubau, Kodru (our two helpers), Anup, I, and Professor Banerjee gathered on the veranda. Our dog spread itself next to our guest, rested its head on his thigh with a, *you don't mind, do you?*

I pointed to the spot where the story was supposed to have been written, nearly two years before; at the base of the Praying Mountains. I read the story to an attentive audience:

I am excited by my closeness to what, until this moment, I have been seeing from the front of my house in Dabi, many miles away. Now, looking back from the opposite direction, Dabi looks even more isolated from up here than I had ever imagined. My house is like a tiny blob, hanging off the edge of the cliff, in mid-air. How weird!

After some thought, I sit up and cross my legs in *sadhna* posture, take a couple of deep breaths, and relax. In my mind, I go back six years, to the night of the first week in September 1947. Since that night, I have been trying to find the answer to the puzzle. My thoughts are being interrupted by the two miracles that happened in our school last Tuesday. *Right, let me get these out of the way, first,* I decide.

The first miracle, was that I was inside my classroom, sitting at my desk, before the roll call. I couldn't recall ever arriving in school on time.

The second miracle was when the maths teacher asked if I had done my homework for the day. I said "no", and before I could recite my litany of excuses, he took me by the right ear, yanked me out of my seat, and dragged me all the way to the principal's office. We entered the office with his hand still painfully attached to my ear, and my ear struggling to stay attached to the side of my skull. He calmly informed the principal why we were there. The principal said politely, but firmly, "That'll do Master Jee. Leave Nihal here. You may go back to your classroom."

'Mashi' reluctantly detached his girly hand from my ear and returned to his proper job. The principal said nothing for a whole *looong* minute, allowing me time to nurse my ear and put it back where God had placed it originally. Then, in his head-masterly voice, he asked me why I kept missing school and not doing my homework. "I want the truth, and none of your fancy stories. I mean it."

I don't know why, but I felt that I could trust him. I told him the truth, briefly. He listened patiently, looked at me with sympathy, then said, "I am sorry to hear you are not in a position to replace your lost exercise notebook. But (an encouraging smile replaced the pitying looks in his eyes) surprisingly enough, your truancy records and absence of homework, have not affected your results as much as I would have feared." He reached into the shelving unit, next to his desk, pulled out a brand-new exercise notebook – the thickest I had seen in my nine-year long pursuit of education. Smiling again, "Here, take this. No more excuses for not doing your homework. Your results could improve considerably if you didn't keep missing school. Right, off you go, back to your classroom!"

Now, let me get back to the questions that my mind won't let go off. All the grown-ups agree that my father died exactly the way we were told by the two ladies in our kitchen, many years ago. But I can't accept it. I know he is alive, and I want to know where he is? And is he coming back home or not?

The memory of that night, when we received the news that my father had died, makes me both sad and angry. I am not bothered much about us having become poor, as a result of his death; that is of course, if he has really died. Most people around us have been poor all their lives. Just look at poor Sukina and her two boys; they are even poorer than us. They, like many of my friends and neighbours, are lucky if they have one square meal a week. If God loves them, then why can't he feed them? One decent meal every other day, would do.

"How many times have I asked you, God, if my papa is alive somewhere? Why do you not answer me?"

The courting song and dance of a bird on top of a rock, over to my left, is distracting me. Oh, how I love the way the man-bird is dancing. The multi-coloured feathers around its neck unfold to resemble a king's collar. Every so often, the she bird comes closer to tease it, and then, quickly moves away. I am mesmerised. All the other birds, bears, leopards, and other creatures in the place are watching silently from their hiding places.

Just as I am getting deeper into the bird's dance-sing-and-tease routine, a picture from my dreams I have seen many times in the past five years, enters my head. I have travelled miles upon miles, on foot, to somewhere far away, in search of my father. I see dead bodies all around me lying in the streets and in the fields of the Punjab. I can't see my father among them. I know my father did not die. I shout out aloud, "Please God, tell me, where is my papa?" After what must have been only a few brief moments, I return to my seat in front of the Praying Mountains.

Now, where was I? Oh yes! On that fateful night, in the first week of September 1947, we had just settled down for the evening meal, in the kitchen upstairs. Khushal and I were arguing over something, and as usual he was winning the argument. I was complaining that he wins only because he is four years older than me. He was going on about him being older than me because he had asked God to send him to earth while I was busy asking God my silly questions. Pushpa, unfazed by our arguments, was humming one of her favourite film songs. Mother was occupied in consoling Anup, baby of the family, after he had touched something hot on top of the hearth. With all that kafuffle in the kitchen, we didn't hear someone knocking on the front door downstairs. It was at their fourth attempt, our visitors told us later, that Pushpa answered the door.

Mrs. Stokes senior, along with her youngest daughter-in-law, followed Pushpa into the house, up the stairs, and timidly hauled themselves on to the kitchen floor. Two women, out and about in those wild woods, at that time of the night, turned our attention away from food. Their body language added to our suspense. Even two-and-a-quarter-year-old Anup, sitting on Mother's knee, forgot about his pain and joined in the silent stare. The daughter-in-law wouldn't take her eyes off Mother's face, which only increased our curiosity. Mama insisted that *'Buajee'* tell her immediately the real purpose of their visit at that unearthly hour, and in such bad weather. It wasn't raining, but the air was clammy, and the landslides were still fresh with deep mud everywhere outside.

It transpired, that the two ladies had come to offer their condolences and were dumbstruck to realise that Mama had no idea of the tragedy that had engulfed her life, and the lives of her children, within the past four days. We sat there, not wanting to hear, nor to believe, what Mrs Stokes was telling us. Pushpa went over and put her arms around Mother, "Mama, don't believe it. It can't have happened." I think she meant it.

Mama and Mrs Stokes had a session of, what felt to us, like hours of questions and answers. Mama, in her inimitable strength of character, was swallowing her grief and distress with far less tears and cries than would be natural in the circumstances. We sat around the hearth, our mouths open, our bewildered eyes drifting from face to face. Our food on our plates untouched.

I wish I could recall something of the conversation between Mama and Mrs Stokes, and what happened after the two women left. Or did they stay overnight? I doubt it. Did we say anything to each other? Did we go to bed, or did we sit up all night? Did we eat, or did we throw our food away? I don't like this black hole in my memory. "Please, God, say something. I am starting to get tired of keeping both my ears cocked towards heaven."

What I have managed to pick up from Pushpa and Khushal's conversations over the many weeks and months since that evening, is that Mrs Stokes informed us that at his place of work, in Theog where he was upgrading a stretch of the Shimla-Tibet Highway in Theog, and building a rest house, Papa had developed severe stomach-ache. In that monsoon downpour, and smack in the middle of the worst communal riots India had ever experienced, Papa was taken to some private hospital, seventeen miles away in Shimla. Doctors there were unable to diagnose the cause. Various treatments were tried and failed. Eventually, after five days of suffering, he died. Attempts were made to contact us, but the one and only road, and most of the telegraph poles between Shimla and Dabi, had been washed away by the torrential rains.

Fortunately, Rup Chand, eldest of the siblings, worked in Shimla at the time, and our two eldest sisters, Vidya and Prabha, were also living with their husbands in town. They were able to visit Papa in the hospital and were also present at the funeral.

That reminds me, something else I've been meaning to ask you. I did put the question to one of our elders in the Church, but he fobbed me off with, 'Oh, Nihal! You do ask some silly questions!' My question is: at the Christian Funeral Services, why do we say, 'Earth to earth and ashes to ashes'? I mean, I've been to two funerals, and I didn't see anyone throwing ashes in the church, or by the grave side for that matter!" *I can wait for the answer, I suppose. I better get back to the original question.* What if, in the confusion of all the killings and the ensuing mayhem, they had mistaken someone else for my papa?

However, our situation was made even worse when we heard that soon after the funeral, Rupchand had also gone missing. His disappearance, we guessed, was caused by the likely pressures from friends of the family, expecting him to take charge of father's business, and to care for his mother and younger siblings. We Indians love giving advice, even where it is not asked for, needed, nor helpful. Worst of all, we suspected, fretted, and feared, that Rupchand had been killed in the communal riots. Mother read the Bible morning and evening and prayed for God to bring her son back home.

One fine afternoon, some months short of three years after Papa's disappearance, Rupchand appeared on the road behind the house with three mules laden with all sorts of goodies. My clearest memory of that afternoon is the large basket of *Dasehri Aam* (the best variety of mangos anywhere in the world) he had brought along with him. I remember nothing of his meeting with Mother, or with the rest of us, or anything else of that momentous afternoon, other than the gigantic basket of mangoes. Oh yes, and a not-a-care-in-the-world-layabout friend had accompanied him.

It has now been three long years of serious disruption to our already shattered and over-stretched lives.
Mama has, at last, received a positive answer to her prayers. The prodigal son has returned home, safely. I

wonder if God knows how short-lived the jubilations and the celebrations have been. The tussle between Rupchand and Mama, for the control of the family affairs, started soon after his return, and is still there. Rupchand believes that the main decisions to affect our future and the development of the little piece of earth we possess, should be entrusted to him. Mama on the other hand – and rightly so, in my opinion – believes that, after all, it is she who owns that piece of land and the house. It is she, who was there when the heavens fell upon us. It is she, who is still jumping through the majority of hoops God keeps putting in our way.

Lately though, during winter months, Rupchand has started earning steady money from tuitions he provides to the children of the few better-off families in the surrounding villages. He is building himself quite a reputation. His natural abilities in music and sports have helped him to make friends within all sections of our community. Among the young sportsmen in the district, he has become the one to beat. Mama and Rupchand still argue, but not as much. However, without papa, the cold winds of debts and shortages will continue to blow through the rest of our lives.

"The End," I said proudly.

"Congratulations Nihal. That is a sad and painful story, but also very beautiful." The professor turned his face in the direction of the kitchen and called out loud enough for Mama to hear, "Did you hear that, *Behan jee (sister)*. You must be proud of Nihal."

"Yes, I am." And that was that.

Chapter 11

The In-between Years

At the start of my fifteenth year on this earth, there was more sunshine, not only around Dabi, but around the entire district of Kotgarh and Thanedhar than we had noticed in the previous years. The most unexpected sermon, by a friend of our padre, in our church, changed my entire outlook on God and the Church. He was the first preacher I had ever met, who had a sense of joy and laid-back approach to religion and God. His sermon was just two stories and a couple of really funny jokes. It was the first time I had seen people in the pews laughing along with the preacher. The first story of his sermon was written by Kahlil Gibran, I think. It goes something like this:

A long time ago, on a Sunday morning, people were gathered inside their church. The priest was busily making last minute checks before the start of the Service. Someone came into the vestry and informed the priest that Jesus was addressing a crowd round the back of the church, in a side street. Guessing that Jesus must have run into the crowd on his way to the church, the priest and the congregation waited expectantly. Then, it is well past the time for the start of the Service. Christ is still outside, speaking to a crowd of heathens.

Finally, the padre loses patience. He goes outside, walks into the middle of the crowd, and calls out for Jesus to tell him that everyone inside the church was waiting for him. Jesus seems to take no notice of the padre. Padre tries again. And again, Jesus carries on addressing the crowd. The padre is now starting to lose his cool. He screams out at the top of his voice to attract Jesus' attention, and points in the direction of the church.

Jesus looks at the padre. Smiles kindly. Raising his hands up, he says, "Blessed are those who do the will of my Father." Jesus smiles in the Padre's direction and walks away from the church.

The young visitor ended his sermon by saying, "God does not belong exclusively to either the Jews, or the Christians, or to the Muslims, or to anyone else. Rather, we together belong to God," he said.

After that Sunday, I started to lose interest in 'our God'. It was not a conscious decision. All that happened was that once I accepted that one did not have to be unhappy and miserable and listen to the boring sermons to qualify to be a good Christian, I began to relax. I don't know how and when exactly I came to accept that my father had really died, but the acceptance further helped to relax me, at last. I started to go with the flow. When I suggested to Jag Mohan that the change in my attitude may be due to me 'growing up', he went into a fit of giggles, "Ha! ha! ha! Nihal, growing up? Ha! ha! ha!" Luckily for both of us, our long-standing friendship got in the way of me strangling him.

I happily started concentrating on more interesting things to fill my head with. Girls came number one on the list. They were far more interesting than anything else I had been aware of thus far on this earth. They were different in so many ways from the way I had been seeing them till then. Luckily for me, I was blessed with the friendship of two members of that species in our small community. One of them spoke more with her eyes than her lips. She had, to quote F Scott Fitzgerald, '. . . the sparkle in her eyes when she talked about something (*or someone*) she loved . . . she was beautiful, deep down to her soul'. She interested me in ways that I could not always understand. Her kind nature and genuine friendship more than adequately compensated for the gradual loss of my erstwhile preoccupations – my mother, and my mother's God. Looking back, I think I was starting to accept that being 'normal' was not as weird as I may have been led to believe. On the negative side, my 'not entirely innocent' interest in things not entirely divine, continued to choke my soul with the string of *religious* guilt.

Jag Mohan used to console us both by reminding us of some stories we had heard about some Roman Catholic priests and nuns. How they had been found having sex in holy places. There were also some stories doing the rounds about the cruel way some nuns treated children in orphanages. And we knew plenty of stories about Imams, Mullahs, and Pandit jees, of course, for how they used their positions in the community to exploit children and women for their personal gratification. He would say, "If God doesn't know what these people are up to, then how would he know what thoughts you and I have in our minds. And we only have thoughts. You worry too much about God, Nihal. We are doing nothing wrong."

I still went to church regularly, said prayers, enjoyed singing the *ghazals*, *bhajans* and the Psalms to Punjabi music. But now, I was concentrating more on music and rhythm, and the social interactions than the meaning of words. I was the first one in our church to be a regular Lesson reader on Sundays, at the age of fourteen. At sixteen, our padre entrusted me with teaching the Catechism to my peers in preparation for Confirmation. To a mixture of surprise and shock in equal measures in the community, I was invited by our padre to preach my first sermon in our church just before my seventeenth birthday. I still grimaced and contorted at some of the Bible readings. I have no explanation for why anyone mistook me for a 'pious' Christian boy. Perhaps they knew something about me that I didn't know about myself, and I still don't.

At home, I continued doing my full share of nightly family prayers. The prayers were still interspersed with brief silences, during which, the person saying the prayer wondered, who or what to pray for, next. Occasional interruptions by the cat or the dog, or someone calling out from above or below the house, provided welcome breaks from struggling to find something intelligible to say to God. Alongside my commitment to the Church, I freely joined in with our Hindu friends and neighbours in celebrating their religious festivals. Sham Lall, a Brahmin boy of Loshta and I, regularly led our school assemblies in singing songs of religious and national interest, right to the end of our high school days.

Having celebrated my fifteenth birthday, I began to wonder what it would be like to be grown up. One noticeable change in my life was the very gradual disappearance of my anger and frustration with Mother's draconian discipline. My frustration with what I believed to be her unreasonable demands on our time and boyhood freedoms, had started to melt away. I was starting to understand what she had been through, since Papa's death. I was also aware that her nightmare wasn't over yet. There was also a realisation that although Mother was very religious herself, and her Old Testament God was still important to her, it was also equally important to her to be caring, kind and generous towards neighbours, irrespective of their religion, or caste. Even the paid helpers (servants) were treated with respect in our household.

Mama too had started to relax, all round. Both Anup and I felt that since Khushal's escape into the Indian Army, our leashes had gradually been growing longer. I still could not understand though why she had to thank God all the time.

Nor could I come to terms with why she thought that the 'Angrez were wonderful people'. Her, 'Angrez this and Angrez that' never failed to rile me up. "Mama, don't you know," I would bristle, "it was your wonderful Angrez Tommy, who kicked our papa for walking on the Mall in Shimla, when he was no more than fifteen? *Their* Mall in *our* Shimla?"

I would remind her again and again, that it was her 'wonderful Angrez' that had twice sent our papa to prison for defending his own freedom.

I would remind her of the massacre that the 'Angrez' General Dyer had caused in Amritsar, and many other examples of the Angrez Sahib's cruelty towards, and ill treatment of, our Indian brothers and sisters.

I knew of Dyer's depravity from one of our neighbours, a universal 'uncle'. He was an educated and well-informed, intelligent person. He had told me so much about my father being a freedom fighter. He told me, how on 13 April 1919, a crowd of many thousands of men, women and children, were celebrating the Spring Festival in Jalian Vala Baag, in the city of Amritsar, in the Punjab. Colonel Dyer, temporarily given the title of General, had deceitfully convinced his masters in London that the festival celebrations on a bright spring afternoon, were a front for a politically motivated gathering against the British Raj. He was determined, now with the full backing of his government, to set an example of the British determination to crush all opposition to the colonial enterprise. Dyer's soldiers blocked all but one exit out of the walled garden. He ordered his troops to fire and keep firing until ordered otherwise. All this time, there was not a bullet, nor even one single brick thrown from inside the walled garden.

At the final count, over three hundred unarmed men, women and children were counted dead. Some of the dead were reclaimed from the well, where they had jumped in, in panic. More than 1,200 were seriously injured. The general proudly counted and recorded, that it took only 1,600 bullets for him to accomplish his mission.

When I went to college in Amritsar a couple of years later, I learned that the House of Lords in London, applauded Colonel Dyer. They wanted to bestow honours and titles upon the killer. An elderly Sikh gentleman who had lost three members of his family, including his mother, in that massacre, told me that it was Mr Churchill, with a majority vote in the parliament, who prevented Dyer from having his temporary rank of General, made permanent.

He also told me that the English language news media, all over the British colonies and in England, had set up a fund to offset the loss that Dyer was to suffer due to being denied the rank of a British General. In 1974, when I found out that most bishops in the Church of England, were also members of the House of Lords, that simply helped to confirm my doubts about the Church's claims upon the 'Eternal Truths' of God.

Lately though, even Mama's 'Angrez' couldn't light my fuse, as often as they used to. With my usual childhood stubbornness and a strongly felt need to avenge the real and the imagined injustices visited upon my father, and upon millions of other Indians, by the 'Angrez' sahibs, I continued to find ways to resist everything that had anything to do with the British Raj. I refused to learn the English language any further than was required by the education system. To me, anyone wanting to teach or to learn English in India, was a British stooge. I believed that, like my father, I was a true patriot. I ignored and derided the Indian slaves, and gladly paid the price.

In the meantime, life in Dabi carried on as usual. Milk deliveries to Thanedhar in winter months were still as bad as before, but now, for some strange reason, the chilblains didn't affect the shape and size of my feet to the same extent as in the previous winters. My encounters with imagined leopards and bears had also come to an end. Sad, really. Just think of all the exciting, exhilarating, and thrilling stories you could be reading in these pages. Or, not, had the leopards been real.

More and more people in the Kotgarh/Thanedhar district had started upgrading their homes, building larger ones. Some had even registered their children in private schools in Shimla. From only four big apple trees nine years before, we counted seventy-nine fruit-bearing trees on our little plot in Dabi, alone. We were working towards planting many more in the near future. This allowed us to hold back more of our eggs and milk and fresh vegetables for our own use. At long last, I was in a position to test the claim, that eating raw eggs helps to make a young person big, strong, and virile. Twice a week, first thing in the morning, I would crack one, sometimes two raw eggs directly into my mouth (one at a time, I hasten to add). Every morning, I would do some press-ups, pull-ups, push-ups, and sit-ups. I did become stronger, I think, but sadly, the eggs and all the 'ups' did nothing to change the size and shape of the skinny 'me'. Virile? I didn't know what the word meant.

All these exciting and helpful changes somehow failed to take away the deep sense of isolation I had always suffered from. I hated every moment of every dusk in Dabi. A feeling of doom and gloom, and an inexplicable sense of loneliness and isolation would grab me by the throat. I can't say why, but I never could share that dreadful and most haunting feeling with anyone, not even with Jag Mohan. Most evenings at home, I would find myself staring at the dying embers of the daylight over the eastern horizon and wishing to be dead before the dark night could touch me.

In my final high school year, I decided to start my own business enterprise in order to earn some cash to add to the family coffers. Luckily for me, the youngest of the three Stokes brothers lived in the direction of Thanedhar, about half a mile away from Dabi. He had set aside a large plot of land near his house, for vegetables galore. He had neither the need, nor the desire to market them. These were mostly fed to his cattle, horses, and other herbivores. I approached him to see if I could buy anything that was surplus to the needs of the animals, at a discounted rate – 'a very discounted rate', I emphasised. First, he laughed, then looked at me seriously, gave me an affectionate pat on the back of my head, and invited me into his study for a cup of tea. "Are you serious? Have you cleared this with Rupi *bua*?" he asked.

I nearly added to my list of truthful lies. Instead, I told him the truth. I wanted it to be a 'pleasant surprise' for Mama. He understood, he said. While listening interestedly to my version of our family news, he carried on scribbling in his notebook. Ten minutes later, the cook served tea and yummy biscuits. Over our *chai-pani*, I shared with him my school progress in general, and told him about my dream – the transport business. I expected him to ridicule the idea, but he didn't. He appeared genuinely interested. *Chai-pani* finished, we made our way out to the vegetable patch, on the east side of the house. It was nearly as big as the whole of my Dabi.

"This is it. What do you think?"

"Wow! Can I pick as much as I want?" I asked quite excitedly.

"Well, as much as you can carry, of course. Your *kiltu* (a large, cone-shaped cane basket with shoulder straps) won't take more than ten kilos," he guessed. "There should be enough here for your purpose, once a week. The plot is re-seeded as and when necessary," he continued. "This should last through to the end of autumn." He suggested a flat rate of one rupee (sixteen annas), per *kiltu* – approximately 1.04 annas per kilogram – which, I was to pay only after I had sold the first lot. "Good luck. Let's shake hands on the deal then, shall we?" He will instruct the relevant members of his staff, he said, to help me pick 'the best bits'.

Long summer days allowed me time enough to return from school, collect my *kiltu* from home, go to Mr Stokes's place, pick a suitable selection of vegetables, fill my *kiltu* up to the brim, and strap it onto my back. Through summer and into early autumn, I carried between ten and twelve kilos of produce in my *kiltu,* all the way to Kotgarh, once a week. On my business trips, the total daily mileage totted up close to fifteen miles.

My regular customers in Kotgarh consisted of my schoolteachers, a bunch of clerks at the forestry offices, half a mile further past my school, and occasionally, the local doctor. At other times, I sold my vegetables, only half a mile away, in the shops in Thanedhar. Profit margins were good, which encouraged me to run my supply trips, back and forth through my final year of high school, and into the start of the following summer.

Mama's reputation for being an uncompromisingly honest woman, and a stickler for details in all things, came in handy when selling our milk, eggs, fresh vegetables, and an occasional cockerel or hen, to pay towards our education and other daily needs. The sense of pride we thus felt in being the sons of *Rup Dei* (Goddess of Beauty), made up for a lot of negative feelings that we sometimes harboured against 'Rupi' the harsh, God-fearing mother.

In November of 1955, I was sent away to the school hostel in Kotgarh, to allow me time away from household chores, in preparation for the final year of the matriculation exams. My memory of those months is a little foggy, and I can't say with confidence, as to how and where exactly I used my freedom from 'home rule'.

I do have a clear memory of the excitement of the fifty-mile-long, dangerous journey though, to our Matriculation Examination Centre in Shimla, in the first week of March. The road went over the mountains, along the deep gorges, through thick forests, small farms, and was only wide enough, to accommodate the width of the bus. Including the pupils and two teachers, there were at least forty passengers on a twenty-two-seater bus. The bus was a Government Transport's elderly, arthritic vehicle. Twenty-two miles out of fifty were mostly over patches of snow and ice in the road. The first bus broke down twice before it reached a point where there had been a small landslide in the road the week before. We all dismounted, put our luggage on our backs and negotiated a dangerous quarter-mile slippery slope to reach the bus waiting on the other side. The entire journey of fifty miles took nearly eight hours before delivering us a mile and a half below our final destination, the YMCA in Shimla.

During the exams, the weather had taken a turn for the worse. We shivered all of one mile to the centre on the mornings of exams. At the end of exams, most of us were running out of whatever little 'extra-expenses' money our parents had given us. Due to adverse weather conditions, there was no hope of buses running between Shimla and Thanedhar. Maya Ram, Dwarka Das and I decided to make it on foot. We packed our beddings, books, clothes and everything else we possessed. The YMCA cook packed enough rotis with dryish potato and spinach curry saag to last us more than two days. We put our luggage on our backs, and before daybreak, we left Shimla on foot.

On the first day, we walked little over eighteen miles to Theog. At night we shared space with some stray dogs, in a sheltered area under the veranda of a roadside shop. The dogs saved us from dying of hypothermia, but the smell of food in our luggage did cause a few scary moments during the night. Following morning, we set off from Theog before daybreak. Just before sunset we arrived twenty-two miles away, in Narkanda. We walked into a shop front, opened our leftover food packs and ordered three tumblers of jaggery-sweet tea. Chomping and talking, all at the same time, we were wondering whether we were fit enough to continue our journey home? Or would we have to be content to find a sheltered corner to spend our night in freezing Narkanda at 9,000 feet above sea level. Our respective final destinations from Narkanda were: Dwarka eight miles, Maya Ram nine-and-a-half miles, and mine was exactly eleven miles.

We were halfway into our final meal of the day, when someone shouted, "The Shimla-Thanedhar bus has just arrived." We left our much-needed food on the table, rushed to the bus stop and managed to squeeze in before most passengers could alight. An hour later Maya Ram and Dwarka got off on the road above Dwarka's village. Twenty minutes later, the bus dropped me in Thanedhar. I put the luggage on my back, and accompanied by the ghosts, the Banshiras, and the many invisible/imagined/real leopards and bears, I arrived home to a hot dinner. We sat up late into the night, listening to my tales of adventures, and my take on the unintelligible process of the examination system.

I passed my Matric with a 3rd. The principal, Mr Wilson, described my result as a 'very disappointing under-achievement'. I couldn't understand what the fuss was all about. I had passed, and that was that. Strangely enough, Mother said nothing, either.

While waiting for the results, I had secured a part-time job with a local shop owner who ran a fruit-and-potato business on the side. Mother allowed me to keep my wages for myself. For the first time, in my living memory, I had pocket money of my own to share with a couple of my less privileged friends. Made me feel good. This is what 'doing good' is all about; it is about being selfish. So, be selfish, I say, and seek your happiness in making someone else happy.

Chapter 12

Adulthood Begins at Sixteen

At the end of high school exams in March of 1956, I sensed that my fetters had been broken, and the shackles of absolute obedience to 'home rule' had been removed – all within reason, of course. I did do a few odd jobs to earn a few bobs, in order to not be a burden on my family. I did my fair share around the house, too. Away from the eyes and ears of my elders, I also made a few unsuccessful attempts at being a 'man'. The thought of the fires of hell, and the sharp fork of the big man in the red leotard, saved me from the temptations.

In my world, we were allowed about two years of 'teenage', followed by one year of 'adolescence' (two, if you were lucky), and then, fast-forwarded into adulthood. There are two incidents from the start of my 'fast-forwarded' adulthood that have provided me with material for many interesting conversations over the years. The first of these, was my first unaccompanied visit to my sister Pushpa and her children in Kandagoi. Kandagoi was then a tiny community of half-a-dozen hamlets, scattered on a hillside, in Kullu district, about twelve miles away from Dabi, and across the river, Satluj. Pushpa and her husband owned a piece of forest in Kandagoi, which they were slowly converting into an apple orchard.

With Mother's permission and blessings, I set off from Dabi about half an hour before dawn, with an old army rucksack on my back, full of a substantial picnic lunch, a fresh leg of lamb, plus some other goodies for Pushpa and the children. To let the leopards and bears in the vicinity know of my presence in their world, I whistled and hummed as I walked. In case I came face to face with one of those beastly neighbours – something we always feared and expected at certain hours of the mornings and evenings in the woods – I carried a solid bamboo stick and a six-inch bladed knife with flick action button. *I will sort them out,* I kept trying to convince myself, every step of the way.

First two miles of my journey over a gently sloping, narrow cattle track took me through small patches of dense woods, villages of upper and lower Shathla and a few small apple orchards, to the village of Shaut. Then I dry-skied over the rough and rugged downhill dirt track for a mile and some yards to the village of Kirti. Another couple of miles over a rocky terrain, helped me reach a jeepable road in Sainj. The gently sloping road took me to the far side of the river Satluj, in Luhri, approximately 3,500 feet below the two points of my departure and my destination on the day.

About four hours after leaving Dabi that morning, I walked the shaky suspension bridge over Satluj and crossed over to Luhri. Said "Hello" and "How do you do?" to the shopkeepers and other locals I had met on my two previous journeys to Ani through there. Half-a-dozen mule drivers were busily scurrying around, sucking on their *hookas*, *bidis*, and cigarettes. They were carrying out last minute checks on the mules and their loads, before setting off for Ani, a small trading village, eight miles away.

I visited the four shops, chatted with anybody I could find in the place, paid a visit to the cobbler behind the 'high street' shops. Some minutes past midday, I ate my packed brunch then smoked the first of the three cigarettes I had pinched from Rupchand's winter stock the night before. Then stretched out for a quick nap on top of the rice sacks in a shaded, cooler corner of my favourite shop. I had barely begun to doze off when I heard the ear-piercing screams of a woman. I opened my eyes and saw the wife of the shopkeeper standing over me with my bamboo stick in her hands raised above her head, ready to strike. Her husband was next to her. They must have read, in my panic-stricken eyes *What the hell have I done, now?* The husband explained calmly that a cobra was making its way towards the top of my head, only inches away. I jumped off the sacks and landed clumsily on the concrete floor, in front of the screaming woman. With three strikes of the stick, she dispatched the poor snake to RIP.

I landed awkwardly on the concrete floor. A sharp piece of knotted wood on the floor caused a deep cut into my left calf, six inches above the ankle – I still have the scar to prove it. Blood spurted all over the floor. The shopkeeper kindly attended to my wound and finished off with a dirty bandage on my leg. His killer wife washed the floor. The entire population of about twenty souls gathered around to witness the drama. Standing around me, they exchanged tales of their own encounters with 'cobras' and other species of snakes in those hot and rugged surroundings.

In the meantime, a steaming cup of sugary tea and some fresh *pakorhas* were brought in from the café next door, which I was not allowed to pay for. A quick face and mouth wash with cold water, and I was on my way to Dalash, a five-mile plus steep climb to the top of the hill.

Middle of May can get pretty hot around Luhri, as the heat bounces off the steep, rocky hills on either side of the river. Just over three hours after leaving Luhri, climbing mostly between 45 and 85-degree angles, surrounded on all sides by nature's 'Arts and Crafts' exhibition, I arrived in the little village of Dalash, a mile past the top of the hill. A hospitable shopkeeper welcomed me with a fresh cup of tea. We shared a cigarette between the two of us while his wife introduced me to the culture of the place and made me feel proud with tales of the popularity of my brother-in-law among the locals. He had been head teacher of the local high school, but two years previously had moved away to another high school twenty miles away. She told me a few tales of my sister's resilience in the harsh circumstances of the place and her kind and helpful nature. Rested and refreshed, I finally set off on the last leg of my journey.

Pushpa lived with her five children, about a mile further up, on the other side of the rocky ridge. By the time I left Dalash, the evening shadows were stretching over the surrounding landscape. After twenty long minutes of leisurely walk over the rocky dirt track, surrounded by a swathe of hills and terraced fields and small hamlets for miles around, I entered the cornfields. Bamboo stick in my sweaty hand, ready to hit the bear 'on the nose' – as advised by the experts – should one dare to get in my way. Whistling, humming, talking aloud to myself, I walked through the fields, in a state of semi-consciousness. Only once did I hear a minor bear family disagreement, from a safe distance to my right. Had the bears dared to test the power of my bamboo stick, you would, in all likelihood, not be reading this story now.

At long last, I was out of the fields, and onto the rocky ridge. Couple of hundred yards up along the track I plonked my posterior onto the smooth top of a large boulder. I was not a regular smoker, but while taking in the smells and sounds of miles and miles of empty spaces before me, I smoked my second immorally obtained cigarette. Lost in the pleasures of soothing solitude of the place, I remained on top of the rock far longer than originally intended.

By the time I entered the thick, dense Pitch Pine Nature Reserve of Kandagoi, light from the clear blue skies above, was struggling to penetrate through the thick, green canopy of treetops. I was not at all certain of the narrow mule track that lay uninvitingly ahead of me. I feared that a few inches this way or that, could deliver me into the thick undergrowth on the lower side of the track.

I heard sounds of someone chopping wood a few yards up the hillside, to my right. Relieved to know that I was not alone in that scary wilderness, I called out, "Hello! Anyone there?" No response. I called again, and still no response. I waited a long ten seconds and tried again, and still nothing. It began to dawn on me that the sound of the contact of an axe with a log of wood that I was hearing, was too constant to be real. I stood still, took a few deep breaths, relaxed my neck and shoulders, slapped my cheeks, gripped the stick firmly in my unsteady, sweaty right hand, and pressed the button on the torch light in my left. The torchlight refused to respond. The woodcutter was still there and moving parallel with me.

'Fire in any shape, size or intensity, is the surest way to deal with the ghosts,' I recalled. I struck a match. Sparks flared into a flame and then, it went out. Struck another, then another. Soon, the matchbox was empty. Night was becoming darker with every strike of the matchstick. I kept moving forward unsteadily. And, as I looked up to check my way ahead, ten feet in front of me, was a stark-naked young couple walking towards me.

Seeing two humans in that situation should have comforted me. Instead, I shouted in an unsteady voice, accompanied by exaggerated gestures of both hands, "Who are you? . . . Wh . . . wh . . . what the hell a . . . a . . . are you doing here . . . at this time of the night? Wh . . . wh . . . what happened to your clothes?"

"Don't be afraid. You are safe here." They moved closer. I froze to the spot. "We don't want you to get the wrong idea. We just don't wear clothes."

I tried to appear unafraid and in control. "I am not afraid, and I was not making any judgements," I said in trembling voice. "I am just surprised to see you naked and carrying nothing with you at all . . . who are you, where do you live?"

The woman replied, in a calm, soft voice, "I am Eve, and this is Adam. Many millennia ago, we lived in a place, called the Garden of Eden." She took Adam's right arm in both hands and leaned her head onto his shoulder. Adam picked up the narrative.

"One day, our boys told us that God had spoken to a couple of men in the place and told them that Eve and I were a bad influence on our community. Everything that was wrong with the world was down to Eve and I having disobeyed God." He looked at Eve, caressed her cheek, held her closer, tenderly.

"Since then," said Eve, "we've heard that some descendants of those men, in that community have written books, blaming us for allowing a snake to mislead us into eating a fruit that they said, we had been instructed by God, not to eat. And that, they said, led to the downfall of the world from the Grace of God."

I interrupted, with my hands up, "Yeah, yeah, I know . . . all about the books and the other stuff. But who are you?" *Why do I feel as if this is a normal conversation?*

Something is seriously weird about the whole thing. They must have read my mind.

"We truly are the Eve and Adam, from the Garden of Eden. Except that we were not called Eve and Adam when we lived there." She took Adam's right arm in her hands again, rested her cheek against his muscular biceps. "He doesn't believe a word of our story." She looked up at Adam. Even in that overwhelming darkness, I could see both of them clearly. She looked at me with a disappointed smile in her beautiful, brown eyes. "Mind you, I can't blame you for not believing us," she added, thoughtfully.

Adam gently placed his hand on her shoulder. "Maybe, we were expecting too much, too soon. Give him time. I think he does want to believe us."

"I don't know about that. I've read the story of Adam and Eve. Both of them ate the fruit for which they got thrown out of the garden. But that was centuries ago! How come you are still alive? You . . . Adam and Eve?" Burning my eyes into Adam's, I said, "You hardly look a day older than me?"

"It is not often we get a chance to speak to someone who would listen to us, let alone someone to believe us," said Eve. She sat down on the ground next to Adam's feet. Adam joined her on the ground. I looked around, noticed a small log of dead wood in the middle of the path a couple of yards in front of them, and sat down on it. The magical tenderness, in the way they looked at each other was melting me into a slobbery figure of sixteen-year-old mush. I thought I was falling in love with that unbelievably beautiful and innocent looking Eve. I could not take my eyes of her tall, lithe figure, delicately wrapped in smooth, silky skin.

"Now, let me get this right. You are Adam and Eve?"

Adam interrupted, "We prefer, Eve and Adam."

"Fine, Eve and Adam. So, you are the first two humans God created following—"

"No! Eve interrupted. We are two of the many who made a living from farming and hunting in a beautiful large oasis in the middle of a desert. We don't know from where or how we came to be living there, but we all lived in complete harmony with each other. At some point, a small group of men started to separate men from the women." She picked up a dry twig from the ground in front of her, twisted and turned it between her fingers. Looking at Adam, sadly. "There was an environment of conspiracy and intrigue about those men," she said.

"No doubt about that," he added.

"The stories we used to tell our children and grandchildren before bedtime," Eve continued, "were now being used by those men, to persuade the tribe, that the stories were factual. That, while out and about with their animals, and working on their farms, God had been talking to them, and telling them everything about himself and his world. This God had chosen them, they said, to communicate his messages to the rest of the human race. Those, who did not believe them, they declared, would be punished by God in the fires of some place called 'Hell'. And those who believed them, would be rewarded by God with never-ending life in some place called 'Heaven'."

"Heaven is the place where God lives, according to them," added, Adam.

"Before long, all the decisions were being made by this small group of men." With a tinge of anger in her voice, Eve said, "Women had to obey, or else . . . Eventually, all the men and women caved in, and stopped protesting. My Adam here and I, we didn't agree with those empty heads."

Adam said with a deep sigh, "Even our two sons joined the 'Men only' club. So, when our children were grown up and settled, Eve and I decided to take a break from our unpleasant neighbours and explore the world outside of our community." There followed a long silence.

Eve finally broke the silence. "You look like an intelligent young man, and we know you like to ask questions. Don't ask me how we know, we just do," she said. "Ask yourself, why would God put a tree in the garden that bears the fruit of the knowledge of right and wrong, and then, tell us not to eat that fruit? How on earth would we know the difference between right and wrong unless we ate that particular fruit first?" She shrugged her shoulders.

"We never saw a 'tree of the knowledge of right and wrong' anywhere on that piece of land," said Adam. "Neither was there a 'tree of life' that anyone had ever seen. But everyone round the place started saying, 'But if God says that there is such a tree then there must be.' How gullible and unintelligent can people be. It was that small bunch of men who said that, not God."

I had been sitting for a while without moving a muscle. My mouth open and my unblinking eyes lustfully fixed on Eve's youthful beauty. I must have looked a perfect village idiot. In my dreamy state I heard myself say, "Must be amazing to see God face to face and hear him speaking to you, up close!"

"We never heard or saw God face to face ..." they both said in one voice.

Next, I found myself standing at the spot where the dirt track pointed in the direction of Pushpa's house. *How the hell, did I get here?* I had a faint image in my head of me having a conversation with two strangers in those

140

dark woods, seconds before. In my sub-conscious mind, I knew that something very weird had happened between me entering the woods and then standing on that dusty piece of earth.

Through the thick veil of darkness my torchlight, with its bright beam, led me safely down the dirt track to Pushpa's house. Her paid home help answered the door. It was only a few days later, when he was telling me about his father's near-fatal meeting with the ghosts in those woods that my own picture started to unfold in my head, little by little. It was days before I filled the canvas with the above narrative.

The second unforgettable experience during that first year of my adulthood had nothing to do with ghosts. It was about sharing of my father's musical talents with our Christian and Hindu neighbours in Ani. Ani was a small trading village, about twelve miles away, in Kullu district. Now, the place is smothered under the thick smoke spewed out by numerous cars and buses and small trucks ferrying tourists back and forth between the planes and the mountains through the village.

In his younger days, Papa had composed the main Gospel accounts into narrative poems and ballads *(Katha)*, and set these to Indian classical and folk music. When our Canadian parish priest, who took keen interest in Indian music, became aware of the fast-disappearing tradition of *Katha*, he started looking for opportunities to get a team of musicians and a small choir together, to stage the *Katha* in public. After protracted discussions, we chose Ani. There was, and still exists, a small congregation, originally baptised and churched by the Salvation Army, and later handed over to the Anglican mission from Canada. The church in Ani was in the charge of our padre. It was agreed that staging the event there would express our support for our lesser privileged and isolated Christian and their Hindu cousins. I don't think it was an evangelical endeavour – we were not at all preachy Christians.

Some weeks later, in the early hours of a Wednesday morning, at the tail end of the Indian summer, my brother Rup Chand, Padre Peel, a young man called Anand Chandulal, (who, many years later, became a bishop), and I, set off from Kotgarh on foot. On our arrival, twelve plus miles away in Ani, our team was joined by the local pastor, who was himself a reasonably competent musician, and some of his musically gifted sheep. After a few days of rehearsals, we were ready for the big night.

On the appointed evening, approximately two hours before the staging of the *Katha*, we were having our evening meal in the church guesthouse, when someone noticed a man skulking in the dark shadows on the dirt track beside the church. We called him out into the flickering light of our two kerosene lanterns. He came over to where we were and explained that he had been sent to inform us that Ezekiel baboo, a middle-aged, stone deaf, and highly revered hunter in that part of the world, had gone to a village across the river from his house that morning to help rid the village of a leopard. The leopard had killed some animals there in recent weeks. When he did not return from the hunt after dark, the villagers feared that he had either fallen off the side of the sheer cliff or been killed by the leopard.

Katha was postponed to another night. A few local young men were engaged to spread the news of the postponement, into the surrounding villages. Our group went to join the search parties, seriously risking their own lives on that dark, steep, rocky hill. I was left to wash up and keep an eye on our possessions. I protested not but hated every moment of the rest of the lonely, unadventurous, scary night. The river below the church eerily interrupted the stunning silence inside that 'neighbourless' guest house. My bedroom looked like a four-screen cinema, with indescribably ugly, horrid images from the Book of Revelation dancing on the four walls in the flickering dim light of one kerosene lantern. After breakfast the following morning, I rushed off to the hunter's place, to join my team four miles away, in Navy.

On my arrival, I was told that within half an hour into the search, a member of the search party led others to where he had found the body of the hunter. From snippets of overheard conversations at the funeral, the following afternoon, I put my story together. Which is, that some members of the search party suspected that the man must have already known where the body was. Suspicions were further fuelled by the most unlikely position in which the body was found. "One cannot tumble down a steep hillside and suddenly come to a stop in a squatting position, with the entire weight of the body resting only on a point of the forehead against the rock," suggested someone from a neighbouring village. There was also a small wound in the head, which, some suspected, could possibly have been made by the entry of a bullet.

No one could think of any reason why anyone in the world would wish to harm the kindly hunter. The general consensus of opinion was that the whole thing could have been the result of an unfortunate accident. There were a few hypotheses, but no clear evidence of a crime. The hot climate of the place and absence of facilities for storing a dead body safely for more than a few hours, made it impractical to reach the nearest police station many miles away. Neither were there any witnesses, no reason to suspect a crime, only hypotheses and conjectures. Padre presided over the Funeral Service, and the body was buried in accordance with the hunter's religion.

Few days after the funeral, we staged our *Katha* at the church in Ani, and were delighted by the response we received from both the Christian and the Hindu communities. Large majority of them were led there by only the dim light of kerosene lanterns, and many had walked many miles over dangerous dirt tracks to join us. It was worth all the effort on our part.

Chapter 13

The Enemy Camp

Hubau was only a few days older than me. He, along with his widowed mother and his two brothers, had been living in unimaginable poverty all their lives. Hubau was not quite nine when one evening his thirteen-year-old brother did not return home from work. No one had seen or heard of him for over a year. We all suspected that he had run away to the planes in search of a better life.

One sunny September afternoon in 1950, Hubau and his mother were sitting on the veranda of our house. Hubau's mother said to Mama, "My Hubau here is a very clever boy. Do you think he could be of some help to you round the house? You could, maybe pay him a small wage in return? I can't meet the needs of my two boys from my tiny plot of land anymore."

After some silent calculations in her head, Mother said, "I cannot afford servants any longer. Considering that your situation is far worse than mine, at the moment, Hubau could be good company for me. He could help me out with the household chores the best he can, while my children are in school." A mutually satisfactory monthly wage was agreed between the two mothers. Hubau's mother hoped that he might even learn to read and write with us. "He is a quick learner," she said, and wrapped him in a look of deep affection.

"You are an educated woman. You will take better care of my son than I can." Mama took the hint. The matter was settled. Hubau, at the ripe old age of ten years, some weeks, and some days old, had obtained employment as Mama's 'chores boy', and would be living and eating with us. He was never expected to do anything more than I could. I often felt that Mama was kinder to him than she was to me.

Before long, he settled into the Paul family like a member. He remained with us much longer than we could have anticipated at the start.

On a pleasant October afternoon in 1956, over our afternoon meal, I suggested to Mother that with Anup and Hubau in Dabi, I would not be missed much if I went away for teacher training. Or some other proper job in one of the cities, somewhere on the planes. Soon after the end of the Raj, the job of schoolteacher had become very lucrative in India. The government had made education compulsory from the age of six I think and was opening schools all over India. To attract young men and women into the job, teachers were being offered free training, good salary, and air-tight job security.

I had also had a good think, I said, about what our padre had suggested in one of his sermons, while I was away on my holiday with young Adam and Eve, a few months before. I was thinking of speaking to him also about his idea, soon, I said.

Hubau and Anup sat up in utter shock, as if struck by lightning. Anup nearly dropped the corn on the cob he was leisurely chewing at, into the fire pace. Mother, on the other hand, appeared completely unmoved by the news. She asked, with her piercing eyes locked into mine, "Are you sure?"

"Sure, of what?" I asked.

"Sure, that you want to follow the padre's advice? That's what."

"Well, I am thinking about it, seriously," I assured

her.

"You must spend some time in prayer, before making the final decision," was Mother's simple advice. To me, it was my decision I honestly didn't believe that it had anything to do with God, as such. I was only interested in exploring the suggestion at that stage. God would let me know if he didn't agree with me, I imagined.

"What are you sniggering at, Hubau?" Mother asked.

"I am trying to picture in my mind, Nihal following the padre's advice!" He sniggered at me sideways.

Mother's reaction was, silent ecstasy hesitatingly expressed with a smile, fully exposing her right upper front tooth that had been eagerly trying to say 'hello' to her chin for weeks. We had tried every trick in the book to persuade her to have the unsightly tusk removed. Her fear of the doctor's pliers – we didn't have dentists up in the mountains – had prevented Mother from putting her looks and long-term comfort first. Once, when Anup tried to persuade her to visit the hospital about it, Mother's reaction was, "I might just as well go down to the blacksmith and have him pull my tooth out."

In the kitchen, "God will bless you, I'm sure," she said in my direction, calmly, and carried on expertly manoeuvring her food from side to side in her mouth. There was no "Wow that is wonderful news!" Or "I am so excited. Come here, give me a hug!" Or, even the simple suggestion, "Come, let us slaughter a lamb at the altar of the Lord, and invite our tribe of the Lord's chosen to celebrate with us." None of that nonsense. She simply had no experience in expressing her feelings and emotions.

The following afternoon, sitting in the corner of the veranda for afternoon break from our daily chores, I told Rupchand about my conversation with Mother the evening before, emphasising that nothing had been finalised in my mind, yet.

"That is great news, Nihal." He looked delighted. "But make sure, you first get some university education. We desperately need properly educated padres in the Church. A padre should be able to speak to people in all walks of life."

Mother sounded uncomfortably suspicious. "Why? There are plenty of padres we know, who didn't even finish high school. Why does Nihal have to have degrees to do his job properly?"

"Yes Mama, I too know some of them. That is precisely why I am suggesting that Nihal should have, at least, a graduate degree before going into some seminary." He turned to face me. "There are more and more people now, in all walks of life, who are educated and better informed than my generation. You must be able to speak at their level." He looked at Mother for her reaction. Mother seemed in deep thought. Rupchand continued, "There is an interesting story in the book I am reading presently. It is very relevant to the way some Church Ministers preach to the general public."

In Rupchand's story, a man was walking along a river. He saw a monkey jump into the water. As he watched, the monkey pulled a fish out of the water, and put it on the branch of a tree. The man approached the monkey and asked it, 'Why did you do that?' The monkey replied, 'I am saving the fish from drowning.' "The point of this story, is that unless you know what other people are about and what their needs are, you can't know what is best for them." He looked at Mother for her reaction.

"Where are we going to find the money to support Nihal in a hostel of some good college, or university, in some far away city? We have barely started to dig ourselves out of the pit your father had dropped us in. It is not that long since we started to remove the burden of debts from our shoulders," Mother retorted in shaky voice.

"We will find a way, Mama. Income from the apples is improving each year, and I am sure Nihal will be careful with whatever money we can afford to give him."

"Be careful and decide wisely. That's all I want to say." She quickly wiped her tears, as if they were something to be ashamed of. Stood up, picked up her knitting basket, and went over to her favourite spot next to the apricot tree.

Two days later, I went to see the padre, and explained to him our one big hurdle in the way of realising our joint dream, at that point in time. He agreed with Rupchand and sympathised with Mama's doubts and fears. After a brief discussion, he promised to look for some sponsorship to cover, at least, part of the cost of my further education.

Five weeks after my conversation with the padre, Mama, Rupchand and I, had a brief meeting with him after the Sunday Morning Service. Ironically, I was standing on the very same locally quarried, well-trodden piece of rock, where a little over six years before the then padre had prophesied that I was heading in the direction of hell fire. Now, standing on the same spot, in conversation with my present padre, I seemed to be heading in the opposite direction. Our padre had managed to secure a sponsorship to supplement my higher education costs. He also informed us that the then Bishop of the Diocese of Amritsar, keenly supported my intentions.

In view of the fact that it would be my first time away from home, in a faraway city, it was agreed that we check with my sister Prabha and her husband, Dyal Singh Rathore, who were living in Amritsar at the time. See if they could take me in as a paying guest and introduce me gently to the city life. In the meantime, Padre Peel offered to handle the enquiries regarding my entry into Dayanand Anglo Vedic College (DAV) in Amritsar. At the time, it was one of the best institutions for higher education within the Punjab University.

"That's settled then," Mother said in her customary matter-of-fact voice. She expressed no curiosity, or anxiety at the thought of her teenage son going hundreds of miles away, to a completely unfamiliar environment. She made her way to the vicarage veranda, and cheerfully accepted *chai-pani* from the padre's wife. Mother's behaviour on that day reminded me of the time, when my elder brother Khushal had come home from Thanedhar one late afternoon, four years previously. He announced excitedly, that he had joined the Indian Army. Mother looked up from her cards – sun or rain, she spent a good hour or so playing a few games of patience, every afternoon on the veranda – unperturbed by what to us was a shocking announcement, her ear cocked up, she said, "Go on then, tell us more."

"You know, I cannot find a proper job around here. So, when I saw the Army Recruiting Officers at the Government Rest House in Thanedhar, I spoke to one of them. He took me in to the doctor. The doctor gave me a medical examination, weighed me, took my measurements, and I've been selected."

"But you are still eight months short of your eighteenth birthday!"

"I told them I was eighteen, and they believed me!" Khushal said proudly.

Mother returned to her cards, rearranged a few on the

rug, while the rest of us stood around with bated breath for her reaction to the news. Engrossed in her game, Mama asked, "When will you be going to wherever it is that you have to go for your training?"

"Five days from now." He explained that the new recruits had been advised to travel to Shimla by early morning bus from Thanedhar, on the following Monday. At the bus station in Shimla, they would be met by some Indian Army people, the Indian Army would look after them from there on.

"We will have to fix you up with some clothes and travel bedding. Not going to be easy at such short notice."

On the appointed day, two of the other recruits went along the main road above our house, escorted by weeping mothers and teary sisters, aunties, and some neighbours from their respective villages, all the way to the bus station in Thanedhar. In our house? There obviously was some extra activity relating to Khushal's departure, of course. When the time came for him to leave, Mother gave him a gentle hug, assuring him of her love and support, and the blessings of God. Then she said to him, "Go on son. You don't want to miss your bus. Make sure you write home regularly ... Remember what I have said to you all along? Your breeding will be judged by your behaviour! Go on, now." At the end of the veranda, Mother gently placed her hand on his shoulder, as if to push-start him on his way. Hubau and I accompanied Khushal to the bus stop and bade him farewell on behalf of the entire community. On our return, Anup told us that only after Khushal and the two of us had reached the road above the house, did Mother have a brief sniffle.

In the context of my preparation for Christian ministry in India, DAV College would have been the last place to be seen anywhere near, let alone making it the base for my further education. Hence, the advice of my parish priest, enthusiastically supported by Mother and Rupchand, caused many a pious eyebrow to reach giddy heights. Fortunately, the people whose opinions mattered to me, were either delighted, or uncritical. The wise neutrals chose to wait, in hope.

Dayanand Sarasvati, later prefixed with the title 'Svami', was a Hindu reformer from Gujarat. He had hoped to introduce to the Indian masses, Vedic Scriptures as the only source of true Indian wisdom. In order to achieve his ambition, he established a few educational institutions, based upon the fundamentals of the Vedic spirituality and education. Due to lack of organisational skills and funds, the first few schools he opened, did not last long.

Eventually, in 1885, he succeeded in getting his message across – now matured by time and experience – to a group of people in a series of meetings and lectures in Bombay. Thus, the first, proper *Arya Samaj* (Society of Noblemen and Noblewomen) was formed with a membership of only a hundred individuals, including Svami jee himself. He refused all requests by the members to become the president or guru of the Samaj. He wished for the Samaj to be a society of equals.

Following the meetings in Bombay, *Arya Samaj* attracted intellectual and open-minded people from the Hindu, Muslim, Christian and Sikh population. As the Samaj progressed and its teachings became more widely known, people began to draw conclusions from its 'Ten Basic Principles'. And as is often the case, the conclusions were not necessarily based upon facts. The opposition found its reasons for their suspicions in the statements of some ill-informed, fanatical followers of the Samaj.

Svami Dayanand's emphasis on the removal of the

caste system, of child marriage, of inequality of material possessions, removal of glaring inequalities in social and educational conditions, and his opposition to polytheism were misrepresented by the religious wing of the Hindus. His unequivocal condemnation of beliefs in animal sacrifice, ancestor worship, pilgrimages, priest craft, iconolatry, prophets, and the Avatars, were viewed with deep suspicion by the followers of the mainly theistic religions in India. Hence, the Muslims, the Christians, and the Jews began to see him as an adversary.

Therefore, the news of a young man going to study in an Arya Samaj college, in preparation for Christian ministry, was seen by many as if I was walking into the enemy camp in broad day light, under my own colours.

I arrived in Amritsar at the start of May1957, and lodged with my sister Prabha and her husband, Dyal sing. Dyal was a senior civil servant in the department of the Indian Post and Telegraph Services. They lived, with their adopted son, in a government house, large enough to accommodate me without any space issues.

In the college, there were only two types of boys: those that came from English-medium private schools and gathered in small groups in the shade of the trees on the college campus. They conversed in both Punjabi and English. The other 98 per cent of the student body came from government local schools, and the surrounding villages. They spoke only Punjabi. The day-to-day Punjabi language is extensively sprinkled with words that my mother and her God did not approve of. Which meant, that not wanting to speak English, unable to speak Punjabi, and totally unfamiliar with the culture of the entire State of the Punjab. In a nutshell, I had no social life whatsoever.

One afternoon, a tall, handsome, sophisticated-

looking Sikh classmate of mine – let's call him Harnam
Singh – came up to me in front of the principal's office,
where I was sheltering from the scorching sun. Harnam
belonged to the English-speaking crowd. We shook
hands. He asked me in Punjabi, "Why are you always
hanging around in your own company? Don't you know
someone in the college, apart from yourself, that is?"

"I come from the Shimla hills," I replied in Hindi. "I
don't speak Punjabi well enough to confidently hold a
conversation . . ." Before I could finish, he jumped in.

"What about English. You can join my friends during
free periods!"

"I don't want to speak English," I said, feeling ill at
ease.

He put one hand in his trouser pocket, scratched his
chin with the other, a quizzical smile dancing on the
corners of his mouth, he said in Punjabi, "Welcome to the
land of Guru Nanak Sahib, you *Paharhi* sister fucker!
Sorry, sorry. No offence meant. It's just the way we speak
Punjabi." With exaggerated emphasis on 'Punjabi'. He
pursed his lips, squinted his eyes, and studying my face
thoughtfully, he asked, "Where exactly in Amritsar do
you live?" I described the route from the college to the
Post & Telegraph colony. He lived in Model town, with his
parents, he said, and my sister's place was about halfway
between the college and his home. "Tell you what, after
our last period, I will come with you. If your sister has no
objection, I'll take you to my place. Introduce you to my
ma and pa and some friends."

"All your friends speak English and Punjabi, and I
can't speak either!"

His *ma* didn't speak a word of English, he said, but *Pa*
spoke a few languages quite fluently. "You will get on well
with them. Best of all, where you are concerned, they both

speak 'clean' Punjabi."

"In that case, yes please! I would love to meet them."
I nearly wet myself with excitement.

Two hours later, during *chai-pani* at my sister's place,
Harnam warned me, that hanging around on my own
would make me an easy target for some village goons.
"Trust me, you will be bullied seriously." We agreed that
I would visit him the day after, for a sleepover, subject to
his parents' permission, of course.

As soon as Harnam (my new and only friend in the
entire State of the Punjab) left my sister's place, she lost
no time in following up on the purpose of his visit. "From
tomorrow, as soon as you get back from college, please
read two paragraphs of any speech by Nehru jee in our
newspaper. Also, listen to his speeches on the radio,
whenever you can. Read aloud the newspapers to me and
also to yourself, regularly," she advised firmly.

"Why Nehru's speeches?"

"Because Nehru jee speaks English, even better than
the English themselves," she stated, proudly. Go and get
an English Dictionary from the book shop in town. Less
than twenty-four hours later, I became, only very
reluctantly mind you, the proud owner of a copy of the
'Concise Oxford Dictionary'. It cost me half my monthly
allowance. To justify the cost of '*this thing*', I memorised
ten new words and their meanings every day, used them
in conversations, mostly with myself. Seven days a week,
I faithfully read two, sometimes three paragraphs of
Nehru's speeches from the Daily Tribune, persistently
and unsuccessfully mimicking the great Pundit jee.

My efforts to learn the English language were
regularly spied upon by a nosey neighbour. He had seen
me delivering my famous speeches to the uncomfortable
and miserable-looking young man on the other side of

the wall mirror, in our hallway. Other times, the nosey neighbour caught me out delivering my speeches, (in Nehru style) to the crowds behind a large, framed print (of a very European looking, blue-eyed, blond Jesus of Nazareth) on the wall of the living room.

Word got out that Mrs Rathore's brother 'is a very clever young man. He is preparing to be a politician, and practices the delivery of his speeches, diligently'. Less gullible neighbours added some elements of humour and imagination to my methods of learning the language. The very large lady next door told the neighbours, "Poor Mrs Rathore! Her brother is not right in his head. He is always talking to himself." Of all the neighbours, she was probably the closest to the truth.

With time, my resistance to learning the English language began to weaken by what my brother-in-law, and his elderly friend, told me about my father. My father, they insisted, never hated or despised the *'Angrez'*. "Your father never hated anyone," my brother-in-law said to me on numerous occasions. "Your father spoke good English himself," said the friend. "He simply did not want the British to rule him in his own homeland."

Both of them pointed out that my father was convinced, that had the Angrez not been helped by our own Indians, due to our disunity and religious divisions, the Angrez would never have succeeded in colonising India.

I had heard similar comments at different times from others, who had known my father. My brother-in-law added, "Your hatred of the Angrez and their language, will only hurt you, Nihal, not the Angrez." Before long, my dubious and forced conversion to the English language was complete. With the help and support of my sister, brother-in-law and Harnam, and my own persistence, it took me about six months to be reluctantly accepted as a member of the English speaking 'upper class society' of the college.

I was pleased with my success in the new venture. I could see the obvious benefits of my hard work. Deep down within myself though, I struggled to come to terms with the sense of having betrayed my father's sacrifices, and the sacrifices of every freedom fighter in all the colonies, the world over. No matter what anyone said, I could not, and I still cannot see how any nation can justify taking away by stealth and force, what naturally belongs to another. Colonialism can have no justification in a 'rational' and a 'culturally moral' society.

I enjoyed two wonderful years, as the specially privileged 'Christian friend' of the college community of Swami Dayanand. The principal of the college had gone out of his way to make me feel not only welcome, but also a very special member of his college community.

Unfortunately, due to my so called extra-curricular activities, I managed to secure only a 'respectable' pass in Hindi, English, Punjabi, philosophy, political science and psychology. Unbeknown to my sister and to the bishop in Amritsar, some of my new-found freedoms and friendships, had led me dangerously close to self-destruction. In my attempts to be accepted fully into the affluent Punjabi community in town, I nearly got sucked into the wrong crowd of seriously 'bad boys'. Had it not been for Harnam and his wonderful ma and pa, I would have sunk in the quagmire of 'un-kosher' high life, which, at the time, had seemed far more exciting than the boring job of a padre.

In the event, I thought it best, without giving anything away, to move out of Amritsar to some faraway city in India, for the remainder of my university education.

Some days after my return home from Amritsar, Mother, Rupchand and I met with the padre outside the church, in Kotgarh. At the end of a brief discussion Mother agreed that the university of Allahabad would do. And off she went for her post-Service *chai-pani,* to wash down the taste of the sermon, I guess.

Chapter 14

Ganga, Jamuna, Sarasvati

In the summer of 1960, I moved to Allahabad (original name was Prayag, but re-named by the Mughals as Allahabad) in Uttar Pradesh, for the remainder of my further education. I enrolled myself, for a two-year BA degree in philosophy, psychology, History of Education, and Hindi literature, at the Presbyterian Ewing Christian College, on the banks of the river Jamuna. The padre used his connections to arrange my stay at the Seminary of the Oriental Missionary Society, approximately six miles away from the college. I was to live, sleep and eat in the seminary, attend all their chapel Services, plus one lecture every morning, before going on to the college.

After a journey of three days and a little under three nights, in some lop-sided buses that spouted more smoke than a small volcano, three different trains – two pulled by coal-fired, and the third one by a diesel engine – I arrived in the 'city' of Prayag on the thirtieth day of May in the nineteen-hundred-and-sixtieth year of our Lord, as they say. In those days, train journeys in India offered endless opportunities for interesting conversations with complete strangers. I learned more about the life and cultures of India on my train journeys, than I could ever have learned from the mobile phones and laptops that are now undetachable items to every traveller's body.

Once in Prayag, I soon realised, that no two cities in India could be further apart culturally, linguistically, and in almost all other ways of human interactions, than Amritsar in the Punjab and Prayag in Uttar Pradesh. Prayag has a spiritual significance in the lives of Hindus that is only a few notches below Varanasi and Hardwar. The city is blessed by the presence of three holy rivers, namely, Ganga (Ganges), Jamuna, and the mythical river Sarasvati that flow through its soil. It is firmly believed by every devout Hindu that the river Sarasvati flows through the city in its invisible, spiritual form.

Since the final decade of the twentieth century, much scientific research has been undertaken to establish the status of this mythical river. Research suggests that there may have been an actual river Sarasvati in the area, probably 4,000 years ago. Interest in the research was sparked as far back as 1893 by the inquisitive mind of an English engineer, while riding his horse along the seasonal River Ghaggar, in the deserts of Rajasthan. But little or nothing was done to establish the truth or otherwise, until recently.

Due to its ancient past, Prayag holds special significance in the cultural and religious traditions of the Hindu religion. The *Kumbh mela* takes place every twelve years, in four Hindu pilgrimage sites, Prayag being one of those sites. In Prayag, the secondary *Kumbh,* known as the *Magh Mela*, is celebrated annually, at the meeting point of the three rivers. The celebrations attract huge crowds during the month of January. According to Wikipedia the 2019 *Magh Mela* attracted the greatest numbers anywhere at any world festival. The University of Prayag, commonly known as the 'University of Allahabad' being one of the oldest and among the most prestigious educational institutions in Asia, adds to the importance of the city.

The first two years in Prayag were comparatively

quiet, but very stressful. The stifling heat of the city and the choking piety of a seminary, run by a group of 'hallelujah' evangelical Christians, were bad enough in their own merits. Combined with that, were the temptations of the secular life of the city for a dubiously pious eighteen/nineteen-year-old village boy. I was continually oscillating between being a 'normal, ordinary young man', and a 'holy and pious born-again-Christian young man'. The anxiety and stress caused by being Jekyll and Hyde, did affect my emotional and physical health to some degree. Riding a third, or fourth-hand rickety bicycle over the roads that were littered with more potholes than a builder's sieve, was more fun than pain. But dust and smoke from passing vehicles on the roads caused my sinuses to flare up at the start of each summer. I suffered sore throat, watery eyes and terrible headaches. My own, and that of the seminary's false piety and presumed holiness, piled up burden of guilt on the back of my poor soul that nearly turned me into a 'hunchback of Allahabad'.

About six months after I moved to Prayag, the old Canadian bishop of Amritsar retired, and we had the first Indian bishop in Amritsar. The new bishop and I had never met, but from day one, he refused to answer my requests for a meeting with him. A few weeks before my final BA exams, the padre and I wrote him separate letters, again, requesting a meeting to discuss the possibility of my preparation for ordination. Again, no reply. I wondered if I could enrol for a master's degree at the university, while waiting for the bishop to 'learn to read and write'. The family and the padre agreed. So it was, that, in July of 1962, I began my studies for a two-year postgraduate degree in philosophy, with one paper in psychology.

Moving from college to the university brought me in contact with a different environment, new friends, bigger library, and all that only half a mile away from the seminary. Ten months on, and only a few days before exams, my normal sinus trouble became aggravated by a four-day-long mild dust storm. For the first two papers (three days apart), I struggled through the full three hours each time. For the third paper, a friend's father, a practicing medical doctor who had been taking care of my medical needs for some time now, insisted on giving me a lift to the exam centre. He dropped me outside the Senate Hall and waited in the car. Some minutes short of an hour, my wet eyes, sore throat, high temperature, and throbbing headache stopped me dead in my tracks. One of the invigilators and a student helped me out to the car. My friend's father took me back to his house. He put me on medication for a week. It did ease my headaches and watery, itchy eyes, but I failed to complete my exams and missed a whole year of my life.

I returned home to Dabi and immersed myself in my favourite vocation, the little apple orchard. At the end of the day in the orchard, I would wash up, have a hurried snack, and make my way over to Madhur and Gosain's digs in Thanedhar, for music sessions.

Madhur was the Assistant Inspector of Horticulture for the area. He played classical stuff on his violin at a fairly high level and could belt out Bollywood songs and folk music to entertain audiences at weddings, village fairs and private parties. His roommate, Gosain, a science teacher in the local high school, played sitar at a novice level. I joined them with a pair of *Tabla* at the lowest novice level. Most Sunday Services were followed by *mehfils* (musical gatherings of family and friends) at Rupchand and Urmila's place, couple hundred yards from the church, in Kotgarh. We never charged a penny for entertaining the crowds.

Towards the end of November 1963, I returned to the university. I found myself a room in the annex of a Presbyterian church hall, at a very reasonable rent, halfway between the seminary and the university campus. Relief was instant. Being in a non-holy, normal environment, communicating with only the 'ordinary/normal' children of God, I felt free to make friends with some wonderful people, both inside and outside of the Church circles. I was also able to concentrate better on my studies.

On a sunny Friday afternoon, in December of 1963, I stepped out of the classroom, at the end of a very entertaining and informative lecture on Greek philosophy. Outside the door I ran into a young man. He introduced himself as Ashraf and wondered if I would join him for a cup of tea in some café on the high street. My curiosity advised me to accept the stranger's invitation. Over tea, he asked me if I could find time to help him improve his English. I said my knowledge of the English language was fairly limited, but would gladly do what little I could, to help him. We shook hands, and a wonderful friendship was born. From then on, he addressed me as 'Nihal bhai'.

His village was an hour's bicycle ride away. Once we had got to know each other better, I let him have keys to my room. He could rest there during long gaps between lectures. Ashraf introduced me to his two childhood friends and classmates at the university. Now, I was blessed with the friendship of open-minded, spiritually aware Hindus, Muslims, and a young Christian man. Eight hundred and seventy-eight miles away from home, they became to me my surrogate family.

If I had to pick one significant moment of interactions between me and my friends at the university, it would have to be Ashraf's twentieth birthday. He wanted to celebrate his birthday with his friends in Prayag. The parents of our Hindu friend, Vishnu, suggested that we use their home for the occasion, while they were 'conveniently' away for a couple of days, at their daughter's place in Lucknow.

On his big day, Ashraf, Vishnu, and I took over the kitchen for the afternoon. In view of the fact, that one of our numbers was 'strict vegetarian Brahmin', we decided upon two vegetarian dishes with rice and chapattis and some Indian sweets for afters. Three Muslims, two Christians and two Hindus ate in the traditional Muslim manner, from one large *thali* (metal plate), in the home of a Brahmin.

Through free and frank interactions with people, who were interested in seeking the truth more than 'we know it all' attitude of the strictly religious, I was learning more about my Christian spirituality; something, that one could not imagine happening in a seminary of 'born-again' preachers. For example, a Hindu professor I had become friends with at the university, loved Jesus Christ so much that whenever he spoke about Christ, his eyes would well up. One day, he said to me, "Paal sahib, before you speak about Christ in your creeds, you must feel him in your heart." And another time, "One would think that Jesus Christ is a brand of toothpaste or shaving cream, the way some stupid Christians talk about him in their sermons." This was his reaction to a radio broadcast by a world-famous American preacher, earlier that morning.

I was still struggling in the shallow, murky waters of religion. The Church Services still bored me to sleep, or made me lose sleep, depending on the text of the sermon and the state of mind of the preacher. I was aware of the painful inadequacies not only of my own religion, but of all the other religions I knew anything about. I felt strongly that we all needed to work and learn together. Others had something to teach me and I, them. That dream could be achieved, I was convinced, only if we tried to seek and to understand 'God' together. We needed to stop wasting our time trying to impress the others with, 'My Daddy is Bigger than your Daddy' virus.

One Sunday morning, I invited my professor friend to join me at a Church Service. He responded, "Why would I want to do that?" He had been to church many times in the past, he said. "Paal sahib, the churches replaced the real Jesus Christ with their own homemade Christ, a long time ago." As an afterthought, he added, with a smirk, "Real Jesus Christ speaks to us heathens in the streets."

In my second year in Prayag, still at the seminary, I was making rounds of *Kumbh Magh Mela* one afternoon, hoping to save the souls of some heathens. I targeted a group of about twenty sadhus, all sitting on the ground, in a circle. I gave a copy of the Gospel of Matthew in Hindi to the one I presumed to be their Guru. He took the Gospel from me respectfully and invited me to sit down next to him. I took it to be a sign of my success and promptly sat down in eager anticipation. He placed his hand on my shoulder, and with a forgiving and loving smile in his big, brown eyes, he said, "Son, Jesus was the greatest man that ever lived on this earth. If you follow his lifestyle, you will not need to preach about him. People will see you and want to know him."

He made perfect sense, but I wasn't yet ready to relinquish my conviction in the superiority of my beliefs over the beliefs of any who did not agree with me. We chatted a bit more. He pointed to a group of young girls we could see playing in the winter sun of Prayag. "Those children, they are poor and some of them are orphans," he said. "They are slaves of the *'Pujaris'* (Hindu priests) inside those temples. Talking about God does not make you holy." He was outraged by the complicity of the police and the priests in 'the evil practices' of child sex slavery. As I stood up to move on, the sadhu said to me with a knowing smile, "Next time you give a Gospel to a complete novice, give them the Gospel of Mark. It is likely to be the closest to the facts about Jesus."

In the ensuing months and years, that sadhu's words took me back to an afternoon in the autumn of 1957, in the bishop's office in Amritsar. On that afternoon the bishop and I were discussing my forthcoming Service of Confirmation. A rich farmer in the Punjab – a Sikh gentleman – came to see the bishop, to discuss the possibility of 'becoming a Christian'.

"If being a Christian means to be like the young couple that have been working on my farm over the past twelve years, then I want to be a Christian," he said to the bishop, in a voice loaded with genuine emotion.

Don't get me wrong. I was not anti-Church or anti-Christianity. I was only anti-religions. Take for example, Hinduism. It had been a uniquely spiritual culture for many centuries. The four castes – Brahmin, Khshatri, Shaivya, and Shudra were originally designed to classify and categorise the Indian society into four sections. Caste classification was based on each individual member's aptitude, interests, abilities, and levels of spiritual and intellectual developments. Thus, enabling each member to make their full contribution to the welfare of the whole Hindu society. If a person born into a Shudra family had the aptitude, interests, and abilities of a warrior, then that person would be a Khshatri, and not a Shudra. And this applied to all castes equally.

At some point in the history of Indian thought development, the community of priests hijacked the wonderful caste system to establish their superiority over and above all other castes. Like the leaders of all the other religions, they turned the caste system on its head, to their own advantage. Soon, a child born to Shudra parents remained a Shudra, irrespective of its aptitudes, interests and abilities. Shudras became the 'slave' caste, with no rights, no equality in any aspect of human life. Even the shadow of a Shudra became unholy overnight. Religion once again destroyed what was a unique, excellent social and spiritual classification of a society.

The leaders of all major religions and their followers do not like questions that they do not have the answers to. They start jumping up and down, claiming that the questioner is insulting their god. That their god requires them to avenge those 'imagined' insults. One is not permitted even an innocent enquiry for wanting to make sense of something that was written in an obscure past, by men of dubious character, writing with their own agenda in mind. The questions are answered by hanging on the cross, by burning at the stake, or by raping and selling the children of the questioner into slavery and chopping the heads off anyone who appears to not agree with the 'defenders of faith'. All this, and more, because they cannot defend the indefensible.

The god of each institutionalised religion needs his 'faithful followers' to defend him and his honour. These are people who pride themselves in taking over the lands of their neighbours and slaughtering them with impunity. This god cares only about the descendants of a friend of his. Another god does not permit any member of the human society to disagree with his 'chosen favourites'. If they do, then this god lets his 'chosen favourites' burn them alive at the stake. There is yet another god; to defend his honour, this god chooses sexual deviants and cowards to rape women and children. He encourages them to torture and behead anyone they don't like.

In asking questions, in not believing everything someone tells them to believe, one is simply using the three basic instincts of *curiosity, exploration* and *adventure*. The three instincts we are born with. These must be the gifts of the god who we believe has created us. The fact that religions deny the use of these God-given gifts, says a lot about the institutionalised/organised religions' inability to cope with The Truth.

For genuine believers in God (whatever image of God one has), choice is simple; which should come first? That which God instilled in us, or that which men imposed upon us?

All through this period, while diving in and out of different images of God, a faint picture kept running though my thoughts; a picture where God has no shape, no name, nothing that I could see clearly, but it was there, nevertheless. The picture was powerfully drawing me onto itself. But socially, culturally and traditionally, I still needed the Church and its religion. I was still afraid to let go of God of the Holy Books. "What makes you think that all followers of our religion over centuries have been wrong, and you alone are right?" This was a challenge that I could not put to one side and forget. Yes! *What if I am wrong? What then?* A scary thought, indeed.

Halfway through my MA final exams, I received a telegram from my padre to say, that the Bishop of Amritsar had unexpectedly broken the silence. Without a word of explanation, he had written to my padre, asking him to advise me to apply to the Bishop's College, Calcutta for admission for a three-year 'Bachelor of Divinity' course.

Although the sinuses problem returned just the same as before, I didn't do too badly. A good overall second class, and a record-breaking 92 per cent in the Shankaracharya's Advaita Vedanta, made up for my many un-scholarly hobbies. On top of that, I had also had the pleasure of learning, as a Christian, to interact freely and openly with the spiritual heritage of my 'Hindu' and other cultures from around the world.

Couple of days after the final exams in Prayag, I made my way back to Dabi, to bask in the cooler shades of the mountains, and to get on with preparations for entry into what I had been told was the most prestigious theological college for the Anglicans in Asia, at the time. Although my application for registration was well past the 'apply by' date, the principal kindly allowed me late entry without an Entrance Exam.

Once again, the 'religion' ego started muscling into my thoughts. Prestige, privilege, and authority associated with the profession of priesthood are not to be scoffed at. A boy from the hills, going to be one of the very few padres in India with a postgraduate degree, and the title of 'Padri Sahib'! Umm, was not an easily conquerable temptation, I confess.

Chapter 15

The Giggler

I had another session of bragging in our Dabi kitchen. Bragging about what it was like to be the first one from those parts of the hills to have completed a master's degree?

"Tell me something about Allabad," asked Hubau.

"It's not Allabad. It is Allahabad," I corrected him. "I have told you all about Allahabad you need to know for now. And I prefer to call it by its original name – Prayag. Sorry, I am going to Thanedhar to meet my old friends. See you later."

I was dying to catch up with my friends, acquaintances, and accomplices from the past. After trawling through the high street of six shops, two cafés, a barbershop, a butcher, and a cobbler, I caught up with a small group of my old accomplices in one of the cafés, for a tumbler of tea. Sipping, slurping, gossiping, and swearing, we were guffawing, like hyenas on a binge. Through the corner of my left eye, I noticed a familiar face at the entrance, eagerly looking in. "Hi everyone! Can anyone here help me transport a dozen large sacks of animal feed and some other stuff to *Madhu ban* (forest of honey)?" he enquired. As he stood there, waiting for a response to his query, our eyes met across the five-yard-deep screen of smoke from different brands of tobacco and 'other things' spewing out of the lungs of a dozen customers.

I called out, full of excitement, "Jag Mohan?" and

jumped out of my seat, spilling tea all over the front of my trousers. Jag Mohan flew in, took my hand, and with exaggerated movements of his entire body, squeezed it so hard, it hurt.

"What are you doing here, you silly ...?" I asked. "Your sister told me, only this morning that you were at the new place you've acquired, in Koel."

He explained that he had unexpectedly returned home, only that afternoon to shop for some essential supplies. We hugged vigorously, like two long-lost lovers. We laughed and giggled – Jag Mohan always giggled. We ordered more tea. Jag Mohan said brief hellos, how-do-you-dos, shook hands, slapped a few backs, and had his back slapped in return.

Materially, Jag Mohan was far better off than any of us in the café, but he treated everyone as his equal. Everyone loved and respected him. His servants were fond of him, because he mucked in with them, whatever the job. I enjoyed his company because we clicked from day one. Our friendship was further strengthened by a close bond between our mothers who were of similar age and had grown up under the same roof – my mother had been fostered/adopted by Jag Mohan's grandparents when she was about three years old. In the not-too-distant past, they had shared much in common, including poverty. We exchanged quick notes about some familiar and mundane things over sips and slurps of boiling hot tea, in stainless steel tumblers. One of the customers in the café offered to take care of transporting his shopping sacks. Jag Mohan gave him some money and left the matter in his hands.

So much had happened since our last meeting. Jag Mohan had married and was the proud father of a little boy, he told me. He had put on some weight. In my case, I had actually lost a few ounces, or maybe a full pound. I noticed that he was not walking around with a ball of wool under his left arm and the knitting needles clicking at nineteen to a dozen – Jag Mohan was the only male person we knew in our world who did knitting. My last memory of him was from when he stood by the bus to say goodbye to me on my way to Prayag, five years ago. At the time, he was knitting a cardigan for his mother. Oh, and another very important change from the old days – now, he was wearing shoes; an expensive-looking pair at that. We soon realised that a quick 'hello' and 'how are you?' were pitifully inadequate. We sent a message to our respective mothers, letting them know that I was going with Jag Mohan to his place, and may stay there for the next day or two. "They will understand," we agreed.

An hour later, we arrived at his place, *Madhu ban*. There was excitement all round. Jag Mohan and I were offered the bay window seats (a guest privilege) with outside views of many country miles. His parents and the three younger sisters stationed themselves in the chairs, opposite. I ducked and dived through a very entertaining and light-hearted evening conversation that made me feel really important.

They all wanted to know what subjects had I studied? What was it like being at the university a thousand miles away from home? A barrage of questions. The sisters were more interested in what I thought of the city girls. Did university boys have girlfriends, and had I found one yet? They teased me about bringing home an Allahabad bride with degrees.

The family's stand-in cook, Sumni, served the evening meal earlier than usual. Savitri *masi* (aunty, on mother's side) advised one of their paid helpers to make up two single beds in the upstairs south-facing conservatory. After the meal, as soon as was socially acceptable, Jag Mohan and I retired to the conservatory. Sitting there on the beds, we briefly brought each other up to date on the history of the past five years. He was more interested in what he wrongly believed to be my far more exciting life in a faraway city, than his own life, surrounded by mountains, valleys, forests and rivers, and tonnes of clean, fresh air.

I told him about my college and the university. How I had enjoyed my time there. Especially the weekly picnics with my friends, on the banks of the river Jamuna. I shared some bits of gossip about the Oriental Missionary Seminary's attitude towards their Indian 'Christian brothers and sisters in the Lord'.

The student body at the seminary fluctuated in numbers, anywhere between six and eight, each year. They represented different parts of India. The medium of teaching was English but, generally, half their numbers were unfamiliar with the language. During my three years there, we had one seventeen-year-old who had very little grasp even of his own mother tongue. I recall his brother telling us that the seminary was the only place that would take him in. In the outside world, he had no chance of getting a proper job. He was not alone in that category of 'priest-to-be' in any religious community, anywhere in the world.

"That reminds me of the question I have been meaning to ask you for a long time."

"Fire away," I said, guessing what the question might be.

"What on earth possessed you to want to become a padre? You don't even believe in God. You have always had problems with religions. You, a priest? Doesn't bear thinking."

He took us back to the school days when I spent more

time in telling silly jokes about the padres, pundits, and the mullahs, than doing my schoolwork. He went over some of the jokes: the one about the bishop, who was kicked repeatedly by the wife of a poor village preacher under the dining table (she had meant to kick her husband to stop him from asking their guest, the bishop, if he would like a second helping. There was no food for second helping). And the one about the *mullah* who always stammered on the word 'Akbar', and its hilarious consequences on the worshippers in his mosque. The best one, he thought, was about a Pundit jee, who had had too much to drink before the marriage ceremony he was officiating at. Halfway through the ceremony, Pundit jee dozed off and went face first into the ceremonial fire, in front of him on the floor.

"I do believe in God. It is what we say about God, that makes no sense to me. We talk about God as if we created him. To me, God is, and always will be, an unfathomable mystery. What worries me, is the lack of the strength of conviction I seem to have about what I think I really believe. At one point during my seminary days, I had even started joining in with those happy, clappy, 'know-it-all' preachers in Allahabad."

Jag Mohan listened intently.

We were distracted by a soft knock on the door. I opened to let Sumni in. She had brought a pot of tea, with proper China cups and saucers, fresh hot *pakorhas* of aubergine, sliced potatoes and spinach leaves, and a bowl full of homemade mint and yoghurt sauce on a silver tray. She placed the tray on the table between the two beds. With a mixture of unease and familiarity, she stood back. Her eyes darting from face to face, while playfully fiddling with her right earring.

Jag Mohan nodded a 'thank you'. Sumni turned

towards the exit. At the door, hand on the handle, she turned round, and reminded me that it had been nearly two years since our last meeting, near Dabi. "Look at you! You are a full-grown man now." She shot a mischievous wink at both of us, and with deliberate slowness, stepped onto the stairs and shut the door behind, softly. Our ears followed the sound of her unwilling footsteps labouring down the stairs.

An hour later, Sumni returned to collect the empties. "When are you two going to call it a day?" She placed her hand on my head and ruffled my hair. "It is good to see you, again. Jag Mohan babu jee is always talking about your school days." She picked up the empties and hurriedly disappeared down the stairs.

The following morning, we joined the rest of the family for breakfast of ghee *paratha*, with *aloo ki sabzi,* and mugs of fresh Darjeeling tea, all the necessary ingredients for a refreshing start to a beautiful day. There was hardly any conversation. No 'thank you' prayers, no list or requests and instructions to God for the rest of the day. After breakfast, everyone in Madhu ban went about their business, with, 'Ah! Thank God for another lovely day'. Fifteen minutes later, I was in Dabi receiving Mother's instructions for the day ahead.

In the evening, I returned to Madhu ban, and was informed that due to some problem on the farm, Jag Mohan would be returning to Koel the following day. His father suggested that I join Jag Mohan there and "Spend a few days together in Koel, without the rest of us hanging around." We happily agreed.

The following daybreak, Jag Mohan turned his face towards Koel, and I towards Dabi. Two days after that, I left home in the early hours of the morning and headed to join Jag Mohan across the river Satluj. First four miles plus were down the steep and rugged dirt tracks through woods, terraced fields, and tiny hamlets; the next two miles were over the new Shimla-Tibet Highway, leading to the river crossing near the village of Nirth. I had only once crossed the same river, in a rickety chair attached to an overhead wire, a few miles down from my present crossing. The wire was secured to a wooden post at either side of the river. At closer examination, the post on my side was unreassuringly leaning slightly to one side. The post across the river looked more like a tree stump sticking out of a rock. Due to some heavy showers in the mountains the day before, the river looked and sounded angry. I was forced to make a deal with a crafty shepherd. If I agreed to carry his soaking wet lamb in my lap, he would tell his son on the other side, he said temptingly, to pull the two of us across.

Across the river, I had another two miles plus of narrow, undulating, rocky dirt track to navigate. The wet lamb had left a large brown, odorous stain on the entire front of my shirt and trousers. Hour and a half later, I stood at the front door of the only house in sight, on a large, sandy plot of land. Jag Mohan, his wife, the little boy, and their workers were waiting to welcome me. Jag Mohan showed me to the outside washroom. One of the young men gave me two large buckets of warm water, and a complete set of Jag Mohan's clothes.

Wash down was followed by lunch, followed by a few turns on 'forbidden' hubble-bubble. We concluded the afternoon with a gentle stroll down to the river. The evening meal was consumed in relative silence, largely out of consideration for my tiredness, I presumed. After some casual chit-chat about most things under the sun, we yawned our way to bed.

The following morning, thundering dark clouds threw

all the soaking wet cats and dogs from the skies onto our dry earth. During a short break in the downpour, Jag Mohan's wife suggested that we catch some driftwood along the northern flank of the flooded river.

Halfway through the exercise, the heavens opened again. We were soaked through to the skin with the angel pee. For the next three days the showers continued, with short breaks in between. Each morning after breakfast, we went down to the river with our ropes, and landed a good catch of driftwood every time. Afternoons were spent on chores around the house and tending to the needs of the many animals. After late evening meals, Jag Mohan's wife and the eldest helper joined us for a few card games, before bedtime.

On my fifth and final morning in Koel, Jag Mohan and I went for a quick walk down to the river after breakfast. On our return, his wife handed me a neatly packed lunch for my journey home, and a glass of fresh orange juice, each. Halfway through the drink, Jag Mohan asked, "Do you remember the heavy snowfall of 1950/51, when we nearly lost you by the rock of *Dhaklambu* (Bergenia)?"

"How can I ever forget the experience of dying repeatedly, in one short space of time?" We reminded ourselves that despite the crippling poverty of our childhood, those bad old days, nevertheless, had gifted us with some wonderful, exciting memories.

Chapter 16

The Encounter with Sita

Standing outside the front door of Jag Mohan's house in Koel, we transported ourselves back to the winter break from school, many years ago. A week or two into January, In the winter of 1949/50 we were snowed under six feet deep in Dabi, alone. "It was the highest snowfalls in the unwritten history of our world." Narsi said so.

First opportunity Jag Mohan had to visit us in Dabi since a week before the snow fall, was towards the end of January. The time must have been around 9.30 a.m. He had virtually run all the way from his home, through the woods and patches of deep snow. He dragged himself up through the snow-covered vegetable patch below our house. Stopped in front of the chicken coop, breathless. "Namaste, *Masi jee* (aunty)," he greeted Mother inside the coop. "Where is Nihal?"

"There, son! Sitting on the veranda." Mother nodded her head in my direction.

"Thanks." He strode up to where I was exaggeratedly nursing my wounds, basking in the bright winter sunshine, and thoroughly lapping up the rarest of privileges; being spoiled by everyone in sight. He flung himself onto the wooden floor beside me and started to check my nearly frostbitten toes on both feet.

Still huffing and puffing, he said, "Primi told me yesterday about your meeting with Sita."

"Jag Mohan," Mother called out, "before you two girls settle down to chattering, would you like to make tea for the three of us?" Jag Mohan dashed into the kitchen, a few minutes later, re-emerged with three tumblers of tea. He took one over for Mother. All this time he hadn't taken the rucksack off his back. He took the rucksack off, dropped it in front of Mother.

"Mama sent these walnuts for you." And rushed back to me.

Mother opened the bag. "Son, please thank your mum from me for these lovely walnuts. Your mama is — "

I cut in, before Mama could embarrass us with her ramblings of gratitude. "You want the whole story?" I asked.

"Yes, every bit. I said so, didn't I," he said impatiently, and sat up against the wall, facing me and the morning sun. I was reclining against the timber structure that sheltered the hand-mill at the northern end of the veranda. I related the tale of my adventure. About a week after the snowfall, we had run out of all the basic rations in the house. Mama, Anup and I were the only ones here. Rupbhai had been stranded at his friend's place on the other side of Kotgarh. Khushal was in the school hostel. Being the man of the house for that week, I had to go to the shops. My feet were so swollen with chilblains that I ended up wearing Rupbhai's army boots . . . I paused to allow the significance of the size of the boots to sink in.

"You went in those big clappers, in that snow, all the way to Thanedhar? Sometimes, you can be incorrigibly stupid ... Sorry, I am only joking."

I was enjoying the tales of my own heroism too much to take an offence. I continued:

Yeah! I rubbed a handful of Vaseline on my hands and feet, put on two pairs of thick woolly socks, pulled Rupbhai's trousers over mine, put on his boots, and put my woolly jumper over my *khaddar* shirt. I wrapped

Mama's *chadru* (a woollen shawl) over the jumper, put on the gloves Mama had knitted for me for last Christmas, and set off for Thanedhar.

I put my shopping bag over my shoulder and stepped out of the house. Struggled through the deep snow up to the road. When I hit the road, I was in the well-trodden furrow down the middle, all the way to shops. Underfoot, it was just one thick slab of ice. On either side of me, reaching nearly up to my shoulders, was the lovely, clean, white, crispy, crackly snow for miles. I put my shopping list in a certain order and fitted the list into the tune of the song that Pushpabua is always humming and singing, lately. You know the one that goes, *Jal re deepak, Jal re jal x 2; Ambar men ghanmaya kaali, kaali nisha daraane vali; Andhkaar ki kali pyali . . .* (Stay alight, oh lamp, stay alight x 2. The sky is darkened by black clouds, the dark night is frightening, and the cup of black darkness is full ...) I sang and whistled all the way to the shop."

Singing and whistling warns the beasts of human presence, I reminded Jag Mohan, and they stay out of the way.

"Some people say that whistling is dangerous; it attracts ghosts out of their hiding places," Jag Mohan pointed out.

"I always whistled, and no ghost has attacked me, yet," I pointed out. "I was still singing when I hit the concrete floor outside the first shop front, in Thanedhar. I moved swiftly towards the narrow opening in the wide front of the shop, stuck my head in. Both the shopkeeper and his elderly customer were leaning over the one charcoal fire between them and sharing the pleasures of a hubble-bubble. I said aloud, "Ooh, your floor out here is even colder than the half-mile-long block of ice I have just walked on, to get here." – *Impress, impress.* They nearly jumped out of their home-spun, colourfully-patterned, woolly shawls.

"What on earth do you think you are doing out here, in this weather?" They enquired simultaneously. I explained my reason for being there.

The shopkeeper unwrapped himself and stood up with such speed, he surprised me and his friend. And in the process let out a ... broke wind loudly.

"I am in no hurry," I said.

He took the bag out of my frozen hand. I recited my shopping requirements slowly, through my chattering teeth, one item at a time. He weighed and measured every item generously, wrapped it in a newspaper cone. Then placed the five cones neatly in my bag and handed it back to me.

"Go on home, now. Hurry on son, you hear! If the cold doesn't get you, some hungry animal sure will." I took the bag from his hand absent-mindedly. Handed over the exact money. He returned to his lovingly crafted portable *ungitthi* (brazier), wrapped the warm woolly shawl over his shoulders, and sat down inside the semi-dark and warm front of his shop. As I turned away from the entrance, I heard him say to his customer, how sad he felt for our mother and her children, for the way things had turned out for us, "since the death of their father." Then, as usual, something about the 'Angrez' being largely responsible for the state we were in. They agreed that had father been wise and careful with his possessions, his family would have managed quite well, even after his death. "This boy would not be out here in this weather, that's for sure," added the customer.

I did not wish to hear any more. I moved away and turned my face in the direction of an isolated house, half a mile away, in the middle of nowhere. The voices grew fainter as I deliriously moved my weary, cold body homeward. Not for the first time, my mind was caught up in the mixture of an uplifting sense of pride and a deep, dark sadness and outrage. *What is the point in talking about my papa's greatness and his generosity, when all I know, is the dreadful mess he has left us in?* I wanted to ask my father so many questions, but I was too cold, angry, and confused to know what to say.

On my veranda, I was still talking to Jag Mohan but turned my face in the direction where Mother was sitting. I raised my voice a few notches, "Papajee is just like God; never there when I need him. I really hate Papajee, sometimes."

Mother heard my anger. "Don't speak of your father so disrespectfully," she admonished firmly from behind the bundles of dried grass.

"We have nothing to show for all the tall tales people tell me about him. So why should I not hate him?"

"Because he is your father. That is why." She spoke in a slightly raised voice.

"Well then! *Why* is he *never* there when I need him?"

"Be that as it may, I will not hear another disrespectful word from your lips about your father. Is that clear?"

"Don't get into an argument with *Masi jee*. Tell me more about Sita!" Jag Mohan whispered impatiently.

Ignoring Jag Mohan's impatient pleadings, I asked Mother, "Were we really rich when I was little?"

"Not really. We were never rich," answered Mother. "You shouldn't believe everything people tell you about your father. They exaggerate out of kindness. We were quite comfortable, mostly. We also had a few years in between, which may be described as being better than just comfortable. But in the last few years, even before your father's death, we were doing just about alright."

She took a sad, deep breath and carried clicking her knitting needles. "Your father did have many friends though, some of them rich, and even famous. People respected him because of his musical gifts, and because he was a freedom fighter, and went to jail twice." After a brief silence she added, "Your father was a kind fool."

Her voice trailed into disappointment. After a brief pause, "Well, he is not here, now. We just have to get on with life." It was the first time I had heard more than one sentence of some helpful information about my father, from my mother's lips.

I picked up my story as if the previous five minutes had not happened.

On my way back from the shop, I was too angry and frozen to sing anything, and I couldn't put my lips together to whistle. As I came round the right-hand bend at the rock of *Dhaklambu*, Sita was about twenty yards in front, smack in the middle of my path. Our eyes met. I recognised her from our meeting in Khlawn, weeks before. It was there we first named her Sita.

I don't know why, but I was mesmerised by seeing only her body above the snow line, without her legs. Luckily, I remembered not to run away, or to stare at her. Slowly, I turned sideways to face the Praying Mountains. I pretended that I had not seen her. I could see Jagtu's house, only five hundred yards below, but with deep snow all around and on the roof of the house. No one could have heard me.

"So, what did you do, then?"

Not a lot. From the corner of my right eye, I could see her looking at me. At one point I thought I saw her licking her lips. I was hoping that she would see how skinny I am and leave me alone.

Unable to move, I was vaguely aware of my

surroundings. The sun had popped its head out through a hole in the clouds, somewhere above the tops of the trees behind me. It made the evening look like the middle of the day. The snow shimmered on top of the Praying Mountains before me. I could see the clouds above the mountain tops had turned red and dusky pink, like someone was playing *Holi* (Indian Spring Festival of Colours) in the sky.

"Do you remember Old Sharhu telling us that those shimmering lights come from the fairies and the goddesses, doing their naughty dances in their colourful, shiny robes?"

"Yeah, yeah, I remember," he said impatiently. "They dance to entertain the gods before night sets in, and the darkness covers the mountains," he added excitedly.

"That's it. You're right," I agreed, and continued with my story. Sharhu had also told us that the red and pink colours in the clouds above, were the flames from the fires, that the nasty demons light to scare the fairies and the goddesses away from the gods.

Completely absorbed in that scene, I forgot all about where I was. Suddenly, I felt this comforting sensation of warm fluid, running down the inside of my right leg, all the way to my ankle. My foot was too dead to feel that momentary comfort. Seconds later, the warm sensation turned wet and burning cold on my skin. And then, some more *looong* seconds, and the fluid froze into a long, narrow icicle, clinging to my flesh. To make things worse, I heard a loud sneeze from the trees above my head. The crystals of snow the trees sneezed into the air, floated all around me. I was shaking with cold and fear. From the corner of my right eye, I saw Sita graciously moving downhill on her way to wherever it was that she was going before I appeared on the scene. *But what if she comes back?* I nearly cried out loud.

"I don't think she would have come back," said Jag Mohan, more with retrospective hope than conviction.

Well, I thought she might. I was too frightened to think straight. I wanted to run, but my limbs refused to move.

"Ooooh! fuffff! I feel as if I am right there with you. It is frightening, but don't let me stop you." He shivered all over.

All this time, the eerie silence was growing louder, and more and more frightening. I thought I was going to faint. I could hear the whispering and moaning of the ghosts. Due to the lack of darkness, they had had to remain hidden, and they sounded really angry. I could hear the heavy breathing of the trees, under the weight of snow and ice. With every sneeze, the tall trees shook off more tiny icicles and powdery snow, all over. Sita, in the meantime, had disappeared from my view *It's now or never*, I realised.

I remembered Jesus Christ. You know, I trust Jesus Christ more than the rest of them gods. So, I called out to him. And immediately, I felt him right there with me. My feet started to move in the direction of home. Every time I thought, I rather be dead than walk another step, I would hear Jesus saying to me, 'Go on Nihal, you can do it.'

"Did you really think that you were going to die?" His eyes were welling up with concern.

"I think once or twice I felt that I was. Or something like that. I can't be sure. I was too frightened and cold to think clearly."

"You really are brave, Nihal. I would have died, just seeing Sita standing in my way." He sounded like he really believed his words.

I was as scared of the leopards as any, but I wanted Jesus to be proud of me. The other thing that kept me going, was the thought, that if I didn't get home soon, Mama would come out looking for me, and she could not have left Anup all alone in the house. Then all three of us would have died together – there, in the middle of the road. I had to keep going for all our sakes. When I finally reached home, Mama came out of the kitchen. I saw her face light up with relief, as she greeted me. 'Thank God, you are safely back. I was starting to panic.'

I told Mama that it wasn't God, who saved me, from the leopard eating me up.

"*Masi jee* doesn't like you arguing with her about God."

I was not making an argument. God must have been watching everything that I was going through. The cold, the fear, bleeding from cracks in my lips, my hands, my feet, pissing down my leg . . . dreadful pain, and . . . and . . . all that. Anger started to well up inside of me, all over again. "I don't know which one I hate most; Mama or her God!"

Noticing the change in the pitch and tone of my voice, Jag Mohan suggested, "Shall we have another tumbler of tea?" Ten minutes later, we were sipping piping hot, jaggery-sweet tea.

For the benefit of those who may be unfamiliar with the traditional Indian way of making tea, this brief description may help. Water, tea leaves, sugar/jaggery/honey, and plenty of milk – whatever one can afford – are all boiled together in a pot for longer than may be necessary. This way, one gets every last drop of the essence of whatever is in the pot. I confess, it is not everyone's cup of tea, but it sure keeps you warm in winters, and cools you down in summer (that's what I was told by a wise old man). Don't say you had not been warned.

As we sat thoughtfully, blowing over the tea and slurping noisily, a bright bulb lit up inside my head. "I know why we are stuck in this miserable condition, in this miserable place, eating miserable green mush and dry rotis every day, and nothing ever changes ..."

Jag Mohan interrupted, "Why? How do you know . . . what?" Impatient to hear the revelation.

"Because we keep thanking God day and night. So, he thinks, 'Oh, they are happy. They don't need my help'."

Jag Mohan looked at me over the rim of his steaming hot tumbler, suspecting, I presume, that I had just landed from another planet.

A gradual build-up of a cloud of vultures overhead, distracted us from our theological conundrum. We assumed that the vultures were heading for Jag Mohan's hybrid calf, Kaltu. The poor thing had slipped and tumbled, all the way to the bottom of Manjebon forest, two days before.

Our conversation turned to where exactly the calf had slipped off of the edge of the mule track, and where it had landed, a couple of hundred yards below. Both spots were clearly visible across the stream from where we were sitting on my veranda. Two of Jag Mohan's workers had tried to reach the calf, but snow and ice over a steep hillside thwarted their attempts. We hoped that the calf was dead before it landed among the bushes and brambles down there. I offered my condolences to Jag Mohan for the loss of a handsome animal

Chapter 17

The Tropical Calcutta (Kolkata)

In the last week of June 1965, I arrived in Bishop's College, Kolkata (Calcutta) to commence my three-year degree course in theology (knowledge and science of God), the Bible, the Church History, some basic study of major religions, and anything one can learn about liturgy and rituals of the Episcopal Church.

On the third, or was it the fourth day in Kolkata, the temperature of my body shot up to the maximum, and then refused to climb down below 103 degrees. To make matters worse, the rise in temperature was accompanied by a seriously painful urinary infection. At the time, the stand-in college doctor was a female, and according to the rules of the college, a female person could not be permitted anywhere near the all-male student hostel. Not even under supervision. Hence, I was ferried back and forth by taxi, between the college and my physician.

Tests in the hospital pointed in the direction of my kidneys. Something to do with certain harmless bacteria that normally reside in human gut, but in my case, had chosen to transfer themselves into the kidneys. *And why did they do that?* I think my sudden move from cooler and drier climate, to the very tropical Kolkata, annoyed the bacteria.

After many failed attempts at sorting me out, I was transferred to a nursing home, where the female doctor could visit, and keep a close eye on her male patient.

A three-week stint in the nursing home, and still no

luck. I ended up in the Hospital for Tropical Diseases, in another part of the city. Two weeks in the hospital and I was 'out of danger'. The thermometer readings finally slid down to below 101 degrees. There was also noticeable relief from pain in the kidneys, but I was diagnosed unfit to survive in that climate for much longer.

The college sent a telegram to Rupchand, advising him to get me out of Kolkata. Lying in the hospital bed, I wondered if someone was trying to tell me something. Perhaps, I was not meant to be a priest? I even prayed seriously for God to tell me if he did not want me in his Church. I was now at the crossroads. *Which path must I choose?*

I don't know, if it was for their benefit or mine, but the moment my brother arrived at the hospital, the staff seemed to be in an unhealthy haste to get me out of there, and away from the State of Bengal, itself. Air travel was considered unsafe in my condition. Using his connections in Calcutta, Rupchand managed to secure two, two-tier sleeper seats on the Night Mail Train out of Kolkata. Lo and behold, the miracle: in the early hours of the following morning, my temperature was down to near normal, and the pain in the region of my kidneys had downgraded to 'mere discomfort'.

Two and a half days after leaving Kolkata, we arrived at the train station in Shimla. My sister-in-law had come to meet us at the platform. Standing six feet away, she asked Rupchand, "Where is Nihal?" I had lost all flesh and fat between my skin and skeleton, and my suntan had upgraded to 'proper black'.

However, the fresh air of the mountains, Mother's recipes, and a regime of regular exercises breathed life back into this body. In March of the following year, the padre and I received a letter from the bishop to say that he had written to the principal of the United Theological College in Bangalore, requesting him to register me on the Bachelor of Divinity Course in his college. Although the bishop confessed to having left it a bit too late, again, for the registration at the college. Nonetheless, Bangalore, due to its temperate climate right through the year, he thought, was worth a try. Within ten days (extremely fast for our postal system of the day) I received a letter from the college flattering me by saying, that due to time restraint, I had been accepted without the formality of 'Entrance Exams'.

Towards the end of May 1966, I arrived in Bangalore for another crack at being – what was later seen as 'a pain in the . . . wherever' of the bosses of the 'Church of God' – in India. That was never my intention. To me, my close involvement with the Church was an opportunity to do my bit towards transferring the Indian Church from its European and American plant pots, into the Indian soil. To have the Indian culture and Indian spirituality at the heart of it; and to use my privileged status to fight on behalf of the poor. And, of course, a chance for me to feed my ego. Although, the latter remained a well-guarded secret from me for many years down the road.

I loved Bangalore, and I loved the college. Bangalore was the 'Garden city of India'. A few months short of a year in Bangalore, Principal Dr Chandran became convinced, that due to my theological position and, "Your problems with what you call 'false piety', you will not make it past the front door of any church, as a parish priest." The only response I could think of at the time, was that perhaps it was time for me to accept the reality of my situation. "How can I preach a religion that I cannot fully believe in, myself? No point in wasting my time and other people's hard-earned money."

Dr Chandran said nothing. An interrogatory smile danced across his face. I asked him why he had never reprimanded me or asked me to explain my 99 per cent non-attendance at the 'compulsory' Morning Chapel Services. Why had he never asked me to explain my frequent absenteeism from the lectures. Two things that no student could expect to get away with? His reasons were highly flattering, but did not sound quite rational to me, at the time.

"Let me put it this way," he said in conclusion, "If you are right in your theological disagreements with the Church, then you have a responsibility help us see the error of our ways. But, in case you are wrong, then the college may be able to help you change your mind. Either way, the only reasonable solution to the problems of what you describe as 'Churchianity', is to stay the course." I could not argue with that.

At the college, we regularly came in contact with people from overseas. They were either on the teaching staff, or students in the college, or missionaries studying one or the other South Indian languages, relevant to their place of work. They came to the college for short refresher courses. The missionaries represented different countries and varied versions of Christianity and Churchianity. Some were pleasant and likeable, some were so, so. Then, there were others, who were there to share their knowledge and expertise in educational and medical institutions in India.

The last category of missionaries above, made no claims to having been sent there by God to represent his Kingdom to the ignorant heathens, *et cetera, et cetera.* A young English nurse, by the name of Mary Sylvia Bulford was on a short language refresher course at the college. She worked in a village in Andhra Pradesh on behalf of the

British Methodist Society and belonged to the last category of missionaries.

I was impressed by Mary's no-airs-and-graces outlook on life. Over a period of some months, we became good friends. I honestly don't know, even after all these years, what Mary saw in me that convinced her that we could have a happy life together. Even when I pointed out that I had no intention of moving away from India, she answered, "I know. I am not expecting you to." I had very little practice in dealing with female affection, and hoped that with time, I would learn. Sadly, I never did.

We agreed that it would be helpful for Mary to have a holiday at my place and meet the family that she may become a member of one day. Although, most members of my family were scattered all over India, and had their own families, yet we always kept in touch. Mary stayed with a family from our local church, only half a mile away from Dabi. Towards the end of our summer break, we became engaged. A week after that, Mary returned to her nursing job in the village hospital in Andhra Pradesh, and I went back to the college in Bangalore.

Some weeks before the final exams, Dr Chandran invited me into his office for a chat, about my future. Having known me now for nearly three years and having met the then bishop of my diocese at some meetings recently, he had drawn the conclusion that my bishop and I would not make a happy team. "It will be a very uncomfortable marriage," he emphasised. The best thing for me, he kindly suggested, would be, to register for the MTh (Master of Theology) degree at the college, starting the following academic year, in a few months' time. At the same time, in view of the impending retirement of Mrs Paulus, the college could use me as her temporary replacement to teach philosophy to the undergraduates.

I wish I could deny the sensation of the swelling up of my head as we sat in the principal's office, planning and plotting my future. I felt very special that someone of the intellectual calibre of Dr Chandran, and the respect he enjoyed among Church leaders the world over, should consider me far more capable than I had ever imagined myself to be. In those few minutes in his office, I sensed my ego filling the entire room.

While Dr Chandran continued scribbling in his notebook, I sat in silence, thinking. At the start of the second year of my course, Dr Chandran – for reasons known to him alone – had also added a full scholarship to my bursary. I do recall asking him the reason for his generosity, but I cannot recall his answer. Not quite sure why, but not becoming a priest was in some inexplicable way a betrayal of the trust the Dr Chandran and many others, including my friend Jesus, had placed in me. On top of that, it would have broken my mother's heart.

Dr Chandran raised his eyes from his notebook. "Have you received any communication from your bishop about when and where you will be ordained? Do you know which church you will be attached to, in your diocese?"

"No, I have never had any communication from the new bishop, and we haven't met yet. He has been in the diocese less than a year," I replied. The diocese, I tried to explain, was huge in land mass. Some of the churches and the institutions up in the hills of Jammu & Kashmir and Himachal could take more than a day to reach, even by car.

Dr Chandran was incredulous. All final-year students, he said, were fully briefed by their respective bishops, months before the final exams, each year, "And you don't even know, where and when you will be ordained?"

"What do you think? Should I go and see the bishop?"

I asked, confused, and embarrassed.

Reading my mind, Dr Chandran pointed out that the final exams were less than twelve weeks away, and my return journey between Bangalore and Amritsar would consume six days, at the least. He offered to phone the bishop that very morning. Early afternoon of the same day, I received a message from the principal's office to say that my bishop would be glad to see me in Amritsar, any time within the next ten days. I rushed to the Cantonment Railway Station. Fortunately for me, I grabbed the last remaining ticket for a two-tier, second-class sleeper on the train to Delhi, in two days' time.

After three and a half days inside three separate trains; Bangalore to Madras, change in Madras for Delhi, and from Delhi to my final destination. I arrived in Amritsar well in time for late breakfast. I *oooh'ed* and *aaah'ed* in a tricycle rickshaw to the office of the bishop's secretary. She escorted me into the bishop's presence who welcomed me kindly and observed that I looked exhausted. The secretary was advised to show me straight into the guest room, in an adjoining building. The bishop suggested that I let the secretary have the bill for my travel costs, plus 50 per cent to cover all eventualities of a long train journey, including the cost of my cigarettes. All my meals were to be served in the guest room, until the following afternoon. As I was on my way out of his office, the bishop asked if the rumours about me saying that I was not a Christian were true. "You want to tell me what that is all about?"

"Well, … Bishop … I say that in the context, where being a Christian means being 'Christ-like'. Sadly, for me, I am a long way off the mark." I thought I saw a smile dance across his handsome face.

He waved bye with, "I look forward to our meeting

tomorrow after lunch." My welcome by the bishop, was in complete contrast to my fears and suspicions.

At the end of a day and a half in the very comfortable guesthouse, delicious meals from the bishop's kitchen, brought in by his very pleasant and chatty Canadian secretary, I was summoned to the bishop's office. At the conclusion of our formal meeting, which lasted well over two hours, he asked me, "I've heard that you don't believe that the Bible is the Word of God. It that true?"

"I am sorry, Bishop, but I cannot find any reason to believe that God would promote and inspire literature that is, especially the Old Testament, clearly biased in favour of one small tribe in the world, and against the rest of God's Creation. In the Bible, God does not come over as a Just and Loving Father of his Creation." I offered my apologies for being a disappointment to him and expected him to send me packing home. To my surprise, he smiled, advised me to put more effort into studying the Bible.

He stood up from his chair, took my hand and said, "I shall look forward to ordaining you in my diocese. Have a safe journey."

Some weeks later, in the middle of May 1969, I had completed a three-year degree course in theology, and a few other subjects, to the satisfaction of all concerned.

Chapter 18

Made It, at Last!

A few days before the end of my three-year stint in United Theological College, Bangalore, I received a letter from my bishop, advising me that my Ordination Service to diaconate was to take place in Amritsar on the twenty-fifth day of May 1969. On my way from Bangalore to the Service in Amritsar, I was to spend two days in retreat, at the House of the Brotherhood of the Ascended Christ, in Old Delhi. I followed the advice to the letter and arrived in Amritsar with twenty-seven hours to spare.

At some point during my retreat in Delhi, I had been informed that the archdeacon would be presenting me before the bishop for my ordination. I hung around the place all day, waiting to be called to meet the archdeacon. My wristwatch said 8.00 p.m., and still, no sign of the archdeacon or any hint of our meeting. I took myself to his residence. All the lights inside the house were on. I knocked at the front door. The archdeacon's wife answered, and after a brief explanation from me, she pointed to the bedroom door. I could see through the fly-netting, the archdeacon was resting on his bed, still in his suit and dog collar. I knocked at the door and asked if he wouldn't mind me interrupting his rest. He invited me in. I politely enquired what was he going to say, when presenting me to the bishop the following morning, when he knew nothing about me? I suggested that perhaps we ought to postpone the Service until he had had time to interview me properly.

The very tired-looking archdeacon shuffled off the bed, came over, placed his hand on my shoulder, and pushed me gently in the direction of the dining room. Invited me to sit down, asked his wife to please brew some tea for us. He then proceeded to tell me that my anxieties were unfounded. He did not need to interview me. He had known and respected my father. He knew my entire family, he said. He could not think of any reason why I should not be ordained. I did not take the compliments seriously but reasoned in my head that I would do well not to get into an argument with the old man. I had presumed, mistakenly, that being the only candidate on that occasion, all the preparations, including miles of distance that many had travelled to be there, were all for my benefit. I apologised for the interruption, bade him goodnight, and left without waiting for my tea.

On the following afternoon, I was ordained deacon of the Episcopal Church of India, Burma, and Ceylon in Christ Church, Amritsar. The Service turned out to be an occasion, far greater in terms of crowds than I could have imagined in my wildest dreams. All because the bishop had managed to fit the Service into the final day of the Diocesan Synod. I did not feel at all embarrassed, when towards the end of the Service, the bishop introduced me to the large gathering, as the future bishop of the diocese. My ego was on the ascendency. At the time, I may even have believed that it had all to do with God having chosen me especially, to put the Devil where he himself had failed to put him, since whenever.

On the same evening, I boarded the train for Shimla. I had been posted there to Christ Church on the Ridge, as the trainee Branch Manager – normally referred to, as assistant curate – under the charge of the Rev George

Harish. Briefing me about my appointment that morning, the bishop pointed out, "I am sending you to Shimla, but I must warn you, Padre Harish will either make you with his sincerity, or break you with his 'befuddled-ness'. He is always busy, doing nothing."

I had known Padre Harish as a pleasant, even-tempered, and exceptionally hospitable parish priest. In the previous six years, on my way to and from Allahabad University, and lately, to and fro between Dabi and Bangalore, I had often stayed at the vicarage, as one of his many 'regular' guests.

Padre Harish was in his fifties. There was more than a hint of innocence in his disarming boyish smile. His inability to make his mind up about anything, and his infuriating interest in unnecessary legal details, were matters of common knowledge, and gave cause for mirth and suicidal thoughts among his colleagues and parish officers. During my fifteen months of apprenticeship under his wings, we had a few arguments over the fact that I had not a clue what I was expected to learn about managing a parish. In all that time, the Parochial Church Council (PCC) met only once, and I first heard about that meeting, the day after.

On the other side of the coin, there was much one could learn from him about material contentment, and generosity beyond belief. He was forever loaning small sums to people, some of whom he knew had no intention, or ability, to repay. And all this from his own pocket. During the summer months, his cook was instructed to prepare one extra meal at every mealtime in case an acquaintance or a stranger turns up unexpectedly. Tales about how he had helped certain members of his family into education, and beyond, were heart-warming and inspiring.

Shimla had been a significant and popular hill station during the colonial times. Since the Independence of India, it was now open to the 'Natives'. Crowds from the planes descended (rather, ascended) upon the little town, throughout the summer months. It was uncanny, how so many strangers managed to arrive at the vicarage at mealtimes, with stories of how the hotel they had booked into, had let them down at the last minute. And how so many of them knew someone in George's family related to someone in their family. He knew that a considerable majority were lying, and still, he invited them to join him at the table, and at times, even offered a bed for the night. In modern terminology, his vicarage house was a 'free-half-board-Inn'.

During my time with him, one of those 'sleep over' guests disappeared with the bedding and a few other items before we were out of our beds. George's response? After breakfast, he went out to the shops, and bought replacement bedding, 'just in case!'. Over the years, I have had reasons to thank him for what little I learned from his sense of contentment, and openness to God.

Due to her extremely dim view of long-distance train journeys, Mother could not be present at my first Ordination Service in Amritsar. Hence, for my ordination to priesthood, the bishop kindly conceded to my request, and held the Service in Christ Church, Shimla, only fifty miles away from Dabi. The Service took place on 31 May, (Whit Sunday) 1970. To Mama, the Service was the fulfilment of a long-cherished dream. To me, it was a small way of saying 'thank you' for her courage and determination in motivating us, her children, to pursue our dreams, regardless.

The congregation did us proud by laying on a generous feast for the entire crowd of over three hundred people, including a group of some 'non-Church' friends (from the Divisional HQ of the Indian Army, half-a-dozen lecturers from the University College, and a group of local artists). Attendance of 'non-Church' friends was the richest icing on the cake that I could ever have wished for. They were there, first, because George Harish had established good working relations with our non-Church community in the town, and secondly, because he supported me in encouraging their participation in the social, spiritual, and intellectual life of our church, and the community at large.

After completing her four years on duty in India, Mary returned to England shortly after my appointment to Shimla. Mary's elders and friends tried to persuade Mary to forget about her future in India. After a year-long furlough in her hometown of Todmorden, Mary returned to India on 5 September 1970. Ten days after that, we were married in Christ Church, Shimla. The church was packed to capacity – nearly three hundred people. Once again, a sizeable minority were from outside the Church community. Our Youth Fellowship, with age range between seventeen and forty, took over the reception arrangements. The YMCA in town provided free accommodation with breakfast, for the twenty guests from out of town.

Exactly eleven days after the wedding, Mary and I moved to my first Branch Manager's job in the Parish of Kangra. The priest's house (vicarage), a small bungalow, was hidden among the lush semi-tropical woodlands at the bottom of the 'Mission Hill' a couple of hundred yards away from the nearest house. To the front of the house were the green hills and small farms reaching half a mile down to the Kangra river. Halfway between the river and top of the green hills across, ran the narrow-gauge

Pathankot-Joginder Nagar railway line. To the left of the vicarage were the Kailash mountains with white glistening tops right round the year. In summer months, temperatures inside the corrugated tin-roofed vicarage easily touched forty degrees. The sight of the white Kailash mountains through the living room windows, served as psychological air-conditioning system.

One of my predecessors from the Punjab had planted a tree each of mango, small and large lemons, mulberry, and a dozen banana plants round the bungalow. There were plenty of wild fruits to add to our own collection. We never had to buy fruits, jam, chutney, marmalade, and pickle etc.

The parish roughly covered an area of 1,500 square kilometres, with three churches. In addition, there was a Church family here, and an individual there, spread out in far-flung villages. I remember visiting a schoolteacher's family in a village, on two occasions. It took three different buses, and over three hours to reach them. Luckily, most others were within a one-bus journey.

The three churches in the parish were: St James at the top of the hill, in Kangra; fourteen miles away, was St John's in the Wilderness, in Dharamshala; approximately ten miles away, was the Army Chapel in Yol Cantonment. Kangra Church had a small hospital and a High School for Girls, attached to it. Views from the church were stunningly beautiful. Immediately to the south was the wooded slope all the way down to the river, half a mile away. Across the river were flat plateau of farming land and villages, leading all the way to Dharamshala. Beyond and above Dharamshala were the Kailash mountains. South-west were open spaces, and wooded hills beyond.

St John's Church in McLeod Ganj, Dharamshala, was less than one half mile from the palace of the Dalai Lama, and literally in the wilderness. It had been a British garrison church at some point in the past and had now been out of use for some years. During this period, the monkeys and the lemurs in the vicinity had been using the roof of the church for their track and field sports. Large number of slates from the roof had been removed and broken. After many hours of cleaning and scrubbing the inside, and if my memory can be trusted, we discovered a marble/slate floor under the ankle-deep mud and sludge.

Three-month long determined efforts to get some hippies into the church, were rewarded with the presence of about twenty of them – a couple with their guitars – at our first Christmas in the parish. From then on, a small number of local Christians joined the mostly fluctuating hippy congregation at our bi-monthly whatever-time-the-padre-could-get-to-the-church late Morning Services. Hippies were mainly of American origin and congregated around the Dalai Lamas residence and the Buddhist temple nearby.

Worship with a hippy congregation was an experience, worlds apart from normal Sunday Services in a traditional 'Church' environment. Freedom of Spirit with a group of free-spirited – some highly educated – young men and women, keen to know, to learn, and to question, must be every priest's dream I presume (or should be). Since moving away from Dharamshala, I have longed for that experience. My attempts in Manchester, in the mid-seventies, to set up something similar in an empty church building near the university were keenly desired by many, but unfortunately 'laughed' out of touch by Church leaders. I tried again when I moved down south to Essex. Again, the younger generation from outside the Church seemed eager, but the thought of holding Services without a Prayer Book, was received like a heresy by the Church leaders.

In my second year in the Chelmsford Diocese, the outgoing Warden of the Chelmsford Diocesan Retreat Centre in Pleshey invited me to lead a 'Day of Silent Prayer'. Someone had mentioned the word 'yoga' with reference to the Day, purely by mistake. Some weeks leading up to the 'Day of Silent Prayer', the bishop's chaplain phoned a few times to tell me that many clergy persons in the diocese had expressed angry opposition to what they considered to be misuse of their Retreat Centre for teaching foreign/unchristian religion. The bishop wisely ignored the protest.

The retreat was well attended and well received by all present. All meditations were based entirely on refreshing our relationship with God and with the world we inhabit. Feedback to the Day mentioned nothing unchristian in any aspect of the Day. But even if it had been leading a retreat on yoga, it would still be about the unity/union of body, mind and soul. How is that *unchristian?* When we deny ourselves knowledge of anything that exists outside the Sunday School Curriculum, we deny ourselves the opportunities of growing up in Faith.

Meditation is about learning to chew and digest our own fresh fruit from God, and not eat the fruit that was masticated by someone else many centuries ago. Meditation is about *feeling* before *knowing*. Meditation is about *seeing* ourselves as we are – unique, precious, and one with all others, hence one with God. And much more …

Let's get back to Kangra. The small chapel in the triangle in Yol Camp, was within the boundaries of an Indian Army post. This too had been out of use for some time. Initiated, and diligently followed through by Colonel Richard Manhas' regiment, the chapel was renovated and decorated for our first Easter Service there, in 1971. The toned-down Anglican Service to suit members of various denominations was repeated bi-monthly and at 'festivals and special occasions', thereafter.

On the first Easter Sunday Service, the chapel was full. When it came to the Holy Communion, there were only seven takers. The rest, as it transpired, were our Hindu friends, and members of 'other' churches. As a result, at the end of the Service, I ended up with the chalice full of red wine. Col. Manhas, who had supplied the wine for the Day, called out, "Reverend, your cup is too full. I better help you out." He came up, and with practised ease, nearly emptied the chalice in two gulps. With his usual cheeky grin, he handed the chalice back to me, and whispered, "Don't look so worried, Nihal. I am not driving. My driver will take you back home after lunch."

The friendship of Jennifer, wife of General Prabhu, and that of Colonel Richard Manhas and his wife, Pam, proved to be invaluable in so many ways. During Mary's pregnancy, Pam ordered strawberry plants from some faraway place. "Mary, being English, is bound to love Strawberries," decreed Pam. The way Richard and Pam cared for Mary and Shobha during my frequent absences from home, was a great source of comfort to us.

In the parish, religious life of 99 per cent of its inhabitants centred around half a dozen or so Hindu temples. In the month of January each year, the small town of Kangra attracted over a hundred thousand pilgrims from all over India. Being a Christian priest in a town and district, such as this, turned out to be an honour and a privilege that Mary and I had not imagined possible when we first arrived. During our four years, we were blessed with a sizeable congregation of our Hindu neighbours at Christmas, Easter, and 26 January (Republic Day) Celebrations, each year.

There was just one little snag to my involvement with non-Church members of our community; only in the initial stages, mind you. A small number could not understand my direct involvement in the social and religious lives of our 'non-Christian' neighbours. Picture the scene:

On a breezy January afternoon, a small number of the Parochial Church Council members call upon their presbyter (vicar) at the vicarage. "Don't you think Padre sahib, the time and energy you are spending with the non-Christian people, could be better spent in the church?"

"I'm sorry. Am I neglecting my Church duties, you think?"

"No, no, no! No one is accusing you of doing that, Padre saab. We just think that as you have more than enough to do in the diocese and in your three churches here, as it is."

"Thank you for that. You are very kind. I am only trying to set up facilities for badminton, table tennis, and some safe board and card games, in order to distract our young neighbours away from other, less attractive hobbies. The Town Council has given me the keys to the library building for the purpose, because hardly anyone ever uses it. The Council has also offered to bear the cost of creating a badminton court, or two, on the land in front of the building. They will also provide all necessary equipment to kick-start the project."

"Have they? That is unbelievable!" Some sounded pleasantly surprised, while others, not so sure.

"Yes! They have, and we should be grateful. But you must let me know if I get side-tracked from my Church duties; especially if you notice me changing my religion." We tittered, laughed, and brought the meeting to a close with *chai-pani.*

As soon as we had the facilities in place, people could see how keen our young men were, in making use of them. Sadly, the culture of the place, at the time, did not expect similar facilities for the women. Certainly not outside of educational institutions. In addition, the support and affection their padre was enjoying, in return for his involvement in the community outside the Church, meant, that any opposition and suspicions on both sides soon ceased. Mary and I enjoyed over-the-top hospitality from our Church and non-Church communities alike.

Most civil servants, including the police in the district, and the army officers at the Yol Cantonment, 99.9 per cent of whom were not members of any church, frequently embarrassed me by going out of their way to get involved with Church, or other general community projects that I was trying to initiate. It was an opportunity for learning to be a Christian without any boundaries.

The minister of the church in town was now expected to be present at all the town celebrations, not only the civil, but the religious ones too. It was, for me, I believe a slow, and occasionally painful way of continuing to 'learn, rather than to teach. To live, rather than to preach' form of Christianity.

Chapter 19

In Danger of Becoming 'Normal'

In the 1970s, the sister of the Dalai Lama, was the principal of the Tibetan Children's School in Dharamshala, which I had visited on a few occasions. I recall a couple of brief conversations with her during the visits. In collusion with the wife of General Prabhu, she kindly arranged for me a private audience with His Holiness. I was not really keen on the idea. I have never been comfortable with titles of 'Holiness', 'Highness', 'Majesty' and such like. More out of respect for the kind ladies than excitement about meeting 'His Holiness', I accepted the offer.

On the appointed date and time, I arrived at the palace complex, in McLeod Ganj. A young monk escorted me to the front door of the palace. The Dalai Lama stepped outside to welcome me with a warm handshake. The spiritual leader of millions, fêted and honoured by leaders of many nations, and loved by millions from around the world, was treating me, an ordinary parish priest, as his equal. He led me into his austere living room and pointed me to the three-piece settee, and then came over and sat next to me.

The Dalai Lama had heard something about my contacts with the hippies and wanted to know how I connected with them. He made me feel as if my work with the hippies was somehow more significant than his own influence on their lives, and the lives of millions around the world. I can think of no 'religious' leader – someone even only halfway up the holy ladder – who would receive a low-ranking priest of another religion, into their plush offices, in the way that the Dalai Lama received that insignificant (compared to his own status) padre into his austere palace. A clear indication of our need to be open to the wisdom and spirituality of the 'non-baptised', the 'non-churched' and the 'not yet born-again' children of God.

Years later, in September of 1990, I had the opportunity to compare my visit to the Dalai Lama in Dharamshala with the leader of another religious tradition. Although, the Patriarch of Bulgaria and his archbishops welcomed me with open arms, as 'our guest from England', the emphasis on protocol and the attention and money bestowed upon the 'garbs of elegance' of the 'Servants of the young man of Nazareth', clearly deprived the occasion of any sense of spirituality. Most people in Bulgaria, at the time, were living what we would generally describe as 'well below the poverty line'. My interpreter for the day suggested that the money invested in the vestments of those four religious dignitaries could have fed half the population of her small town for a week.

Back to India. Teething problems of the Church of North India (a union of seven protestant denominations, inaugurated on 29 November 1970) in our diocese, were getting worse by the day. A small number of us were unable to prevent ourselves from getting sucked into the financial, legal, and administrative quagmire that had engulfed the newborn United Church in our diocese. The pressures of running around the sub-continent on 'pointless' important meetings, spurious court cases that were initiated by a small bunch of senior members of the erstwhile Anglican Church, were visibly affecting our small group of the 'don't know when to give up' fighters. As Honorary Secretary of the Executive Committee of the diocese, along with the parish responsibilities, my physical health and, who knows, mental health too, was on downward journey.

Mary, either did not know how to, or simply did not wish to complain. She was left alone in the vicarage, with our small daughter, for days, sometimes weeks, without the facility of communication with the outside world. We both seldom knew where, or for how long, I was going to be away. Pressure from many friends and from my own conscience, was piling up for me to change our family circumstances, sooner, rather than later.

Flicking through the pages of a book in my living room in Kangra one evening, I came across a brief essay on Francis Bacon. He was quoted having said, '. . . the institutional religions we have inherited are the result of precision guesswork, based upon unbelievable data, provided by those of questionable knowledge.' That got me thinking. Although, we are all meant to be, yet only a significantly small number of us ever acknowledge that we are 'unique and free in spirit'. At the same time, we also have an inherent need to belong within an organised community, which, in the case of a large majority of the human population, happens to be their religious community. Most of us don't choose to join it. We are either born into it, or are forced, coerced, tricked, and even bullied or threatened into joining it.

Over the years, religion becomes part of a person's social and cultural psyche. I was born to Christian parents, brought up within the Church. That is why I felt part of the Church. Many significant memories of my life's experiences, both positive and negative have their origin within that global institution. And, in spite of the

Church's shortcomings, its dubious and false claims to possessing final and complete knowledge of 'God', there are some individuals within the Church, who clearly express the true spirit of Christ. Therefore, the safe option for me was to carry on with what is familiar and easily accessible, however incomplete and unsatisfactory I may have thought it to be.

I have managed, very inadequately, I am sad to say, to continue to explore my natural freedom *to be* whatever it is that I am meant to be, within the context of the total existence, both inside and outside of the Church.

To claim complete and absolute knowledge of something we call All in All, the Alpha, and the Omega, the Omnipotent, and the Omniscient; Creator of all that was, is, and ever will be, is clearly self-contradictory. It doesn't make sense. We can't even know everything about the person of our own child, how can we then claim to know everything about the Person of God? I was finding the recital of the Creeds, more and more difficult. Nevertheless, as a priest, I still felt obliged to follow the rules. I could not come up with a satisfactory answer to the question, "How come you alone are right, and billions of people around the world, over many centuries, are all wrong?" The fear of *What if I am wrong?* kept me bound to the belief system of the Church.

I put my intellectual and spiritual needs to one side, and within reason, continued to be faithful to the teachings of the Church. I would console myself, that by not walking away, and continuing to seek answers to my own questions, I was helping my fellow sojourners too. I hoped to help, at least a few, who needed the Church socially; like I did but intellectually and spiritually wanted to be free to think and to learn. I wanted to find a way of joining the 'Living Mystery', while continuing to be a member of what is obviously a social, cultural and a political institution. God, as a 'Mystery' is likely to be the ultimate, all-encompassing reality. Church, and all other religious institutions are purely human, and by their very nature, divisive.

My private audience with His Holiness, the Dalai Lama, had helped to confirm my doubts about the institutionalised religions. Working among the hippies in Dharamshala, their frequent comings and goings in and out of our home in Kangra, and my close contacts with our Hindu, Muslim, Sikh, and Buddhist neighbours throughout my life, continued to stir up my struggle between 'Christianity' and 'Churchianity' between 'Faith' and 'Religion', and between the 'Real' and the 'Made up'. Surely it would be far better, I thought, to *live* the Gospel than to *preach* the Gospel. I mean Jesus himself only preached one sermon in three years of his ministry. Nevertheless, preaching being the easier option, I continued to preach.

One afternoon, I arrived home from another one of those 'important' meetings in some far away part of India and knocked on the front door. Eighteen-month-old Shobha came running into the living room. She saw me through the fly-net door and called out to Mary in the back room, "Mummy, that uncle is here!" Words cannot describe the hurt I felt. Now, call to attend to the needs of my wife and child took on urgency. I had to find a way to spend more time with them, while continuing to sort out my relationship with the Church and the 'Great Mystery'.

Not long after the untimely death of the first CNI Bishop of the Diocese of Amritsar, in 1972, we were at the Diocesan Synod meetings in Jallandhar in the Punjab. At the end of a long day, I was summoned to attend a gathering in the school hall, a hundred yards away. Inside the hall I saw through my bleary eyes, a crowd of human forms floating in the thick clouds of smoke. Out of the clouds emerged Padre Mall, a senior presbyter of the former American Presbyterian Church. He pulled a chair over for me near the main entrance, and reminded the gathering that, on the following morning, the Diocesan Council would be required to submit nominations to the General Synod, for the election of the next bishop of our diocese.

Looking me in the eyes (barely open), he informed me in an over-the-top official tone, "We have decided to put your name forward to the Electoral College of the General Synod. Our diocese needs a young and energetic bishop; someone who will be able to deal with our corrupt and incompetent Church leaders." To be fair to the Church leaders, most were neither corrupt, nor incompetent. Many had simply not been trained adequately for the job, some were too nice or wise and cowardly to waste their time fighting the baddies.

My immediate reaction was: *Ummm ... I will be the youngest bishop in the history of the Indian Church.* I humbly congratulated myself. But a voice in the depths of my soul screamed out, *no, no, no, don't be foolish. You are not ready yet to be a bishop – good or bad. Period.*

Hoping that the inner voice would calm down by the opening meeting of the following day, I advised the group inside the hall, to say no more. "I am not sure," I said. "I need time to think." I said I was tired and, without another word, made my way back to my bed in the student hostel, where most delegates to the Council were housed.

Inside a mosquito net, a thin mattress on a rough string bed, and in the same clothes that I had been wearing over the previous two days and nights, I slept like a log (whatever that means). I had no change of clothes with me simply because, two days previously, I had been called out to resolve a dispute between a village evangelist and the local police, in a village hundred miles away. The dispute took more than a day to resolve. It was too late for me to go home to change and be back in Jallandhar in time for the start of the Diocesan Council.

The morning after my invitation to Bishopric, I slithered and tumbled out of bed. After a cold shower, I felt like a new man, even in the sweaty, old gear. There was no excitement and no doubts. I knew I had to say "no" to my dream of being the youngest bishop in India. Those who thought that I was ready, had to be mad. At the start of the morning's proceedings, I told them so. Suddenly, I was no more the popular young man of the night before. I had, in the words of a senior colleague, 'let everyone down'.

At the conclusion of that Diocesan Synod in Jallandhar, Isa Das, a wise and much respected elder of the Anglican communion in that part of the world, drove me away to his home in Chandigarh. We spent the best part of the night taking stock of the Church scene. He had no doubt in his mind that those, who wanted me to become their bishop, were looking for someone to stand up for them and give them a voice. That is exactly what I had been doing, he believed. "Our problems are crying out for a bishop with patience, wisdom, and experience." He was honest enough to express his delight over my decision to say no to the purple shirt.

When I arrived home, the following afternoon, the first thing I did, to prove to myself that I was starting to grow up, and happy to be 'normal', was to book a week's holiday for Mary, Shobha and myself at the Diocesan Guest House in Dalhousie. A week in the hills of Dalhousie, over a hundred kilometres away from Kangra, away from the chaos of 'Churchianity', seemed the ideal place for a short break. Thanks to my bank manager, we could just about afford a self-catering break in a small, one-bedroom bungalow, a hundred yards away from the main guesthouse.

Shobha Rani, Mary Sylvia (back)
Nihal and Pavan (front) 1983

Aimee Paul (Daughter
of Pavan and Shalini)
2004 -

Chapter 20

The Final Nail

On our arrival in Dalhousie, we ran into an Englishman by the name of Peter Hiscock, Mary his wife, and their two sons. They were staying in the guesthouse. Peter had recently been appointed chaplain to St Stephen's College, Old Delhi. During late afternoons, we would make our way through the wooded paths onto a nearby road. The children loved the freedom of being able to play unrestricted in the middle of a road. Their occasional friendly encounters with small groups of mountain ponies, and mules ferrying goods between Dalhousie and the surrounding villages, added to their fun. We were able to indulge uninterrupted in long conversations about the different cultures, socio-political attitudes, systems of education and the Church scenes, both in India and in England.

During one of those leisurely conversations, I happened to mention that the institutionalised religions had failed entirely in seeing the unity of all existence. And in my view what unites all existence, or is at the heart of it, is what we call God. Founders of each religion have created a deity that fits into their own need to control the masses. 'Our God does not like the *others* to disagree with us.' Solution is simple, 'Accept my religion, or go to hell.'

Peter appeared intrigued and wondered what else was there about religions that I don't like?

I mentioned my thoughts, about how the wandering

preacher of Palestine had disappeared, and in his place appeared the 'King of Kings', 'Lord of Lords', very God of very God, begotten, not made ...'. Most daring 'takeover' of all times, I thought. It seems like we don't care who Jesus and what his life's mission was all about. If he doesn't agree to fit in with Emperor Constantine's ambitions, then we will design our own God – Three in One, and One in Three.

Peter fixed his eyes into mine, and said softly, "I am listening, but not sure where you going with this."

"Have you ever read any of Kahlil Gibran's writings?" I asked Peter.

"I have heard of him. But no, I have not read any of his books, yet. Go on, what were you going to say?" Peter said keenly.

"He has written some beautiful parables and stories. I don't remember the exact words, but this should be close enough to one of my favourites."

Long time ago, there was a rich, young farmer. He was well read, with interest in architecture and religions. One day, when his servants came back from their shopping trip in the nearby town, one of them gave the young man a page torn out of a book. He explained that on the high street in town, a stranger was preaching some new religion. Some local young thugs beat him up and tore his book into shreds. "I picked this page as the wind blew it past me. I thought you might be interested."

The young man read the page. It said something about 'all the believers were one in heart and mind ... they shared everything they had. Some even sold their homes and land and placed all the money at the feet of the disciples ... which was then distributed to anyone who had need of it.'

The young man enquired if anyone knew who and where these people were? Did anyone know what they were called? No one had heard of them. He became obsessed with 'these people'. He had to know and find them. Eventually, he left his home and set out in search of the people who happily shared everything they had.

Many miles away from home, he ran into a man in a small town who knew nothing more than that 'these people' he said were known as 'Christians'.

The young man moved on. After many more weeks, by which time he had run out of money, his clothes and shoes were in tatters, he came on to the top of a small hill. A mile or so ahead his eyes fell on a large building headed by a tall tower. He recalled having seen drawings of similar structures in one of his books on architectures.

He forgot his hunger and thirst and headed keenly towards the building. By the time he reached his target, the sun had warmed up and the heat was stifling. He felt weak and hungry, moved into the shade under the spacious porch, and sat down on the steps that led up to the entrance of the building.

Just as he was starting to dose off, he heard voices from inside the building. He thought he heard someone say the word, 'Christians'.

He forgot all about his hunger and thirst. He jumped up, ran up the steps, pushed the huge door open, and started up the aisle in the direction of the man decked in out-of-this-world shiny robes. The man was delivering an address from an extensively ornate platform, near the front.

The man on the platform stopped mid-sentence. He stared in disgust at the dishevelled, dirty young man. The young man felt the eyes of everyone inside that vast and beautiful place fixed on him. He heard the whispers,

"Who is he?" "Look at him, filthy, dirty," said another voice. One man came out of the pews and stopped him physically. The dirty, filthy young man shouted joyously, "Are you Christians? I've been searching for you for months."

Couple of big men grabbed hold of him. "Look at yourself. How could you come into the house of God, looking like this?" They pushed him out and shut the door behind. He fell face first onto the hard floor of the porch. As he lay there, crying, he sensed the presence of someone next to him. Slowly, he lifted his head, looked up. Through his tearful eyes he saw the figure of a man standing next to him. The man's hand stretched out to help. He took the hand and stood up. The man asked him, "Why are you crying?"

The young man briefly described the whole incident through sniffles. "Calm down, young man. At least, you got inside there. I have been standing here since this place was built, and they won't even let me in through those doors."

The young man wiped his tears. Looking closely at this kind stranger, he retorted, "You hardly look a day older than me, how could you be standing here for centuries. Who are you, by the way?"

The kind stranger smiled, "I am the one they worship in there."

"Wow! That is some story. Makes one stop and think," said Peter thoughtfully.

"All I am saying is, why can't we accept Jesus for who he was, and still is: an example of human love and service? Get over the MDBTYD (My Daddy is Bigger Than Your Daddy) syndrome, and let him into the Church?"

At the end of our brief holiday, we promised to keep in

touch. Whenever I happened to be in Delhi, I would visit the very hospitable Hiscock family, on the premises of St Stephen's College, in Old Delhi. A few minutes in Peter's study, and the conversation would invariably turn in the direction of finding a way of serving God and the people, without getting sucked into Church politics. It helped to talk to someone who had no personal stake in the Church in India. Peter suggested that I ought to pursue my interests in the academic field, for a couple of years, at least. We agreed that Mary and Shobha needed more of my attention than I had given them hitherto. My doctor in Kangra was always pestering me about my health. "Padre sahib, please slow down. With your lifestyle, you won't last long," she admonished me, with annoying regularity.

In the meantime, Dr Chandran had continued to find ways to get me back to what I guess he thought was the only thing I might be able to do with some degree of competence. In early 1971, he wrote to advise me to accept the offer that he said I will be receiving from Hamburg University in Germany. Week or two later, I received a letter from the University of Hamburg, advising me of the date etc. for the registration at the university. I was expected to be accompanied by my wife and child. All travel costs, our expenses in Germany and the cost of childcare and education, our travel to India and back once a year would all be paid for by the university, and a few other extremely generous offers.

I wrote back to thank them for their generosity, and promised to let them know, "as soon as I am able to free myself from my job in India, for three years."

In the sinking sands of our Church business, and my dreams of indigenising the Church, and fighting for the rights of the 'excluded' members of our society, I soon forgot the university. Two years down the line, I received another letter from Hamburg University informing me that since they had not heard from me, all this time, they were withdrawing their offer. "Should you change your mind, we will be happy to reconsider." I had decided to slow down, even thought about changing parts of my routine, but had no plans of abandoning my dream. Certainly not within the foreseeable future.

My lack of enthusiasm for a desk in the corner of a university library across the oceans, was being nurtured unintentionally by Mary's ability to calmly take things as they were.

After the General Synod of 1973, I made my way out of Old Delhi by the late evening train and arrived in Pathankot about 2.00 a.m. The first bus to Kangra wasn't due for another three hours. I chose to wait within the noisy security of the train station, as opposed to the insecurity of the quieter bus station, only a short walk away. I stretched out on a long wooden bench on the platform, and soon dropped off to sleep.

Twenty minutes before the first morning bus to Kangra, I was jolted out of dreamland by the blaring of a horn from a passing vehicle. With the luggage safely attached to my back, I ran all the way to the bust station, got in the queue, purchased the ticket, hopped onto the bus, found a seat, and sat down to prepare an outline of . . . some sort of sermons for the three Sunday Morning Services in the parish. The three-hour bus journey from Pathankot was largely spent in deep sleep, except for a couple of tumbles off the seat, at sharp bends in the road. I arrived home with an egg-shaped lump just above the right eye. Time enough for a quick wash and change of clothes before the first Service of the day.

After conducting the 8.30 a.m. Service at 8.50-ish, in

Kangra, I literally ran down to the vicarage for a rushed breakfast. My trainee priest colleague (assistant curate) Prem, insisted on carrying my suitcase as we ran to the bus station. I hopped on to a moving bus. Prem threw the suitcase in after me, which landed safely at my feet. A kind stranger offered me his seat for the fourteen-mile journey to the church in Dharamshala. A three-quarter-hour long Service in the Church of St John in the Wilderness ended around lunchtime. That was followed by a brief intellectual/spiritual conversation with my hippy congregation outside the vestry, while waiting for my bus to Yol Camp. The lemurs and the monkeys watched us curiously from the top of the church roof and the trees, above our heads.

I caught the 2.00 p.m. bus for the 'whatever-time-I-get-there' Service. I was greeted by a packed church in Yol Camp at few minutes to 3.00 p.m. Just before sunset General Prabhu's driver dropped me outside the vicarage in Kangra. For the first time in years, I spent one hundred and sixty-eight hours with my wife and daughter, interrupted by only a couple of church meetings.

Peter Hiscock had mentioned on a couple of occasions that he was thinking of writing to some of his contacts in England, to make initial enquiries about possibilities of finding some academic interests to lure me away for a couple of years. I said I was not interested.

Then, out of the blue in February 1974, the postman delivered a letter into the church caretaker's hand, with a UK stamp on it. The letter was from someone by the name of the Rt. Revd. Dr Anthony Hanson, head of the Faculty of Theology, University of Manchester, England, UK. I do not have the letter on me, but the following is pretty close to the contents. He had been approached by some people within his academic circles, on my behalf. Based upon the information supplied by them, he would be happy to register me at the University of Manchester for a master's degree in my chosen subject. 'And if that leads to a PhD, all the better', he hoped.

Um ... In theory, it all sounded interesting. I could still keep in touch with the Church. There was just one small snag in the scheme; *Could God manage the Church of North India without my help?* Eventually, my sense of guilt about spending too much time away from Mary and Shobha, won the day. Added to that, the pressure from those, who cared for me and my family, further helped to reach the decision. I wrote to the bishop, accepting his kind offer.

The months leading up to the date of our departure from India, were hectic. We put into motion the process of handing over the charge of Kangra Parish to, whoever. I applied through the central office of the CNI for couple of study grants, both in India and in England.

First, the permission for a two-year study leave arrived post haste. The Moderator of the Church of North India appeared more excited about my departure from India, than I was about my intended research project in Manchester. The process of resigning from the parish was emotionally more painful for both the parish and for me than I had imagined. Handover of the files and folders relating to three court cases, and the many councils and committees was less traumatic than we had expected. All in all, the speed of the handover left me in a spin.

Saying goodbyes to family and friends, sorting out travel arrangements and obtaining passport, visas and so on, was not that simple. Determined not to take the short cut, it took me months and three visits to the passport office (five to six hours each way), in Chandigarh, to obtain my passport.

Chapter 21

Ollie for England

Before we left India, Mary's eldest sister, Joyce, who lived in Todmorden at the time, kindly invited us to stay with her, until we could find a place near the university in Manchester. For our travel, the Soviet Airline was the cheapest in the market. Hence, on 19 September 1974 we boarded an Aeroflot plane in Delhi, on an uncertain quest to the west.

On the way, our flight was scheduled for an overnight stop in Kabul. We landed there late afternoon and were duly led out of the plane into the terminal building. Two official-looking young men collected everyone's passport and disappeared into the terminal building.

After nearly an hour and no sign of the two young men and our passports, our fears and suspicions started to upgrade to anxiety. There was talk of us having become victims of a hijack. "I think we have been had," suggested a Sri Lankan gentleman, calmly.

Finding a public lavatory by chance, gave cause for some low-key celebration, and long-awaited relief to all in need.

Finally, after too many long minutes, since we had been dumped in the middle of nowhere, on a remote, but beautiful piece of earth, a bus and the two officers materialised from somewhere with our passports. The officers handed our documents back and pointed us in the direction of the bus. Soon, the bus started running out of space inside. A five or six-year-old girl, with a strong

Texan accent, about to be pushed into the bus, along with her mother, pointed to the dust clouds approaching the airport at break-neck speed from the direction of the east. She shouted at the top of her voice, "Looook mommy, looook, theyere! (point taken; won't try the accent again) There's another bus coming for us."

The two drivers managed to pull out a few passengers – still breathing – from the first bus and loaded them onto the second one. Some women complained under their breath, that the two pious looking drivers with their 'holier than thou' looks and prayer beads to boot, had touched them inappropriately, while supposedly helping them in and out of the two buses. We heard someone to our left pleading with his wife in whispers, "Those two men won't take kindly to a woman complaining against them." We exchanged carefully camouflaged glances, in support of the husband.

The buses dropped us at the appointed hotel in the late afternoon/early evening hours. We were assigned to our rooms. The rooms were cleaner and more comfortable than the airport experience had led us to expect. Unpacked, freshened up, we locked the doors behind, and without much ado, Mary, Shobha and I walked out onto the street. Before long, we found ourselves on the busy high street. Everyone around the place was pleasant and polite. We made our way to what looked, from the distance, a good place to eat. Five minutes up the high street, and we were standing at the entrance of a busy restaurant. We found a table, sat down, and let the waiter choose our order.

While we were eagerly waiting for our meals to be served, we noticed large metal plates, piled high with fleshy, fresh grapes on top of all the tables around us. The appetising aroma of the food reinforced our need to eat and eat now. We attacked the grapes on our table, as gracefully as a hungry cat attacks a fat mouse, I guess. We were halfway through the grapes, when one of the three gentlemen, who had just finished their meal at the table to our left asked, in the most elaborate and sophisticated Afghan etiquette if we wouldn't mind him retrieving his plate of grapes from our table. We looked round, and to our horror realised that there were no plates full of grapes on the two unoccupied tables, not far from us. We handed the plate over with more apologies than the number of grapes left on 'their' plate.

Next day, we left Kabul late morning, and landed safely at Heathrow just after dark. Kultar Duggal, husband of my niece, Usha, met us at the airport. We made our way to their house in North Acton by the London's famous red bus, in London's famous pouring rain. Usha and Kultar's hospitality brought us in contact with some Indian people in London, which contributed towards making us feel at home, away from home. We stayed with the Duggals, I think, for two days. Then, it was time to make our way up north, via Manchester, to the beautiful little town of Todmorden, astride the border between Yorkshire and Lancashire.

My first encounter with the colour-based prejudice in and around London, at the time, happened outside the Duggals' house. On the morning of our departure to Todmorden, a young cockney taxi driver arrived to take us to the train station. Mary and Shobha were standing by the luggage, on the pavement. He greeted them cheerfully and started to place the suitcases in the boot of his taxi. He was about to put the third and last suitcase in, when he noticed me putting some smaller items onto the back seat, and Usha standing at her front door. The look in his eyes and the sudden contortion of his face, was shocking. He stopped, took the suitcases out of the boot, dropped them on the footpath, got on his taxi phone to his base. He made up some stories about us having too much luggage for his car (completely untrue, of course). We found another taxi with an intelligent, pleasant and chatty cockney driver to take us to the train station. By early afternoon, we were in Todmorden.

In Todmorden, there was a young vicar, by the name of Ollie. On the second day of our arrival in his parish, he came over to Joyce's place to welcome Mary back to her hometown, and to inform her that he had arranged an interview for her with the local paper. On his second visit, two days later, he expressed great disappointment that no Church leaders in Manchester had approached me to see if I could be of some help to them. My explanation, that no Church leaders, apart from Bishop Hanson at the university, were aware of my presence in England, cut no ice with him.

In little over a week, he had made appointments for me with the archdeacon in Wakefield, and a couple of vicars near Manchester, whom he knew to be looking for some help. The meetings and interviews he arranged for me, were helpful in introducing me to some basic ways of the workings of the Church of England, as well as the opportunities of meeting some good people, I would not have met otherwise.

Two weeks after our arrival in Todmorden, Mary secured a nursing job in Manchester for two nights a week. I registered at the university in Manchester. Weekday mornings, Shobha and I took the train from Tod to Manchester, then a bus to the university campus, where I dropped her at the play school. Late afternoons, on my way out of the university, I collected Shobha, and we made our way back to Tod station. From there, we took leisurely walks up the hill, along the side streets, to our temporary home on the corner of Oak Avenue. We were always back well before Mary left for work. On the two mornings after Mary's night shift, we met her halfway up the hill on our way to the train station. Time enough for greetings, and a quick, *see you later.*

Towards the end of November, I visited Ollie to tell him that his efforts had secured me a house, in return for Sunday Services and some other occasional duties, in the parish of Urmston, 2.8 miles from the Manchester United Football Club. He wanted to know if the house was furnished. "No, it isn't, but I have already visited a couple of second-hand shops in Manchester ..." I hadn't finished the sentence, and Ollie was already on the phone to his parishioners. In less than a week, he had gathered enough pots, pans, small items of furniture and a few other essentials to last us a lifetime. We gratefully selected whatever we thought was necessary to help us get through our two years in England. Next, he borrowed a small truck and a driver from the local garden centre. Ollie, the driver, and I arrived with the van in Urmston on a typical Manchester evening in December – the little angels hadn't stopped peeing all day. Herbie, the vicar, welcomed us at the front door of the curate's house on Urmston Road and handed me the keys to the house.

After a week of hard scrubbing, cleaning, and tidying up, between the university and Todmorden, we moved into our new temporary home. Soon after moving there, Mary secured a part-time job in a local cottage hospital. To combat the cold and damp in the house, I purchased myself a large hand saw from a second-hand market in Manchester. With the vicar's permission, I raided the lower field of the two-tier back garden of his large Victorian vicarage. There were a few dead apple trees still standing on their feet, and plenty of dead wood about the place.

With the Manchester winter already with a foot in the door, the small family from the warm climes of India, inside the assistant curate's draughty house, needed all the firewood I could lay my hands on. We could have had a coal fire, I suppose, but a coal fire can't hold a candle to the flames of a proper fire! It took a country boy to feed an open fire and create the flames that perform the dance of Creation.

On my first Sunday in the Parish Church of Urmston, some members of the congregation stared at their new, part-time assistant curate with curiosity. Half-a-dozen Christians made a point of ignoring him, politely. A significant majority welcomed Mary, Shobha and me with open arms, doing everything to make us feel welcome. As time went by, they made our presence in the parish, happy and comfortable.

I fell in love with the northern accent, right from the start. To me, the way people spoke English around Manchester and Todmorden, sounded phonetically more accurate than the other accents I had heard thus far. Apart from the phonetic correctness, there was also the musical quality in the intonation, which made the speaker come across as warm and friendly.

The Church in England being within a different cultural setting, had a different way of doing 'Churchianity', from what I had been familiar with thus far. In comparison, Church in England was like a rich middle-aged man, and the Church in India, like a recently orphaned religious infant.

I felt no sense of discomfort in keeping to myself, what was important to me personally, and sharing with the parishioners, in the best way I could, what seemed to meet their needs.

The way the protocols were maintained within the English society, was impressive, at the first glance. Each person within the institutions, seemed to know their place. People at the lower end did not see it any of their business to question the decisions and practices of the people above them. A priest, in the same way, was trusted, seldom questioned, and believed to have been placed there by God and the Queen. Correct about the Queen, in a roundabout way, but not sure about blaming God.

Looking in from the outside, I was intrigued to observe, that the more the Church appeared to have lost its grip on people's lives, the more Christian the society became. Now, in the present set up, there appear to be more Christians outside of the Church than there are on the inside of it.

The one thing that hit me for six, was the division of human race into many races, based upon people's colour of skin, their ethnicity, their nationality, even their religion at times. I still can't get my head around the fact that the civilised, well-informed, so called, European societies are incapable of accepting a basic fact of life, that there is only *one human race*. They always speak of people of darker skin pigments as belonging to some 'other' race. And in recent years even a Pakistani could be referred to as of a different race in comparison to an Indian. Any dispute or unpleasantness between two individuals or groups of different skin pigments, nationality, religion, or culture is referred to as 'racist' or 'racism'. This is something completely weird way of looking at 'the human race'. I had never imagined, that despite a very negative view of people from outside of the British Isles, the English would divide the human race into different races – seeing their own as being superior to all others. When someone refers to me as being of a different race, I usually tend to respond by saying, "Do you not belong to the human race? I am sorry to hear that!"

The 'vicars' and 'rectors' in the modern Church of England, as I had suspected, have reasonable levels of formal education, both secular and theological. Although, there appear to be too many notable features of its past still clinging on, yet the Church is clearly making some serious attempts at pushing and heaving its way out of the Middle Ages. It is heartening to observe that a small number of Church leaders are genuinely attempting to keep up with the aims and objectives of the young man of Nazareth.

The sense of urgency in trying to keep up with the rest of the world, I found encouraging. The 'class' system – not too dissimilar to the 'caste' system in India – is definitely slithering out from within the Church structures. The colour of one's skin does still seem to affect the decisions of the God of the Churches in England, and in Europe.

Most ministers of the modern Church of England are still living in houses, larger than a vast majority of their neighbours can afford. In my first few years in England, I was hard-pressed to find a rectory or vicarage, that wasn't the largest house in the area, and always in the 'better part' of the parish. I wondered if this significant detail was, and still is, responsible to some degree, for isolating the rectors and vicars from the unwell souls of their patients. My guess is, that in the Middle Ages they must have reasoned, that a man of God, in the business of curing ailing souls, could not be expected to live in a house that looked just like the houses of his patients. A

Church headed by an emperor, could not be served by ordinary men, living in ordinary houses, among their poverty-stricken, spiritually ailing 'ordinary' brothers and sisters. Or something along those lines.

A State transport bus near Kulu. Lucky for me, I was travelling in a Jeep

On way to the mountains of Himachal to fight back the onslaught of arthritis into my body -1993

On way to the mountains of Himachal... 2

Southeast views from the vicarage in Kangra

On way to the mountains of Himachal -3

View from the front of my Dabi house

Northern bank of River Satluj in Rampore

Chapter 22

There's No One Here

At the university in Manchester, I was advised by Bishop Henson to attend lectures on 'History of the Development of Christian Doctrine' and 'Psychology of Religion'.

History of Christian Doctrine was generally stimulating. The intrigues, the rivalries, the head-banging, and the many stories about, '*I don't care about the truth, or about making a mockery of God, or that young chap from Nazareth. I am here to win the argument*' were attention grabbing. During the occasional boring bits, I found myself sneaking into the Council of Nicaea, listening to the great bishops and theologians, vying with each other for the attention and favour of the Emperor, Constantine. Planning and plotting the construction of a 'Jesus Christ' that the emperor and the world at large would be impressed by. On other occasions, I followed Jesus and his disciples, in the back streets of Manchester where they were looking to help the homeless and the hungry. I can't explain why I never bought them a decent takeaway Kibaab or Pizza to share among the twelve of them?

I also had some pleasant chats with Peter. He couldn't understand how, or from where, I got the idea that he was a gate keeper, and also responsible for accommodation of all the guests in heaven. I paid a few visits back home to the meetings of the General Synod of the Church of North India. Once or twice, I found myself at a loose end in some board meetings in heaven, where the Satan wouldn't take his eyes off me.

All those unplanned visits were a relief from looking for the needle of non-qualified monism of Shankar's Advaita Vedanta in the jungles of the Development of Christian Doctrine of Incarnation. Maurice Wiles' book on *Re-thinking Theology*, was right up my street, and so was the approach of some German theologians to the whole question of Christian theology, based upon biblical narratives.

Lectures on the Philosophy of Religion could have been equally interesting and stimulating. My classmates, apart from a layman from Nottingham, were all directly involved in fulltime service of various churches – a Roman Catholic nun, three Methodists, was there also a Baptist, I think...! The electrician and I got on well from day one. To the rest, anyone who had spent too long under the hot sun getting a tan had, in the process, melted away their brain cells. They often gave me the impression that they did not expect sun-tanned foreigners to know anything about Christianity, or about anything of importance for that matter.

It is possible that part of the reason, why they came across to me as patronising, and why I felt uncomfortable in close proximity to them, was down to me being self-conscious of my ethnicity. I probably gave them the impression that I was as thick as they believed me to be. The one thing I knew for sure, was that I did not enjoy their company, which suited them fine. The layman from Nottingham, on the other hand, visited us at home and stayed overnight a couple of times. We were both happy to learn from each other.

Three months into my much-heralded return to proper academic life, Dr Hanson invited me into his study to discuss a structure for my proposed thesis. To my horror, he confessed to never having had anything to do with Indian philosophy, and that he had not heard the name of ... "How do you say it?" I spelt the name, one letter at a time, "S H A N K A R A C H A R Y A" as he wrote it down on his notepad. I felt embarrassed for the man and realised that I should have been more diligent in checking out what was what, before diving into the Faculty of Theology. His repeated apologies for knowing neither the name nor the philosophy in question, only helped to hammer the nail of 'where do we go from here?' into my throbbing head. We talked our way through some names who could possibly throw some light on the path that I intended to tread. I tried my luck with the professor of the New Testament studies. He confessed to having some interest in the philosophy of Swami Vivekananda, but the "other name you mentioned" he had only heard in passing.

With Dr Henson's blessings, I wrote to Dr Ninian Smart at the university of Lancaster. He was the only name I knew of in England, at the time, who was a recognised authority on the subject of Indian philosophy. A week later, the postman pushed an envelope through our letterbox in Urmston, with the Lancaster postmark on it. I touched the envelope over and over, with every fingertip, and put it on the windowsill.

After lunch, I tore open the scroll hoping to receive the revelation that I had waited for, with much longing and expectation. The letter revealed that Dr Smart believed that the proposed subject of research was 'exciting' and that he would love to be part of it. He had penned my name in his waiting list of prospective candidates, the letter informed me. But and this was a big 'but', I would have to wait two full years, before he could join me on my journey towards the fulfilment of my dream.

I put the letter back in its original spot and went out to visit a senior lady of our congregation. Irrespective of the time of day, she loved sharing a small glass of sherry with her assistant curate. Normally, I never have and never will like the stuff, but her genuine interest in India and its culture, which she appeared to have read something about, the very engaging anecdotes she told me about her late husband's job as the owner of a book shop in the centre of Manchester, and the gossip about her 'friends' and acquaintances, made her sherry quite palatable.

By the time I returned home, Mary was back from wherever. I gave her the letter. She read the last paragraph, twice. "So, he has a long waiting list of research candidates," she said with a deep sigh. "You're not having much luck with this thing, are you!"

Trying to inject a note of optimism, I pointed out that the letter did say that he will be free in two years' time. The reality was very different. I had accepted the rejection and knew that at the end of that academic year, we would return to the job that I had always believed to be my destiny. The same evening, I wrote to my bishop in Amritsar. His prompt reply was, "We need you back here, Nihal, but please be patient. I shall let you know as soon as I can sort the mess we are in presently." Not long after, the bishop resigned from the diocese on health grounds, I was told.

Miss Bhan, a retired Director of Education of the state of Himachal, and a well-known kingmaker within the Church circles at the time, wrote to say that the Diocesan Council had decided to send in my name to the General Synod, to fill the vacant chair of St Peter, in the diocese. The council secretary also wrote to convey the wishes of the Diocesan Synod.

My response had to be a, 'No'. I knew in my heart that

I never – no matter how hard I, or others tried – could be the bishop they would want me to be. At the time, all my friends in the Church in India were convinced that the only way back for me was to return as a confirmed candidate for the bishopric of one of the dioceses. My friend and mentor, Padre Jagnath wrote, "Nihal, please accept the reality of our situation, and accept the nomination. Stop being so bloody modest. Why can't you become a bishop?"

Not wanting to be a bishop had nothing to do with me being modest or a 'bishop hater'. My shoulders were too weak to bear the burden of a bishop's fancy cape. My neck was not strong enough to carry the weight of the crown of St Peter on my head. In other words, I was neither holy nor pious, nor did I have time for anyone else claiming to be one. I certainly could not fully accept the Church's interpretation of what the image of God was all about. I wrote to Miss Bhan and Padre Jagnath, "I want to return to continue to do what I was doing before coming to England. Please get me into any parish; anywhere in India, will do."

At some point during my correspondence with the Church leaders in India, I happened to run into the then Bishop of Manchester at the cathedral. During casual conversation after the Service, we had a brief chat about my dilemma. The bishop didn't think it was wise for me to return to India, until I had something concrete to return to. He agreed with my colleagues, who had been pestering me about the fact that in view of the 1960s and 70s migration into England of people of Asian and South Asian cultures and religions, I could make a useful contribution to the community in general. They argued, "you could be sharing your insights with both sides of the cultural divide." I could see their point but the sense of guilt for not doing what rightly, or wrongly, I had believed to be the purpose of my life, was dragging me into the dark mists of depression. Arthritis started to sneak into every joint in my body, and depression into every cell in my brain.

My twelve-month visa was running out. I applied for six months extension to give us time to tidy up our affairs here, before getting back to where I wanted to be. The Home Office wrote back to advise that I did not require extension and could stay indefinitely. That weakened my argument for return home to India.

Some weeks after our brief conversation at the cathedral, the bishop invited me to his office. We had a friendly and helpful chat. He thought that since the people and the vicar of Urmston were happy with me, I might as well stay there a while longer. If the doors in India were still shut on me, we would meet in a year's time. I got back from the bishop's office, immersed myself in the job in hand, with some added responsibilities at the Branch Church of the Parish of St Clements, Urmston. I got down to doing what I liked best – be out there with the people I was paid to be with, and respond to their needs, the best I could. Church can, and sometimes does, help people to care for each other, and in the process, lead a soul here and there towards real God; that's a bonus. I was happy to be part of it, with or without the 'bonus' – after all, I was only a parish priest.

Spirituality, as opposed to religion, is a universal and a constant experience that is shared by all humans, irrespective of which god they believe in. Spiritual experience is there, even when we may not be aware of it. It is like breathing; we breathe even when we may not be conscious of the experience. The experience is there, nonetheless. Faith is based upon spirituality, and it seeks, senses, searches, feels, and infers, but does not claim to 'know'. Religion offers certainty, based solely upon conjectures.

As usual, I kept getting carried away when doing my own mixture of religion and spirituality. After one Evening Service, my vicar gently pointed out that the congregation may not be ready for some of my sermons. More than once, I had been observed thumping the pulpit, by the few who happened to be awake during the sermons. I realised that the authoritative thumping is clearly an expression of the importance that a preacher attaches to his/her words, irrespective of which end the words may be coming out of.

On 21 June, the hottest night of 1976 Mary and I were blessed with a boy. We named him Pavan, meaning, breeze/wind, depending on the context.

In April of 1977, I found myself back in the bishop's office, wondering what he had in mind for me. The bishop understood why returning to India was important to me. He suggested that if and when I could find my way back into the Church in India, "I will make sure that we release you from here, as quickly as practically possible." In the meantime, he advised me to take a look at a few parishes, gently warning that I may have to be content with a 'black parish'. To which I responded – with my natural lack of diplomacy and ignorance of the English sense of humour – "I have not seen any black or white parishes in Manchester, bishop. They are all either green or grey, depending on the weather." He gave me a *I don't know what you are talking about* sideways look. The bishop scribbled a phone number on a piece of paper, handed it to me, and suggested that I call the number, "first thing tomorrow morning."

The following morning, I dialled the number. The

person at the other end of the line, was the archdeacon of the diocese. He gave me addresses of two parishes, and telephone numbers for the respective churchwardens. He cautioned me gently, that I should not take it personally, if the reaction from the 'white parish' happens to be negative. He thought that I ought to visit the 'black parish' first, notwithstanding the fact that I was more foreign to my 'black' British brethren than to the white English ones.

With the curiosity of a cat, I decided to sniff my way to the 'white parish' first. In the little over two years in the white parish of Urmston, there had been no reports of damage caused to any parishioner by my natural tan. *If I can hack it in Urmston*, I concluded, *then I can hack it anywhere*. I phoned the churchwarden of the 'white' Parish of Farnworth, on the outskirts of Bolton. We had a quick friendly chat and arranged to meet the Parochial Church Council in two weeks' time.

While waiting for the meeting in Farnworth, I arranged a meeting with the two churchwardens of the 'black parish', in the south side of the City of Manchester. The churchwardens – a gentleman and a lady – both of Afro-Caribbean origin were welcoming and friendly. The lady warden did the talking, while the male warden and I struggled to get a word in edgeways. The church was far higher on the inside, than it was on the outside – a very 'Anglo-Catholic' church.

I couldn't imagine myself counting the number of candles, checking the exact position of each candle in relation to the Cross, kissing a few books and God knows what else, before even saying the first prayer of the day. At the end of two good hours with the lovely non-stop talk-talk lady and her male colleague, I knew that I would definitely be the *'wrongest' (pardon my grammar)* person for their church.

After the 'black parish' experience, the meeting with the Parochial Church Council of St Peter's, Farnworth, was very different. We started gingerly. Everyone present being over-the-top polite and ultra-sensitive to my tan and culture. I was understandably a little nervous, and uncertain of the ground upon which I stood. After the initial formalities and a chit-chat about the weather – all conversations in England naturally include some reference to the weather – we moved on to some personal and family information about me. The conversation went something like this:

"Did the archdeacon tell you that we don't have any black people in our parish?" They enquired.

"Well, not in so many words, but he did mention something about this being a *'white parish'*. Does that really matter? It doesn't matter to me. I myself am the average of the two. There is no one in Urmston either with a 'permanent' tan, except me, of course. I have had no problems there relating to my work."

"I didn't get that. What do you mean by you being 'the average of the two'? Are you half-caste?" asked a lady in that musical Mancunion tone.

"No. I am full caste Indian, and my wife is full caste English. Our two children are 'double-cast' Anglo-Indians. They are blessed with the best of both." My remarks had the intended effect. I sensed embarrassment and unease all round. I let it sink in.

"As you can see, I am neither black, nor am I white. I am average of the two – brown." I pointed to my face. It took longer to hit the mark than I had expected, but when it finally did, it helped to break the ice. A few embarrassed titters and mumblings soon gathered momentum into a hearty laugh. That was followed by a timely break for some tea and cake – the two great stimuli for social cohesion.

Over the *chai-pani* break, enriched by a chunky cheesecake – my favourite temptation – the former Sunday School Superintendent (SSS) asked plainly, "How do you think you will fit into a parish where there are none of your people? I mean, apart from one Pakistani family, there are no coloured people in the entire town."

"Well ... all people are my people, and all people are coloured. Some of us more coloured than others. If I were to come to this parish, I will still be happy in my brown skin. As you can see." They all looked a bit uncomfortable and suspicious about what I may say next. "The way I see it, to me, you will be Bill, Terry, David, Tracey, Jane, and I hope you will see me as Nihal, vicar of the parish."

"I like that," announced the former SSS cheerfully. The entire Parochial Church Council seemed to agree with him. They nodded and smiled their agreement at me. I felt the warmth of acceptance.

"If we agree for me to come here, I will look forward to having the support of everyone in the Church to help me do my job the best I can. I can't be bothered to spend my time on checking people's pigments before saying 'hello' to them." I guessed that from that moment, I had moved up their list of prospective Managers of the Parish of St Peter, Farnworth.

Date and time were arranged for Mary and me to view the vicarage. One of the two churchwardens met us at the gate and before we even went inside, he assured us, on behalf of the PCC, that we could have the place decorated to our satisfaction, "and don't concern yourselves with the cost."

The large red brick Victorian vicarage comprised of three storeys and a fair-sized basement, with large lawns on three sides, and a cul-de-sac on the fourth. The attic was pretty close to heaven, and would have made an ideal 'study', but at a cost to my arthritic knees. Now, this was in a parish, where the parishioners lived in row upon row of two-up, two-down terraced houses and small bungalows. Most of them with no front gardens.

Some weeks after the meeting, the bishop *installed* (whatever that means) me as the vicar of St Peter, Farnworth. I was expected to lead the parish towards joining the already established Team Ministry in the small town.

The day we moved into the vicarage in Farnworth, the treasurer visited us on her way home from work. She had come, she said, to tell me not to concern myself with the heating costs of the vicarage.

"The diocesan office will not accept that arrangement." I pointed out.

"Nothing to do with them," she said, curtly. "You are not used to our Manchester climate, vicar. With two small children in this big house, you must keep the heating on day and night. You can't afford that on your stipend." The PCC had arranged for the supply of oil to the vicarage house for my predecessor, and it was going to be the same for me, she said. After that, the tank was topped up regularly, usually without my knowledge. I felt obliged to inform the archdeacon about the PCC's decision in respect of the heating costs of the vicarage.

The archdeacon tried to intervene. They made it clear to him that I had not asked them to pay for the oil. "The parish paid its dues to the diocese regularly and in full," they reminded the archdeacon. "What we do with the rest of our money," they emphasised, "should not concern the diocese." And that was that. I apologised to the archdeacon for causing him unnecessary problems.

"What problems?" he said. "I am not aware of any problems here." With a cheeky grin, he patted me on my arm and said, "Don't let it worry you, Nihal. You are in a good place with them."

There were two things about English culture that puzzled me. The first was the pride that some took in their Colonial past (mostly 'working class' older men and some top-hat-men with expensive pocket watches). I could not see any reason for the poorer ones bragging about the 'British Empire'. They didn't seem to have got even the thinnest slice of the 'colonial cake'. All they appeared to have been used for, was to promote the interests of a small number of their masters. They were posted to some of the remotest parts of the world, away from their families; despised by both the empire builders and the natives. Most of them were still living in poverty, tiny little houses with outside toilets.

There were some who would apologise for the Raj. All I could say to them was, "If you were there, then yes, I accept your apology, and hope that you will help others to not be proud of forcibly taking away other peoples' homes and land. But if you weren't there, then let's move on. In the final analysis, we all have something to answer for. Let's hope we have all learned something positive from our past."

The second thing about the English culture that saddened me, was the inability of a sizeable minority, to see any good in anyone or anything that wasn't 'English'. Fortunately, the great majority of the English are nothing like the image most of us had from their colonial past. They are generally as hospitable and civilised as any that I have met in my limited travels.

In the diocese of Manchester, Bishop Patrick was followed by the Rt. Revd. Stanley Booth-Cliburn. He was one of the most humble and down-to-earth men I have ever met in a purple shirt. He was concerned, "Should something happen to you, Nihal, how will Mary and the children cope in India?" And, "I can think of so many ways in which you can contribute to the enrichment of the Church in England, in these fast-changing times."

I happily put my energies and interests into my job in the parish, which, I was enjoying immensely. A parish of just two thousand souls, afforded me endless opportunities to get to know the people at work, at home, in pubs and clubs, and in the tiny shops down the high street. I was seldom made aware of my 'outsider' status. At the same time, I continued chasing the bishops in India, and they continued to ignore my letters.

In Farnworth, I did not have many weddings, christenings, and funerals to conduct but I was flattered to learn that most people appreciated my 'different' way of doing things, especially the Funeral Services. The shopkeepers along the high street appreciated my visits for a social chat, and 'no preaching', they told me. One day I dropped in at the carpet shop. The young owner looked me up and down and returned my greetings with a formal "good afternoon." I sat down on a roll of carpet. I wanted to know if he had been affected in any way by the terrible accident two days previously in front of his shop. After five minutes, the question marks in his eyes were replaced with a kind smile. He said, "My dad started this shop over fifty years ago. I used to be in and out of here every day of the week when I was growing up. I never saw a vicar come into the shop for a chat." He insisted that I have a cuppa with him. It had never occurred to me, until that afternoon, how sitting on a roll of carpet can make up for so many shortcomings in a vicar's life. If they have rolls of carpets in the Judgement Hall, I am going to sit on one of them. Peter might overlook a few of my sins.

Seven years in Farnworth were among the best years of my job in the Church. Most things, including carpets for the vicarage, equipment, and the decorators for the church were donated by a cleaning company in town. Dozens of large tins of paint, for both the vicarage and the church, were donated and delivered to the door by the DuLux depot in Bolton. A top of the range litho printer and ink etc. for printing our own Parish Magazine, were donated by a business in Manchester. Peter Orchard, a Litho engineer, who lived in the parish but never attended the church, maintained the machine in return for a cup of coffee, and some friendly chit-chat per visit.

My 'Indian barbecues' became a hit in the town. I organised the first one as my contribution to the fund-raising efforts in the parish. I had catered for fifty to sixty people maximum. The final count was over one hundred and twenty curious natives. The late comers ended up with just a sausage, or half a burger and one roll shared between two. But they all paid for the full meal and made me feel like I was the best chef in the north of England. For all our parish Bar-B-Qs, the lamb chops, sausages, burgers, and bread rolls were donated by local suppliers except for the bags of charcoal, of course.

One thing I was not aware of, in my first year in Farnworth, was that a clergyman does not *drop in* at even the fund-raising event of another parish, in England. A parish is a clergyman's kingdom, given to him by God. I soon discovered that my actions were seen as a serious disregard for 'clergy etiquette'. I had upset three of my neighbouring colleagues by turning up at their fund raising 'dos'. To me, visiting a neighbouring parish was a sign of friendship and support for one's neighbour. I soon learned to mind my own business.

Chapter 23

The School Tie Religion
In the spring of 1983, I decided to take my chances back in the Church in India with Bishop Booth's reluctant blessings. He had no doubt that I was being selfish in expecting Mary to adjust to life in India, with me seldom being home. We started preparing to return there. If it didn't work out, the bishop said, he would be happy for me to return to his diocese, whenever. My idea was, that if the Church there didn't want me without the purple shirt, then Mary and I would find ourselves jobs outside of the religious confines. I could perhaps fulfil my boyhood dreams of setting up our own business. I had written to four bishops in India, requesting them to find me a job anywhere within the Church institutions.

One pleasant morning in May of 1983, while still waiting for some response from the bishops in India, I was busily looking for the cheapest possible flights, and all the other details associated with a long and final one-way journey. The phone rang. The call was from the Team Rector of Basildon Team Parish, in Essex. He had read something about me somewhere, from which he and his Area Bishop had concluded that I would be the right person for what he had in mind. I said I was on my way back to India. Wished him well with his search and politely put the phone down. Two days later he phoned again and received the same answer as before. Day or two after his last call, the phone rang, I picked up the receiver, it was not the Rector of Basildon, but the call was about the vacancy in Basildon. I answered and said politely, "Thank you for your call, but sorry, I have already said, I am not interested." and put the receiver back.

The rector's voice came over the phone the following morning. He told me that the caller the day before was the Bishop of Bradwell. "Sorry. My sincerest apologies to both you and the bishop. Tell you what, by way of an apology to the bishop for putting the phone down on him, I will come to the interview."

On a sunny morning in June of 1983, I got off the train at Basildon at 10.30 a.m. As I made my way towards St Martin's church, via the town centre, I was gobsmacked by the sight of the number of young families in the place. *Plenty of work for any lucky vicar*, I pondered.

Conversation at the interview revealed that the patch of Basildon that I would be expected to serve, had more than half-a-dozen Infants and Juniors and two Comprehensive schools within its boundaries. Church did not have a great deal to do with the schools at the time, I was informed. Another significant temptation, I thought.

Last but not the least tempting, was the sight at the top of the Church Hill in Laindon. I found myself inspecting a seven-hundred-year-old, beautiful church building that was to be my main responsibility within the Team Parish of Basildon. I had never had the privilege of working in a church more than a hundred years old. Like most people, I love ancient buildings. The social, cultural, political, even some spiritual, history that is imbued into them, is always fascinating. One didn't need a magnifying glass to see how desperately the church building needed major works of repairs and restoration. To have the privilege of restoring that building to its former glory, I imagined, would be like performing a major age-reversing surgery on an old person's body.

Back at St Martin's office, I said to the rector, "Tell you what, I will gladly accept the job, but only on one condition."

He took his time to ask, "And what is that one condition?" With a knowing smile spread across his face.

"I mean no disrespect, but I like to be left alone to get on with my job. If the bishop will allow me free hand, without undue interference, I would like to say, 'yes'."

I think his response was, "You won't believe it," he said. "I had expected you to say something like that. There will be no problem. It's your church, mate. You run it any way you like. Think of it as your 'Freehold Parish'." His sense of humour and the gift of the gab added to the other, more significant attractions.

Thus, on September 6, 1983, I became the Branch Manager of the Laindon and Dunton section of the Team Parish of Basildon, and responsible for St Nicholas Church on the hill. In the first couple of years, the major family issue, was that our children did not like the fish 'n' chips in Essex. "They don't taste the same *down here* as they did *oop north*," they would remind us every time we treated ourselves to fish and chips.

For me, the structural and pastoral problems of the beautiful thirteenth century church, and an enormous parish, were an exciting challenge. Trying to integrate into the Team Parish of Basildon, as an equal member, was, to put it mildly, intriguing and frustrating, in equal measures. It proved to be trickier than initially imagined. But there were plenty of other matters in the parish, to keep one gainfully employed. Demands for the Hatch, Match and Dispatch ministry at St Nicholas Church, due to its position on the hill, were physically, and at times emotionally tiring, but otherwise interesting – even exciting, at times.

Imagine, the church car park is occupied by 'Travellers'. There are no toilets inside of the church building. The nearest one, is in a dilapidated church hall down the hill, a hundred plus yards away. What could be more embarrassing for the poor vicar in that situation, than regularly pointing the female attendees at christenings, weddings and funerals to some bushes at the back of the church. Therefore, connecting the church building to the water supply became priority number one for me. Unfortunately, but understandably, it gave rise to the first signs of opposition to the vicar's interference in 'our traditions and ways of life', as an old-timer repeated with boring regularity.

When I once asked, "Do people in Basildon still go behind the bushes to answer their call of nature?"

His eyes full of utter disbelief and contempt, he jabbed his finger in the direction of the building, "Well, this church has been on this hill for over seven hundred years, and we have managed without the toilets."

Umm! I smiled back at him, "So, do you think the electricity has been in this church since it was built over seven centuries ago?" He stared back at me annoyed and embarrassed. Might be a good idea, I thought, to get this settled, once and for all. "Do you have indoor toilets at home? Surely, you didn't have them seven hundred years ago. Or did you?" He unsuccessfully pretended not to have heard me and turned his attention to his lawn mower. I sprinkled a bit more salt over his frustration. "We enjoy all the mod-cons in our homes, why can't God enjoy a few in his house." Gladly, he did not respond.

On the morning of December 29, 1984, my eight-year-old son, Pavan, (with full support and blessing of his headmaster) and I were on our way to Heathrow airport when I received the news that my mother, back home, had had a massive heart attack the evening before. Just before she died, Rupchand's wife (my sister-in-law) heard Mother shouting in agony, "I have had enough of this, now. Stop this pain or get me out of here!" About four hours before our flight took off from Heathrow, God conceded to her demand, and she breathed her last. Neither of them thought anything of the 4,470-mile journey that I and my son were undertaking to see her alive. Inside the plane, my son chatted up the air hostesses, and told them and a few passengers, that he was going to visit his grandma. I couldn't think of how to tell him that she wouldn't be there.

In Delhi, my nephew used his connections to get us out of the plane and the airport as quickly as possible, and straight into a waiting taxi. As we were getting into the taxi, Pavan asked me if I was some sort of dignitary or celebrity in India. "What made you think that son?" I looked at him quizzically.

"Because we have just walked out of the plane, straight into the taxi with no body asking us any questions or checking our luggage inside the airport!"

I can't recall what stories I made up to explain the most unexpected run through the airport. Once we reached my nephew's house, I gave Pavan the sad news. He took it like a man. But for the next two days he hardly spoke. In the taxi from Kalka to Shimla, the driver asked why we were going to Thanedhar in that horrible weather. I answered subconsciously, "My mother lives there."

Pavan said firmly, "Grandma lived there, doesn't live there, now."

Our seats had been booked on the late evening train from Delhi to Shimla. By the time we reached Shimla, fifty miles short of Dabi, there had been further snow fall, causing snow drifts and imminent snowstorms. Both the driver of the military jeep with all the safety equipment, and the pilot of the government helicopter (both arranged by Surinder bhai, a family friend) advised me not to undertake the journey with an eight-year-old on board. I couldn't leave my son in Shimla with my friends; they were complete strangers to him. I phoned my family to let them know that we could not be present at the Funeral Service. The Funeral Service went ahead while my son and I sat in an empty restaurant only fifty miles away. For Pavan, it was his first encounter, not only with losing a loved one, but also being deprived, in the least expected way, from seeing his grandma.

I have often wondered, why is it that I have so far missed the Funeral Services of all my nearest and dearest family and friends – my father, mother, three sisters, two brothers, one niece, a nephew, and my five best and closest friends in the whole world. Physical distance was not always the reason for my absence from the occasion. Some of the absences were due to misinformation or some completely unbelievable spanner in the works. On the following evening, Pavan and I said goodbye to friends in Shimla and returned to New Delhi.

In New Delhi, I had arranged to meet the then Moderator of the CNI, and a few other Church dignitaries. They kindly arranged my stay for four weeks in the guest house attached to their headquarters on Pandit Panth Marg. Pavan stayed with my sister Prabha in another part of the city, where my sister's husband, who worked from home, thoroughly enjoyed spoiling him. I visited them a couple of times a week.

Meeting with the then Moderator of the CNI, was a wonderful spiritual experience. He was humble as humble can be. One morning after breakfast, he invited me into his bedroom-cum-temporary office. Spending a couple of hours with him, was a revelation. He was the first and the last bishop I ever heard say (these may not be his exact words, but close enough), "It is not the repetition of theological statements and formulae that will legitimise and save the Church, as the Body of Christ. Rather, it is Christ and his way of life that the Church needs to concentrate upon. Sadly, neither the Moderator nor his two bishops I met at the CNI House, could understand why I could not return to India as a bishop"

At the end of my meetings with the Church leaders in Delhi, Pavan and I went up to Dabi. The Remembrance Service for my mother, five weeks after the funeral, was a wonderful tribute to her ability to connect with all parts of the community. Church was full of regular congregation and many Hindu and Sikh friends from all parts of Kotgarh and Thanedhar. A week later Pavan and I returned to Basildon.

The fundraising campaign for the Church, in a 'new town' situation did demand a great deal of compromising of one's understanding of what a 'vicar' is about, and the expectations that the general public place in their 'parish priest'. I kept going into overdrive and getting carried away with what I believed had to be done. Significant majority of the small congregation of mostly over sixties, couldn't understand why a building, that had been in existence for over seven centuries, needed someone from a faraway land to save it from crumbling.

Thirty-five to forty per cent of the church walls on the inside were green with algae. Plaster from the ceiling had started to drop off in small pieces. The insurance company was thinking of withdrawing the cover due to their concern for some safety issues. I think the congregation of St Nicholas did believe me, but religion, is after all about traditions and customs, more than about right and wrong.

On the other hand, appeal for funds and for other practical matters received an enthusiastic response from some individuals inside the relevant department of the Essex County Council, from local businesses, and from the non-Church community in town. A ten-year-old boy from a local school, accompanied by his grandparents, turned up at the vicarage one afternoon. "Vicar, he wants to give you a donation towards your church funds," grandma said proudly. The young lad handed me a cheque for £1.25, made payable to me. And he wasn't the only child to contribute his pocket money towards the appeal.

Unfortunately, the political party in control of Basildon Council at the time, was not inclined to support my plans for the church on the hill. Some years further down the road, political landscape of the borough changed, and that helped me to establish a working relationship with the Council. We even succeeded in getting the church's picture on the District Council logo.

In our Diocese of Chelmsford, one had to get accustomed to different way of doing 'Church' from what one had been accustomed to say, in the Diocese of Manchester. The one big difference being that in Chelmsford, the apparent significance attached to school tie, and 'it is not what you know, but who you know' way of doing Church, appeared more obvious than it had been in Manchester. I kept hoping for someone to prove me wrong, but after little under three years, I concluded that the best way for a man with a tan, who suffered from a 'foot-in-the-mouth' disease, was to relinquish any ambitions of being part of the larger Church. I decided to concentrate on the job in hand. I did not isolate myself entirely from the larger Church, of course. I Just did not make a conscious effort to be involved in things outside my primary responsibilities within the parish.

About five years down the line, there were only the Team Rector and I left in the Team Parish of Basildon. The other had moved on. Under the direction of Bishop John Wane, the Team Rector and I agreed that the Team Parish simply had not worked in Basildon Town. The bishop advised that the Team be dissolved.

Thus, on 1 November 1990, the new Freehold Parish of 'Laindon-with-Dunton' was created by order of Her Majesty, Queen Elizabeth II. In the judgement of both the bishop and the Team Rector of Basildon, it was only right that the Team Vicar of Laindon in residence at the time, be honoured with the title of the first Freehold incumbent of the new Parish of Laindon-with-Dunton.

There were moments in Laindon when I did privately wish for God and the law of the land to allow me to strangle a professional fool, occasionally. Such as, a group of three or four men who regularly incited school children to vandalise and trash the church building. On more than one occasion, when they found me on my own on the hill, they walked past the church chanting, 'Kill the vicar!' Each time I smiled back and then carried on as if they weren't there. Late one night, one of them phoned to say that if I did not remove the gypsy family from the church car park post haste, he was going to 'set fire to your fucking church, and sort you out.' The fact that the presence of the gypsy family was causing me and the Church more problems than to anyone else, had not registered on his 'whatever?'.

I once managed to catch one of my tormentors standing in front of the church encouraging four boys on the roof to remove the roof tiles and throw them onto the graves below. On that occasion, they had removed and smashed over two hundred tiles. I asked him what pleasure could he possibly derive from damaging a beautiful ancient icon that was like a crown on the head of a new town? His response was 'We don't want a 'darky' to be our vicar.' The fact that he had never darkened the church doors in his life, and that I was only trying to save a precious piece of heritage of our town, his town, was beyond him. Lucky for both of us, he was horizontally a few times wider than me.

The 'Travellers' were another potent source of constant headache at the Church of St Nicholas on the Hill. During my twenty-two years at St Nicholas, they cut through large locks and bars on to the small church car park on the hill, on numerous occasions. They would camp there for as long as it suited them. Polite requests to vacate the car park, at least during the many wedding and funeral services were met with serious bullying. Law enforcement agencies were either not interested, or unable to help. Even the children of those travellers were trained bullies. A good number of their trucks and cars had no road tax discs on display. Every time I brought the matter to the notice of the DVLA, they showed no interest whatsoever. The travellers were convinced that they could, and they would get away with most anything. What made the experience even more painful, was the fact that the small 'brainless' group of (four men to the best of my knowledge) men in Laindon blamed me for encouraging the Travellers on to the church car park. Can anyone really be that dim? Or were they using the travellers as an excuse to get at me? More likely, the combination of both.

I am afraid that this will lose me all my non-existent friends within the do-gooding community, but my painful experiences with the travellers, over a period of twenty-two years in Laindon, have led me to lose sympathy for their cause.

13th century St Nicholas Church, Laindon, Essex

Chapter 24

The Trouble with Women!

Vicars/ministers like Ollie are a rare breed in any church, anywhere in the world. Of course, times have changed and many parish priests and bishops within the Church around the world are beginning to free themselves from the slavery to 'It says so in the book'. There is still a sizeable majority of men and, even women, who are convinced that God created women only for making tea and cakes; holding stalls at the church bazaars; flower arranging in the church; cleaning; and attending the Services. Women must respect the low ceiling that God himself had placed above their heads. 'So says the Word of God' they say. In the Church of England for example, since the late 1970s and 1980s more and more men are conceding that women have as much right to be priests as the men. The opposition to women's ordination to priesthood by so many women though, is shocking. Most of these very women blatantly disobey and disregard their 'Holy Scriptures' in so many areas of their personal and Church lives. Some of the male priests who see women as biologically, intellectually and spiritually inferior to themselves in the Church, are pretty henpecked at home.

Just over a year into the job in Basildon, I accepted the invitation from a deanery colleague to join him at a meeting on the subject of 'Women's Ordination'. The meeting took place in a very affluent-looking neighbourhood on the northern outskirts of London.

Everyone present was clear that it was their God-given responsibility to stop this nonsense before things got out of hand and 'damaged the Church beyond repair'.

Including the main speaker and the host lady, there were *seven* men and *eleven* women, altogether. The meeting was led by a bishop. I was given to understand that he was among the leading lights of the movement. The bishop, among many others was trying to save the Church from being irreparably damaged by the 'Ordination of Women'.

Some of my completely innocent enquiries appeared to light firecrackers under the bishop and his followers. He objected quite angrily to 'outsiders' interfering in matters sacred to the Church of England. One of the things that I was wanting to know, was, did the opponents of the ordination of women have some divine logic to support their case?

The bishop replied, "What better divine argument do we need to support our case than to point to the fact that, if Jesus had wanted women to be ordained as priests, he would certainly have chosen some to be his disciples?"

I said, "If we go down that road, then we could find ourselves in serious trouble ..." The host interrupted quite haughtily. "What are you talking about?"

"Well! The Church, all over the world will have to dismiss all the priests, bishops, even the Pope himself, and anyone else who leads and governs the Church. Following this argument, only the direct descendants of the original eleven disciples of Christ can be priests in Church. There will be no one to lead the Services tomorrow morning." I said with a cheeky smile.

"That is utter nonsense, if I may say so. What are you trying to say?" the host lady asked brashly.

"I am only trying to respond to your arguments against women's ordination. Bishop said earlier something about the interference in the affairs of the Church of England by outsiders. I mean no offence but, in England, even Jesus Christ is an outsider. He was a Palestinian Jew."

The lady, sitting immediately to the right of the bishop's chair, aimed her fire at me.

"That is utter nonsense, if you ask me." There was a quick nodding of heads and shifting and shuffling of behinds all around. I sensed unease and some embarrassment among the less gullible-looking campaigners.

"To follow Jesus' example; he did not ordain them. He sent them out to heal the sick, and to support the widows and the orphans. He told them to carry no purse, no spare pair of sandals, no change of clothes, no bookings in hotels and retreat centres, no money for a return fare home. No holidays in Spain or Greece; there is no mention of stipend, or pension funds. He offered them no large mansions, no bishops' palaces where to rest their weary heads at night."

The bishop ignored my sarcastic interruption as if I was not there. He continued to educate his small flock in the basic truths about what he believed to be the true Church of God – the Church of England. This Church was now under attack from people who are completely and utterly ignorant of the 'Holy Scriptures' and had no regard for the sacred traditions of 'the Church of God'.

At 1.00 p.m. sharp, we had a short break for a yummy buffet lunch, followed by tea and coffee, very classy biscuits and my favourite, lemon cheesecake. During the lunch interval, no one except my deanery colleague and two other guests acknowledged my presence in the room with a nod and a smile. After lunch, the bishop left to attend to his other duties.

When the meeting resumed, the largest person in the room (let's call him David) who had been keeping a lid on the tempers of some haughty ones with his light-hearted, timely and intelligent interruptions in the dialogue, resumed the conversation. He said, "Father Nihal, let me get this right. What is your main point against the bishop's argument that if Jesus wanted women to be priests in his Church, then he would have chosen women to be his disciples?"

"My point is, Father David, that if we go down that road, then we must also accept that if Jesus wanted Englishmen, or Indian men, for that matter, to be the priests of his Church, then he could easily have had Englishmen and Indians among his disciples. Since he did not, no one except the Christians of Jewish origin can be priests in the Church."

Most of them stared at me with a, *what in the name of ... is he talking about?* look in their eyes. Only one or two seemed switched on. I wasn't sure if I should say any more. Silence and discomfort filled the air. Then, a demure looking lady, with what looked like a bigger than the original cross resting upon her over-exposed ample bosom, and neatly cut short hair on her head, and well painted face said softly, "You are trying to turn a serious discussion into some cheap and insulting remarks, which have no bearing on the ordination of women."

The gentleman sitting to her left whispered, "I bet he would love to shut down the Church of England".

"Here, here! Jane is right. You are taking the whole debate into unrelated areas," said one of the vicars, looking around with a triumphant expression on his face.

"Did you not understand a word of what the bishop

was saying?" said another female participant with a look of disdain in her eyes.

I put my hands up and promised to shut up. David suggested, "In this small gathering we should be able to discuss each other's points of view, openly and patiently. I am happy to hear Father Nihal's thinking on the subject a little further, if others have no objection." He looked around hopefully.

There was a conspiratorial silence and suspicious looks in the eyes of most participants. Once again, I apologised for having said more than I had intended. One of the participants who had not said a word till then, speaking in perfect Oxbridge accent and soft voice, said, "I am happy to hear you out for a few minutes more."

"I am really embarrassed about upsetting you all. All I will say now is, that to me, Church is a purely human institution, based upon what a significantly small number of the Church leaders wanted in the 4th Century AD. They seemed to have shown little regard for what Christ and his teachings were about. Jesus said, 'God is Spirit and those who worship him, must worship him in spirit and in truth'. If God is Spirit, then we cannot define this God in a few crisp statements. And this God must not be blamed for writing leaflets, pamphlets and booklets that are full of self-contradictions."

I was excitedly congratulating myself, for having hammered the final nail into the coffin of the 'No Women Priests' lobby. The host locked her piercing eyes into mine, her eyes burning with righteous rage, and her finger on the proverbial trigger. *What a sad misuse of two beautiful green eyes*, I thought.

"You seem to have no respect for Christ or for His Church. What do you do, by the way? If you are not a Christian, then what are you doing in this meeting? I don't remember inviting you!" she demanded to know. She had had enough.

"I am sure if we could concentrate our minds on what might be more important to Christ, than on our own prejudices, then the Church could be right at the heart of the English society. Instead of walking away from it, people might start coming back to the Church, to hear what Christ has to offer them."

"Well said, sir, but we must protect the great traditions and the faith that the Church is built upon. It is these customs and traditions and the respect for them that has always put the Church of England at the very heart of this nation," suggested a hitherto silent priest.

By now, the host lady was visibly struggling to hold back her rage. She wanted this ignorant, uninvited guest out of there. "The only way to know what Christ wants is to look at the Holy Scriptures. Paul is very clear on how the man is the head of the woman and therefore woman cannot be equal with man in matters as important as the Church of God," she fumed.

David said calmly, "I am beginning to see Father Nihal's point though. I am also thinking of the words of St Paul in the eleventh chapter of the first letter to the Corinthians. Where St Paul is concerned, when it comes to obeying the instructions of Jesus to his disciples most men and women would not be permitted to hold an office within the Church."

Everyone went quiet, shifting and shuffling in their chairs, and eyes jumping around from face to face, willing me to leave before they changed their mind. The host turned her attention to her handbag, *looking in there for a handgun,* I feared. *It is time to leave,* I concluded thoughtfully.

I stood up, said 'thank you' all round for putting up

with me. I apologised to the host, and to my colleague for causing him embarrassment. He nodded. No one said a word.

David's globular beer belly of Cyril Smithsonian proportions was made to match his personality. Every time he giggled the belly moved in all directions. His shirt and the trousers were constantly struggling to keep his middle from pouring over on to the floor (if you happen to read this, David, you will know, I am only borrowing your words). He followed me out of the room. As soon as we were out of the ear shot of the others, he placed his enormous right hand on my tiny shoulder.

"Thank you for your openness. I think you have given some of us something to think about. It is good to have an outsider's perspective on matters as important as the one we are embroiled in at the moment." He promised to take a fresh look at the whole debate by stepping aside from the Movement for a while.

"Personally, I am neutral to the question of women's Ordination. All I am saying is, that if women want to be ordained to priesthood, it is their business. It should not affect us either way."

We wished each other well and hoped to meet again. I turned in the direction of the nearest tube station, and unnoticed by the passers-by, put my proverbial hammer and nail, safely away.

In case you are not familiar with the C of E scene, I am glad to tell you that the women did win and sadly, like the men, they too are jumping about with joy for having been 'called by God' to the 'sacred vocation'. Wonder why God took nearly one thousand and seven hundred years before calling the women to the sacred vocation? I have only seen middle-aged women priests so far. It's an opportunity, I guess, for doing something outside of the house once the children are grown up. The female element within the ministry can only enrich the culture of the Church.

I wonder when God will start calling women to priesthood in the Roman Catholic and the Orthodox Churches, and in the Anglican Churches in Africa and many other parts of the world? Bible being the 'Word of God', and the belief that one is 'called into the priesthood' by God, do not stand on firm grounds.

Why can't we stop making a mockery of God and accept the way life is. Church is established by men for their own benefit, and we become priests because we want to. Most of us are ordinary men and women. You will rarely come across a priest who is pious and holy in the real sense of the words. We become priests because of what we rightly, and wrongly, believe. Also, perhaps because we love working with people, and the social status that goes with it. Sadly, there are some of us who are paedophiles, and some others seem to enjoy the company of Mafiosos and whoever ... did God call them as well? Why not? After all, how else did they get past God?

The Church is no different from the BBC, from the Football Association, and the like. Yes, it does have some Christians within its boundaries. But then, there are Christians outside the Church as well. Probably more on the outside than on the inside.

Upon his death, my colleague who had taken me to the meeting on the subject of ordination of women and was a dedicated denier of the 'right of women to priesthood', went to heaven. In the Male Reception Hall, there were two queues – one was under the sign that said, 'Henpecked Husbands', and the other sign said, 'Independent Husbands'. The queue under the first sign stretched all the way back to earth. My colleague was the only one standing under the second sign. His next-door neighbour, who had known him and his wife over many years happened to be standing in the longer queue. He called out, "Hello vicar, have you read the sign above your head?"

"Yeah, I've read the sign." The vicar looked embarrassed.

"Should you not be here with us, at the front of the queue?"

My friend retorted, "Shut up, John. Missus told me to stand here."

Chapter 25

Invitation from Moni

On a midsummer afternoon in 1991, the then MP for Basildon, Mr David Amess, was escorting a small group of MPs from Eastern Europe around parts of his constituency. His parliamentary secretary phoned to say that Mr Amess wondered if, after a brief visit to St Nicholas Church, they could drop in at the vicarage for a cup of tea.

"No problem," I said.

Following the *chai-pani* and some interesting chit-chat at the vicarage, on their way out the MPs gave me polite invitation to visit their respective countries in the near future. A few days after that, I received an invitation from Dr Solomon Passy (Moni to his friends), the MP from Bulgaria, to visit his country. A week after that, the invitation was confirmed in a formal letter from the leader of his political party.

In September of that year, I managed to free myself from my parish duties and flew to Sofia (Sofija), in Bulgaria. Moni, the airport manager and a soldier greeted me outside the plane. We went into the manager's office for sips of coffee, while the soldier collected my luggage from the plane.

After a customary thank you and vigorous handshakes, Moni, his friend, and I, got into a car and the driver took us to Moni's seventh-floor flat, eight miles out of the centre of Sofia. He had placed the flat at my disposal for the whole of my stay in his country, while he stayed with his parents in the centre of Sofia. I could hang on to the driver and the car for the duration of my stay out there, if I wished, Moni suggested. In view of the serious shortage of fuel in Bulgaria, I didn't think it was right for me to be adding to the problems.

Moni and his friend stayed over in the flat for the first night. Following morning, Moni took me to the House of Parliament and obtained three official passes. One pass allowed me entry into the House of Parliament, and for the use of facilities therein, such as telephone for calling out of the country, food, and drinks (these items were hard to purchase in the shops). The second pass allowed me access to all public buildings, except sensitive defence establishments. The third pass was for free travel on public transport. He also arranged a rota of interpreters (his friends from the university) to accompany me all day from the moment of arriving in the centre of Sofia to the end of my day, which was usually in the early hours of the following morning. Travel on public transport was far greater fun than sitting in a car for hours, in three to four-mile-long queues, hoping to reach the petrol station before the fuel ran out in both the car and the petrol station.

I was impressed by the energy Dr Solomon Passy possessed, and how he used it in the service of his country. His interest in matters that effected the lives of people on the lower rungs of society was inspiring. I hardly ever ran into a young person in Sofia who did not know and admire him.

Every day, on my return to the flat from the various meetings and visits to places of interest, I would find a tray-full of fresh, tasty homemade snacks in the fridge. That provided me with a late-night top-up and a hearty breakfast the following morning.

Hospitality offered by everyone, who was anyone in Bulgaria, was embarrassingly overwhelming. Equally overwhelming, was the lack of basic amenities all over the country. Walking on a full stomach past long queues in front of empty shops in towns and suburbs, was heart-breaking. Most shopping queues were manned round the clock in rota, by different members of the family. Queues could often last for up to four/five days at a time, I was told. Even, at the end of those excruciatingly long waits, when the supplies finally did reach the shop, those at the back end of the queue, often returned home empty handed.

One could buy most essential items in the shops if one paid in British pounds or American dollars. For local currency, shops were always empty. I insisted on paying in local currency. I could not buy even a cigarette lighter or a box of matches. Which in turn helped to reduce my smoking. I had to wait to run into another smoker, to help me light my pipe. On a visit to a town few miles out of Sofia, my interpreter for the day barged into a shop, said something to the shopkeeper in her language that made him jump out from behind his desk and hand me two new lighters, and refused to accept the money. I left some coins on his desk. She wouldn't tell me what threats, or whoppers she used to bully the poor shopkeeper. With the benefit of hindsight, perhaps it would have been more helpful all round, if I had paid in Pound Sterling?

As is always the case, people did not crumble under the stress of shortages of everything, even the most basic amenities of life. They still held parties, where there was hardly anything to eat or drink, yet plenty of songs and laughter. At a gathering of some politicians in a club one evening, I found myself sitting next to a very knowledgeable and chatty gentleman. Half hour into the conversation I discovered that he was the Prime Minister of Bulgaria. During the entire evening, not once had he, or any other politician, referred to their troubles, in our conversations about pre-and post-communist eras. Everyone was having a good time.

Students at the Sofia university always looked hopeful and, even excited about the future. For some, the one and only dream was 'to get a good degree and go to America'. Once at the university campus, I asked the students about what they had learned from the outside world since the 'Wall' came down. Desire for democracy was the positive import, they said. The negative imports were the fanatical Churchianity and pornographic films from the United States of America.

They wanted something different, something new. During occasional brief conversations about religion and the freedom that a priest enjoyed in the Church of England (generally), they wondered if the Church of England could send someone there to help them change their Church. Unfortunately, on my return to England, I failed miserably in exciting the leaders of my diocese to establish a connection with the young people of Bulgaria.

The one common hero of the young people in Sofia, at the time, seemed to be an Orthodox priest by the name of Dr Christopher Subef. He was a well-known nuclear physicist, I was told. Most people who knew him, gave me the impression that he had become a priest, in order to reform the Church in his country. By all accounts, he was a thorn in the flesh of the Orthodox Church of Bulgaria.

Everyone was excitedly telling me about the embarrassment the scientist priest had caused to the Patriarch and his officials at the Easter Sunrise Service in Sofia that year. The news media appeared to know of his plan to conduct the Sunrise Service outside the cathedral in Sofia, while the official Service was to be inside the cathedral. The Service inside the Cathedral, they said, had the Patriarch of Bulgaria, and about half a dozen of his priests. The Service outside, attracted thousands of worshippers and the attention of international media. A journalist from Bulgaria's National Radio gave me a copy of a video of the outdoor Service. I still have it on the shelf in my study. Unfortunately, it's in German. In Sofia, I did watch the crowds outside the cathedral on another video though.

One afternoon I casually mentioned to Moni if I could possibly meet Dr Christopher Subef. I had heard so much about him, I might as well see him in person. The same evening, I received a phone call from Dr Subef to say that he was going away to some academic meetings, somewhere in Europe (I can't remember where) in the next few hours. But he had arranged for me to spend some time with the Patriarch of Bulgaria and his three archbishops. I was to travel with them in their car, to an 'important' city, a fair number of miles away. I would be staying with them overnight and join them at a 'very important event' the morning after.

I offered some polite excuses for why I could not travel with them that night but would be happy to meet them in the morning. In truth, I was worried about getting squashed between the over-weight, over-dressed Church dignitaries. Dr Subef gave me directions to where I could catch up with the Patriarch and his entourage the following morning. "They will be there taking back possession of an important seminary, from the former communist administration."

My interpreter for the day, Catherina (not her real name) collected me from the flat in a taxi to the train station. We boarded an early morning train from Sofia, bound for Plovdiv, approximately a two-hour journey in the south-easterly direction from Sofia. We missed the start of the event by nearly an hour. With my brand-new VHS camera on my shoulder, I tried to get a closer view of what was happening at the centre of the open-air Service, in front of the seminary. We got pushed and shoved to the back of the crowd by official camera crews and reporters. Luckily for us, one of the archbishops at the front turned round casually, spotted us, came up to where we were being elbowed aside by a large German-sounding cameraman.

"You are our guest from England, yes?" The archbishop asked. I didn't know what to say. I nodded uneasily. "I am Archbishop for Western Europe, please come, follow me." He led us to the front seats. I am ashamed to confess – my ego went into overdrive.

Following the Service, I was invited to join the Patriarch and his entourage in, what was described by Catherina, as 'The Upper Room' where, according to her, "women were not permitted." I suggested to the archbishop that it would not be right for me to leave the young lady outside the building, while I enjoyed their hospitality in 'The Upper Room'. He smiled with a *now, that could be a problem* look in his eyes. He exchanged a few whispers with his other archbishop. Then with a broad smile and generous movement of head and hands in the direction of the room, he invited the young woman to join us upstairs. In 'The Upper Room', someone passed around a strong alcoholic drink. It reached my head before touching the back of my throat.

The poison chalice was followed by an invitation to a private photo shoot. The Archbishop for Western Europe helped the Patriarch from his seat over to the chair on my right. One of the other two archbishops took a couple of pictures with my camera. The photo shoot was followed by some light snacks – can't recall if we had any tea or coffee. Every liquid item smelt and tasted of alcohol. Catherina thought that the Patriarch appeared to be under the influence of *'something'*. I could think of no reason to disagree with her. The whole morning was of great significance in terms of social, political, educational, and ego-boosting experience for me. The spiritual element was entirely absent.

Back in Sofia, fresh from the Patriarch's big event in Plovdiv earlier in the day, Catherina asked if I would not mind accompanying her to the grocery shop on her high street. In the shop I got the impression that she introduced me as her friend and 'the guest of our government'. She bought some basic items for a cake and seemed to receive more than her share of the rations. The cake was to celebrate her and her boyfriend's birthday which happened to be on the same night. I was invited to the party.

I arrived at the party in the house of Catherina's parents just after ten. The parents had handed the house over to their daughter and her friends for the night. There were over twenty young men and women present: joyously dancing and singing along to the record. On my arrival, they cut the cake. Each slice no more than an inch wide. I was offered the widest slice. I couldn't bring myself to accept their generosity. With too many embarrassing minutes, I managed to exchange my thicker slice for Catherina's thinner one.

After birthday celebrations, a taxi dropped me at my flat just before 3.00 a.m. The lift was not working at that hour of the morning. I climbed up the seven floors, then slid straight into bed. I was awakened at 6.45 a.m. by my first interpreter for the day and found myself in the back of the taxi by 7.30 a.m. on the way to an historical site. I must have sleep-walked all day because I cannot recall when the first interpreter left and the second one joined me, neither the name of the place, nor the sights I was supposed to have visited.

From left: Nihal, Sophia, Moni (directly facing the camera) and his friends

Bulgarian Orthodox Church, taking back a Seminary from the erstwhile Communist government in Plovdiv, September 1990.

Patriarch's archbishop for Western Europe on my right

Chapter 26

The Angel Sister

At the start of 1992, I suggested to the congregation that although I enjoyed my job, I was becoming more and more uncomfortable with the language of our Services. To be fair to the Church, I ought to resign from the job, and move on. One of the churchwardens suggested, "it will be helpful all round if you explain your reasons for what some of us have been expecting for some time, now," he said. The congregation eagerly agreed with him.

At the end of six Sunday sermons, I announced, "Well, that's it. I understand you wouldn't want someone like me to be your priest."

The response of the congregation took me by surprise. I nearly fell out of the pulpit. They wanted me to stay. I heard the churchwarden say, "We can all learn together."

What was even more surprising and encouraging, was that my bishop refused to accept my resignation, on the basis, as he explained, "you are privileged to have grown up alongside different religions, faiths and cultures. People in your parish are happy with you. I suggest that you go back to the parish and do whatever it is that God wants you to do."

The bishop's attitude only confirmed that there always were, and there always will be, some Christians in the Church, just as there always have been, and always will be Christians on the outside of it.

Members of the congregation of St Nicholas were generous enough to allow me to leave out, at least, certain prayers and parts of the Services that are clearly an insult to the notion of God, and of Jesus.

One Sunday morning in 1993, during normal intercessions (*'intercessions'* are a long list of gratitude, apologies, regrets, suggestions, requests, instructions, and reminders that we place before God, at some point during the main Services), the person reading the prayers was requesting God to put an end to the war between religious factions in former Yugoslavia. It hit me, *surely God must know what IT is supposed to do there. God should not need us to beg IT to do IT's job.* At the end of the intercessions, I heard myself thinking aloud, *why are we not doing something ourselves to help those people?* The congregation wanted to know what their 'mad' vicar had in mind?

"I wish I knew. We will need to think of something," I responded with honesty and hope. In the coming days, we put our heads together. It being the start of winter of 1993, the one immediate thing we could think of was to send out an appeal into the community for warm clothes, blankets, food and other items for domestic use, and over-the-counter medicines. The response was phenomenal. Within two weeks of the appeal going out, I had to request the then Town Corporation to lend us a warehouse in the parish.

After just one home cooked Indian meal, I managed to secure Bob-the-fireman's support for the project. He offered Firemen's Relief Aid (based in Hadleigh) trucks and drivers to transport the goods to the war-torn areas. All he expected me to provide, was fuel for the lorries, somewhere to lay our heads at night at our destination, and the simplest and cheapest meals for the drivers while out there. While on the road, we took enough loaves and anything that goes inside it to make sandwiches and tea, coffee etc. We slept in the lorries there and back. Bob arranged with Feed the Children – a Reading-based charity – to unload our trucks into their warehouse, on the outskirts of Split, in Croatia. From there, they provided necessary, up-to-date information about the points of need within a few miles. While in Split they loaned us their smaller vehicles to reach the nearby smaller refugee camps, as and when necessary. Their staff even shared the small living quarters with us in Split, on couple of occasions.

Response from across England to subsequent appeals, was a sign of how deeply the majority of human beings care for each other. I was gob smacked by how quickly the *St Nicholas Aid to Children* appeal picked up sufficient momentum to require the use of two warehouses in Laindon, which the Town Corporation kindly placed at our disposal. With continued support of the Firemen's Relief Aid, generosity of businesses and individual members of the community, the project took off successfully. A substantial, surprise cheque from Martin Gore of Depeche Mode, and a long-wheel-base van from his group, helped me to remain financially afloat.

Due to the possibility of being mistaken for a Muslim, I was discouraged from accompanying the firemen into danger areas. Being a coward, that suited me fine (maybe, I am being a little unfair to myself, here).

On our visits to that part of the world, we regularly came across the carnage visited upon the minds and bodies of human beings of all ages and genders by those, who claimed to have God exclusively on their side. There were others, on the other hand, who did not claim to be holy and pious, nor having any knowledge of God. They did what they could, to live and let live, and to support others, as and when they could.

In a refugee camp on the outskirts of Split, while the firemen were unloading the truck into the camp's storerooms, the manager of the camp asked if I would like a guided tour of the camp site, to get a better view of how things work in those desperate situations. A beautiful, smiley girl of about ten followed us around all the way from start to finish. I asked the manager if she knew how the girl came to be in that camp? In short:

Some months before, one dark night, the Catholic village where the girl's family lived, was attacked either by the Serbs or the Muslims. They set many homes alight, killed most inhabitants of the village. In the smiley girl's house, three soldiers made the entire family stand in a circle in the living room. First, they beat up the father and the two boys mercilessly. Next, they turned their attention to the two women in the room. While the three beasts were engrossed in bestiality with the two women, the little girl noticed the door to the kitchen next to her was open. She crept out of the room and out through the back door, into the dark night. Someone found her in the nearby woods after four days, starving, cold and disorientated. They took her to the camp. Her house had been burned down, and she had no idea where her family – if still alive – might be.

When we came back to our truck, the firemen had already gone into the communal area for a cup of tea/coffee. The manager went to join them, I decided to have a few puffs on my beloved pipe. Miss Smiley positioned herself against a tree about ten yards directly opposite to me, watching my every move intently.

I leaned against the tree behind me. Held the pipe between my teeth, and I don't know what made me do that; before filling my pipe, I gestured for Miss Smiley to come and give me a hug – we had no other common language between us. She virtually flew those ten yards between us and put her arms tightly round my waist. I was moved to tears. She calmly looked into my face. One arm still round my waist, she took the pipe out of my mouth, dropped it onto the ground. Kept signalling for me to *'Shushshsh'*. That was the final straw. I gently pushed her away and went to the back of the huts and broke down. Took me a good ten minutes before I got a grip over my slushy self. Finally, I wiped my tears, tried to look normal and came out from behind the huts. The smiley miss was now standing against my tree. Just then the firemen and the manager came out of the communal hut.

I requested the manager to please ask the little girl to tell me what kept her smiling after what she had gone through in her short life.

Miss Smiley, in return asked the manager, "Where does he come from?" The manager told her that I and the firemen were all from England.

"Ask him, don't the children in England smile?" she asked, still smiling.

"Not always. Especially, not many children smile like you do." The manager translated my words to her.

"She says," the manager turned to me, "Tell the children in his England, to always smile." She waved at us all sweetly, turned away and disappeared into a nearby hut.

On another visit to Croatia, the firemen had gone further into the danger zone. I had to stay behind with the warehouse staff and volunteers. During a break from unpacking, packing, and loading the vans and trucks in Split, half a dozen of us stood round a small fire in the center of the courtyard. In temperatures below zero, our hands were firmly wrapped round hot cups of tea.

Someone mentioned the massacre of an entire village somewhere north of Split recently.

A teenager volunteer at the warehouse asked with tearful eyes: "everyone says, there is only one God. Why does this one God set one group of his followers against another group of his followers?" He had escaped out of Sarajevo with his father and little sister. He had lost the entire family on his father's side. His mother had to stay behind in Sarajevo to look after her elderly, disabled mother. He hoped his mother was alive somewhere in Sarajevo, still under siege.

All eyes in the circle fixed on the one person who was expected to know God's mind. I could see them silently urging me to answer the question.

I felt obliged to say something that would hopefully make some sense to a troubled teenager. Feeling ill at ease, I looked toward the hills to my right. I tried to picture the scene of the massacre somewhere far beyond, on the other side of those hills. All that came out of my mouth were words I had read somewhere, *'blessed are the animals, for they shall lead us back to our lost innocence'*. The look in his sad eyes said, 'what does that mean?'.

I tried another angle. I said "God neither starts nor ends the wars. We start the wars, and we alone can end them. Jesus said, 'Love your neighbour as yourself'. When we don't do that, we cause pain and distress all around. If we believe in God, then we must use the gifts that God has blessed us with – the ability to think, to ask questions, to rationalise. Likelihood is, that when we do that, we will not want to harm another person for disagreeing with us. For none of us will see ourselves better than our fellow man. Let me tell you a story."

In the land, not far from here, there was a mighty, young king. His name was The Truth. Everyone within his kingdom had to agree with The Truth. If anyone spoke, what the King believed to be a lie, the King would have them beheaded. No one dared disagree with the King and his courtiers.

By the time the King entered old age, there were not many men left in his kingdom. For they had all been beheaded for disagreeing with him. The only ones alive, were those who made up lies to please the King. The Kingdom finally came to be known as the 'Kingdom of Liars'.

The young man looked into my face thoughtfully for a few seconds, then said "I understand. Thank you."

Thoughtful silence descended upon the group. Our hands were still wrapped round the warm cups, all eyes fixed on the flames rising from the fire in the center. I heard someone say, "Come on lads. Let's get back to what we're here for." We followed him into the warehouse.

Back inside the warehouse, someone mentioned if we could treat ourselves to a Combi and chips dinner that night ... ('Another one, spending charity money on meals in restaurants', I hear you say.) Trust me, evening meal was the only meal of the day we ate during our visits to that part of the world. Rest of the time we scraped a biscuit here, a slice of bread there from the warehouse kitchen. En route, as I said before, we carried our own supply of loaves of bread, sandwich fillers, milk, tea bags, coffee and sugar etc.

A member of the Feed the Children projects suggested to me one afternoon, that while in Split, I ought to visit a nun. She had been working with a large number of young people and many pregnant women in a refugee camp, based in a hotel on the outskirts of the town. She was a midwife, and a significant number of young women in the camp were pregnant. Few pregnancies were within a normal relationship, but the would-be mothers, seldom knew *if* the father of their child was dead or alive. Majority of the pregnancies had resulted from rape. He said something like, "Because Sister is helping all young mothers, irrespective of their religion and country, her priests had refused to support her." He gave me directions to the hotel. After a couple of slices of bread and tea, two firemen and I drove to the hotel with some relevant supplies for teenagers and for mothers and babies, in the back of a small truck.

At the hotel, we made our way into the manager's office. He greeted us warmly and advised us to be patient. "You know, Sister is an angel. She walks more than three miles to come here very early in the morning. She eating quick breakfast, then she going to the mothers and their babies. Some days she helping to deliver two, three babies. Some days, no babies." At this point we were interrupted by a waiter with a pot of tea and some light refreshments. During refreshments, the manager told us more about this 'Angel Sister'.

The sister, he believed had to walk there and back every day in the freezing cold weather. "And I tell you something more about Sister's work. You know, after she finish with the mothers and babies, Sister make five ... how do you say? ... baby boxes and five 'mother' boxes for the first five days for all of them." ... The manager checked his wristwatch, "Sister finish her job at two o'clock and then she come out. Come, I take you to meet her."

We followed him out of the office, through a long corridor, out into the fresh, freezing cold, and sunny January afternoon. We stopped near the mouth of an underground goods delivery tunnel. Couple of minutes later the sister, accompanied by half-a-dozen teenagers, appeared at the entrance with a big smile on her very tired face. I checked my watch. It was exactly 2.01 p.m. We were staring at the face of an angel. Well, if there really are angels, then they must look like that Sister. We were introduced to the Angel, and the manager left us with her.

With some words of English and hand gestures, Sister pointed us in the direction of her storage room on the first floor. We unloaded the truck and carried the stuff to the room. We stacked the boxes up to the ceiling, with just enough room left for her to move around her small desk and chair by the window. Sister showed us what went into each five-day 'mother' and 'baby' box.

On our way out of her office, Sister invited us to join her for free 'late lunch' in the hotel's dining room. We were starving, and gladly accepted the invitation. Over the meal, I asked the Sister if what I had been told about the attitude of her priests in relation to her work with the women, was correct. She smiled and said nothing.

In any war-ravaged society, there are always numerous individuals and groups of all ages grieving for the dead or missing members of their family, yet many do not give up on living, even smiling. And while living, they continue to do whatever they can to help their neighbours.

Here are two more tales, similar to the two you just read, to illustrate my point: The firemen were planning to go into a danger area, later in the day. My presence with them could compromise our safety. I borrowed a clapped-out Luton van and a clapped-out jeep. With help from volunteers at the warehouse, I filled the van with food items, fruits, over-the-counter medicines, and two large boxes of Yorkie chocolate bars. The warehouse secretary gave me directions to the refugee camp on the outskirts of the town, overlooking the Split Olympic Stadium. Bob led me there in the clapped-out jeep. Once we had found the camp, Bob returned to his duties with his colleagues. It took me less than ten minutes to find a small group of teenagers walking purposefully towards my van. A sixteen-year-old girl in the group spoke good English. I explained to her the purpose of my visit. She instructed her friends to pass the word around and to get some men to help me unload the van. She directed me to the community hall on site.

On the way to the hall, she told me that she had escaped from Sarajevo with her father. Her mother and two younger brothers were still missing. She hoped they were still OK. And here she was, none-the-worse when it came to doing something for her fellow sufferers.

Half-a-dozen men came over to help me unload the van into the small community hall. I asked the young lady to find someone to make a list of the number of families in the camp, number of members, and how many adults and children in each family.

She walked up to the desk in the corner, picked a large notepad and a biro, and disappeared outside. It must have taken me and the three men an hour to unload the van into the hall (the other three just sat there and smoked non-stop throughout). We laid out the goods in neat piles on the floor. The young lady, Elana (I don't remember her real name), came over and handed me a cup of tea and the detailed list. "The Camp manager is out for the day. I have made this list for you myself." She had even managed to scribble the gender and approximate ages of children in each family. The triumphant smile in her eyes said, *you didn't think I could do it, did you?* So much for not believing in her competence, in the first place.

The crowds were starting to gather outside the hall. Elana called out details from her list. The three men and I filled the bags accordingly (I had taken hundreds of plastic bags with me from the warehouse). Maria handed the bags out to the families.

During the normal chit-chat, it transpired that one of the three male helpers had been a schoolteacher in Sarajevo. Five months previously he had been caught out in one of the regular bombardments of the city. Rescued from the rubble, he was transferred out of the city, unconscious and seriously injured. He still had shrapnel in his head and his back, he said. He had no knowledge of the whereabouts of his wife and two daughters. "I don't know if they are still alive." Tears streamed down his young face. I could not help sniffling along with him for the rest of my time at the camp.

The exchange of angry words that had unexpectedly erupted among a small group of young men immediately outside the door to the hall, five minutes earlier, had now upgraded into a fist fight, and use of bricks. Elana explained that a small number of 'bad women' were telling some young men that I was favouring some families over others when it came to certain food items.

"But I don't know anyone in this camp. Why would I favour one stranger over another?"

"Please, you must get out of here before those men come in."

"How do I get out? They are right outside the door!" I sensed panic in my voice.

"We will distract them," the young man said. "The window behind us is not locked, and you can slip out through there. Your van is right outside the window." He advised me confidently.

Elana and the young man went over to the door. I

carefully backed towards the window immediately behind me. Slipped out and jumped into the van. Luckily, I had left the keys in the ignition. I turned the key, the van started without any hitch, and I drove off. Two men came running after the van, but soon gave up the chase. After a couple of miles, I hit the main road and turned in the direction of my warehouse sanctuary. After only less than a mile, I came upon major road works. Single lane two-way traffic, controlled by traffic lights. Less than hundred yards on, and the van ground to a halt. It would not restart, no matter what I tried. No luck either in trying to contact the warehouse staff on my CB radio. There were no streetlights, and the winter's evening shadows had started to threateningly slither into the impending dark night.

By now the drivers behind my van, were getting out of their vehicles, and curiously queuing in my direction. Four suspicious looking young men started hovering around the van. Two soldiers, who were in charge of the traffic, came over to check. With the help of hand gestures, I explained my problem to them. Told them I was a Christian priest from England, and not a Muslim. They ordered everyone to get back in their cars and assured me that I would be safe.

I tried the warehouse CB, again. To my surprise and relief, Bob answered the call. He said that due to some safety concerns along their route, the firemen had postponed their departure till the following morning. In shaking, nervous voice, I explained my problem. Twenty minutes later I saw him walking towards me from the opposite direction, accompanied by the FTC (Feed the Children) vehicle mechanic. After a quick fiddling about, the mechanic concluded that we would have to push the van out of the way of the traffic queue.

With the help of some onlookers, we pushed the van to the other end of the road works, where we were received with lots of handclapping and cheers by the frustrated, but kind and patient drivers.

We left the van by the roadside. I jumped into the jeep with my two rescuers. On the way, Bob said, "We were starting to worry about you, seriously. Lucky you, I went into the office for something and heard you calling on their CB."

We arrived at the warehouse to warm handshakes all round and a sizzling hot barbeque, of juicy lamb chops, sausages, burgers, and a few other goodies, all brought in by the British Army Chaplain and half-a-dozen soldiers from the army camp in Split.

Before daylight the following morning, two volunteers went back to collect the warehouse van. It wasn't where we had left it the night before. We never saw it again. We consoled ourselves in the knowledge that it had served its purpose well.

None of the firemen, and many other NGOs (non-government organisations) that I had the privilege of meeting briefly on our visits to former Yugoslavia, had direct interest in religion. I have yet to meet a better Christian than those men and women out there. They did what had to be done, to make this world a better place for all. They did not waste their lives in fighting their fellow man over *'definitions'* of God.

Somewhere in Germany, on way to Bosnia January 1993

Epilogue

Please allow me a few lines to reiterate that I do believe in God, in Brahma, in the Supreme Spirit Paramatma and many other words that we use to refer to the Source and Cause of all that we hear, see, smell, taste, touch, and much, much more. The Mystery of all Mysteries. If we are honest, we also know that there must be worlds beyond our capacity to know. So how can we define, once and for all, that which created the known and the unknown, and the unknowable?

The 'Word of God', if we think calmly - without submitting to those who say, 'Agree with us, or God will send you to hell' - is not possible to be contained and confined to a few pages in an 'obscure past'. Word of God can only be 'Living Word', communicating with every living being, in every generation, and at every living moment, addressing the needs of each living being, in their given context.

The 'Word of God *', of the Jewish, the Christian, and of the Muslim religions* portrays God as an irresponsible, muddle-headed, misogynistic, partisan, vengeful Being. In the Old Testament, His interests are confined to a small group of nomads in the desert. He has no time for the rest of his Creation.

This God creates a *Man* and a *Woman* in *his own image*, and *in his own likeness*, and then accepts no responsibility for their shortcomings? Here is a watch maker, who blames the watch for its malfunctions. Is this how we show respect for our Creator? The Christians and the Muslims have borrowed the Old Testament God, and then redesigned him to fit into their own ambitions for control of the human race.

Think about it calmly; the children of Adam and Eve, if there really were two such individuals, could only have multiplied by either committing incest, which, according to at least, the Jewish and the Christian 'Word of God' is a serious sin. Or, they must have had reproductive relationships with something other than, but similar to, the human species. If they did the latter, then their descendants are not fully human. Hence, only partially representing the image of God. Hence, not fully responsible for whatever is wrong with 'our' sub-human race. Now, whose fault is that, if not 'their creator's'?

Would it not be more sensible to stop trying to outdo each other by designing the best God? Instead, concentrate upon the realities of life. A life that connects everything and every living being in an amazing variety of ways. Seek together, to reach out into the Supreme Spirit – the source of all Life, of all Intelligence, of Water, Earth, Fire and Air and whatever else is out there in the skies above.

Is God a He? Or is God a She? Or is IT, simply 'IT' ...? Who can honestly say that they know what IT is? Pointing to a book and insisting, 'It says so in the Word of God', is a sad reflection on the human race.'

There is so much to learn from every contact we make with our world. When you hold a conversation with a dog, cat, bird, or any other living being, look into their eyes. Their eyes move all over you, and then, they lock their eyes into yours. They are talking to you, communicating with you in love and trust. How much do we know about the dog and the cat?

Watching a dog leading a blind person across busy streets and along overcrowded pavements is a fascinating revelation. You are watching an intelligent, loving and utterly faithful animal, communicating with its human companion. Where does that love and intelligence come from? We priests could learn a great deal from a dog or a cat.

Picture, driving along a road, lined with trees and a myriad of other forms of greenery on both sides. Fumes from your vehicle are damaging the health of the trees and polluting their entire neighbourhood. No matter how many times you drive down the same street, the trees welcome you with a wave, and continue to provide you with oxygen to keep you alive. How much do you really know about those trees?

Take a gentle walk in the park? Look at the grass beneath your feet. You have trodden all over it, every blade still tries to rise up and be there for you, the next time you take a walk in the park. There! look at that bush in blossom, smiling at you. Are you thinking of plucking some of those flowers for your vase in the window, at home? Is your dog contemplating leaving something under the bush or peeing on it? Imagine that both you and your dog have done the dirty deeds. As you walk away, turn around and look at that bush, again. It is still smiling at both of you.

The worlds give in abundance and asks for little in return. Before we start defining what we call the Creator of those worlds, let us learn to understand and respect the worlds this Creator has created. I cannot think of any other way to nurture and to express, our 'faith' in what we call 'God'.

Printed in Great Britain
by Amazon

16457760R00169